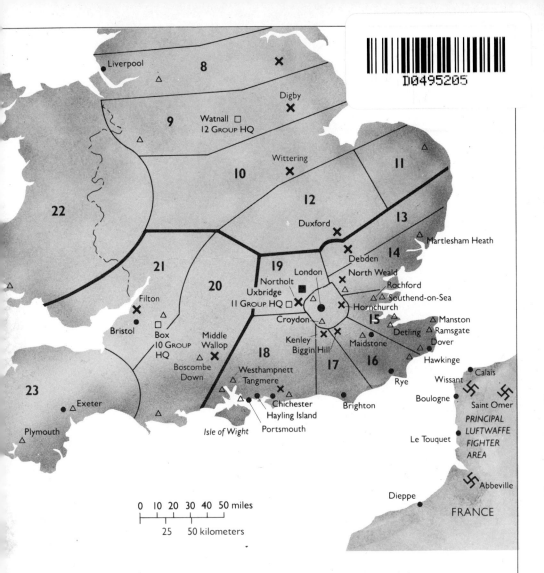

D0495205

THE BATTLE OF BRITAIN

LEGEND

1	Wick	13	Debden
2	Turnhouse	14	North Weald
3	Aldergrove	15	Hornchurch
4	Acklington	16	Biggin Hill
5	Usworth	17	Kenley
6	Catterick	18	Tangmere
7	Church Fenton	19	Northolt
8	Kirton-in-Lindsey	20	Middle Wallop
9	Digby	21	Filton
10	Wittering	22	Pembrey
11	Coltishall	23	St. Eval
12	Duxford		

━━━━━ Group boundary

───── Sector boundary

□ Group headquarters

■ Fighter command headquarters

✗ Sector airfields

△ Other fighter airfields

卐 Luftwaffe airfields

SCRAMBLE

Also by Norman Gelb

The Eight Penny Spy
Enemy in the Shadows
The Irresistible Impulse
The British
Less Than Glory

SCRAMBLE

A Narrative History of the Battle of Britain

by

NORMAN GELB

Michael Joseph
LONDON

First published in Great Britain by Michael Joseph Ltd
44 Bedford Square, London WC1
1986

© 1986 by Norman Gelb

All Rights Reserved. No part of this publication
may be reproduced, stored in a retrieval system,
or transmitted in any form or by any means, electronic,
mechanical, photocopying, recording or otherwise,
without the prior permission of the Copyright owner.

British Library Cataloguing in Publication Data
Gelb, Norman
Scramble: a narrative history of the Battle of Britain
1. Britain, Battle of, 1940
I. Title
940.54'21   D756.5.B
ISBN 0 7181 2687 4

Typeset by Alacrity Phototypesetters, Banwell Castle, Weston-super-Mare
Printed and bound in Great Britain by
Billing & Sons Ltd, London and Worcester

CONTENTS

This book is dedicated to the memory of
HUGH CASWALL TREMENHEERE DOWDING

'After Stuffy was made to retire, the war blew up into a global thing. Great names arose – Eisenhower, Montgomery, Alexander, Bradley. Great battles were won – Alamein, D-Day, the crossing of the Rhine. But they were all courtesy of Stuffy Dowding. None of those people would even have been heard of if Stuffy hadn't been there, if he hadn't won the Battle of Britain. His statue ought to be standing atop a plinth in Trafalgar Square.'

Squadron Leader Sandy Johnstone

FOREWORD

The Battle of Britain was one of the most dramatic and important periods in the history of our Islands. In 1940 the outlook was dark. Although supported strongly by Empire and Commonwealth, we stood alone in Europe to face an enemy who had occupied much of the Continent in a very short period of time, leaving our country in a state of shock. With the fall of France came the loss of many of our forces: the Battle of Britain had begun. The whole country took part in that battle, civilian and serviceman alike, but the brunt of it fell upon the Royal Air Force and in particular Fighter Command, which had few resources; indeed, the experience level of many of its pilots was pitifully low. The battle lasted only a few months, but it was ferociously fought and it prevented an assault upon our country. Thereafter, the opportunity for Germany to contemplate invasion never returned. Britain was given the necessary respite, enabling her to lick her wounds and prepare for the long fight ahead – a fight which was ultimately to culminate in victory, achieved in concert with our Allies some five years later.

1940 was a time of great valour, innovation, dedication to the task and skill, not just in the air but on the ground, with controllers and engineers and all the panoply of support that goes with operating an air force in such difficult circumstances.

Much has been written about these epic times, but I believe this book to be unique in that it is a series of recollections of people who actually took part in the battle, many of whom will continue to echo in the halls of fame and in legend, and it is attributed to them by name. The stories of ordinary men and women as well as the great and brave are blended in such a way as to provide a continuous but personal history of those dangerous and crucial times. It would be easy in such a work to produce little more than a scattering of fragmented memories, interesting though they may be, but the author has carefully and superbly threaded them together to provide a series of crescendos, interspersed with light relief, to give one a feel for the events and difficulties that faced our people. It gives one a sense of the moment.

Air Chief Marshal Sir Peter Harding KCB CBIM FRAeS RAF
Air Officer Commanding-in-Chief, Royal Air Force Strike Command

PREFACE

It was the summer of 1940. A shroud of gloom had settled over the cities, towns and villages of Britain. The future looked ominous. Within a few short months, most of Europe had fallen under the shadow of the swastika. From northern Norway to the Bay of Biscay, from Poland to the westernmost reaches of France, Adolf Hitler's steel-helmeted legions had spread terror and despair, and now were not far away. The Wehrmacht stood poised and threatening twenty miles from the cliffs of Dover and the beaches of southeast England.

The country was braced for a German invasion which most people in Britain were certain would be attempted and which a few, including the American ambassador in London, believed would succeed. Winston Churchill, newly named Prime Minister, made things perfectly clear: 'Hitler knows he will have to break us in this island or lose the war ... If we fail, then the whole world, including the United States ... will sink into the abyss of a new Dark Age.'

The abyss which most concerned the German High Command at the time was something less spectacular but still very daunting to their tacticians. It was a geological trench, the English Channel. Not since William the Conqueror had crossed over from Normandy to seize the English crown nine hundred years earlier had the Channel been successfully bridged by foreign forces trying to invade and conquer Britain. Napoleon had, at one time, cooled his heels in the French Channel port of Boulogne, waiting a full year for the right moment to launch his attack on the English coast. That moment never came.

Hitler was aware of the difficulties. He had hoped the British would swallow their pride and accept with good grace the humiliating setbacks their forces had suffered while trying to hold back the Germans on the continent. He had hoped they would surrender part of their empire to Germany as a gesture to the realities of the situation and agree to back out of the fighting. The British at home would thus be spared the horrors of war which had been visited on the Poles, French, Dutch and others in Europe. The Germans would then go about consolidating their conquests and turning loose their forces on the Soviet Union, which boasted no similar frontier moat to frustrate the advance of the German armoured divisions and which, not long before, had obligingly signed a non-aggression pact with the Nazis.

However, the British had no intention of acquiescing to a Europe dominated by Germany, and certainly not a Nazi Germany. They would not meekly bow out of the struggle, nervously to await the moment when Hitler would cast his eyes in their direction again. If the Germans wanted them out of the war, they would have to knock them out.

Intoxicated with the string of easy conquests his forces had accumulated and enraged by British obstinacy, Hitler thereupon decided to do exactly that. He would pound the British mercilessly, invade their island homeland and force them to submit. The cross-Channel operation would present problems. But Hitler believed he knew how it could be managed.

During their rampage across Europe, the Germans had proved that airpower was a surgical instrument with which to sap enemy morale and destroy enemy resistance. It would be employed just as effectively against the stubborn British as it had been against the Poles, Norwegians, Dutch, Belgians and French. The British, too, would learn the meaning of total war.

There was, however, a difficulty. The British had lost many of their fighter planes and pilots in a futile effort to stop the German advance in France. But though seriously weakened and heavily outnumbered by the Luftwaffe, the Royal Air Force's Fighter Command was still intact. It would have to be eliminated – shot out of the skies or destroyed on the ground – to give Germany uncontested mastery of the skies over England.

Such was the making of the Battle of Britain, the first and only time in history in which a major military confrontation having a critical bearing on the ultimate outcome of a war was fought and decided exclusively in the air. It was a relatively brief episode in the Second World War, lasting a mere 114 days – from 10 July to 31 October 1940. But it came at a crucial moment and it taught a crucial lesson. Despite previous evidence to the contrary, the British showed in that battle that the forces of Nazi Germany, which had subjugated and terrorized so many nations, were not invincible. And they showed that freedom was not necessarily doomed to extinction across the face of Europe.

When their moment came, they mustered both the pilots and the planes to stem the tide. During that historic summer and early autumn of 1940, many of those pilots took to the air in their Spitfires and Hurricanes half-trained, learning survival skills in their first interceptions and dogfights over the rolling countryside of southern England, but not always learning them fast enough. Losses were heavy, leading one pilot to recall afterwards: 'I felt there was nothing left to care about because obviously one could not expect to survive many more encounters.' To cope with hearing a seemingly endless rollcall of friends and colleagues killed or maimed as the days and weeks fled by, the young pilots, most of them barely out of their teens, learned to accept the cruel face of war. They masked with feigned indifference the conviction that they themselves would not escape death or disfigurement, or had their fears overridden by the thrill of being young, dashing and engaged in daily, heroic, life-or-death encounters in defence of their homeland – with other equally aroused, spirited, youthful warriors flying and fighting at their side.

Whether exhilarated by the excitement or half-comatose with exhaustion from going up and down all day from dawn to dusk to meet the German challenge, the men who fought the Battle of Britain fashioned a decisive moment in modern history. Had the Luftwaffe been able to obliterate the RAF's Fighter Command, a German invasion of England might well have succeeded. Freedom's first line of defence against the expanding Third Reich would have been forfeited. By frustrating Nazi invasion plans, the Battle of Britain pilots guarded the base from which the successful invasion of German-occupied Europe was to be launched four years later. Theirs was a memorable achievement.

The Battle of Britain was, however, not won only by the men at the frontline bases who, for weeks on end, were engaged daily in mortal combat with the German foe. Many were shunted in and out of the battle to maintain the operational effectiveness of their hard-pressed squadrons. Some were assigned to less pressured patrol and intermittent combat duty at rear bases. They were held there in reserve by their commander, Air Chief Marshal Sir Hugh Dowding, who never knew whether German tactics would be altered to expose other parts of the country to airborne attack, and who wanted those reserves to draw upon when his men in the front line approached exhaustion. Some were sent up in mostly fruitless efforts to find and attack German bombers coming over at night.

The battle was also won by the ground crew who serviced, fuelled, armed and patched up the planes, often restoring them to combat-ready status to meet new enemy raids within minutes of their landing. It was won by ground control personnel, radar operators, the Observer Corps, which fed a steady stream of reports on visual sightings of incoming German raids, and others who provided essential back-up for the outnumbered and harried fighter pilots and crew.

It can be argued that the Battle of Britain began in France in the spring of 1940 when, with formidable aerial cover, German ground forces slashed through French defences, launched their dash to the English Channel, and commenced the process of crushing or neutralizing the Allied armies which stood between them and the British Isles. But the actual assault on British home defences began after the Germans had, to some extent, consolidated their victories on the continent and could concentrate on their single remaining, defiant adversary in Western Europe.

There were five phases to the Battle of Britain. Between 10 July and 12 August, the Luftwaffe was in action mostly on the periphery of England – over the English Channel and English coastal areas – probing frontline defences. Between 13 August and 23 August, the Germans, their invasion plans in hand, moved on to a calculated effort to destroy the Royal Air Force's Fighter Command, stepping up and expanding their assault on Britain's battered aerial shield during the third phase of the battle, 24 August to 6 September. The fourth phase, 7 September to 15 September, marked the turning point in the battle. The onslaught was shifted to London, which was subjected to the most horrific aerial bombardment any city had yet seen. The final phase, 16 September to 31 October, was the climax of the Battle of Britain, fast and furious at first, but gradually petering out as the Germans, forced to concede that the planned invasion of England would have to be 'postponed', started along the road that led to their eventual defeat and to the end of the vicious Nazi reign of terror.

When I began this project, the curator of the Battle of Britain Museum in north London warned me that battle veterans might be reluctant to talk about the parts they played. And I knew from my own experience that the English are a private people, not usually given to talking about their personal lives. So it was with some misgivings that I first approached those on whose recollections I planned to base this account of that historic moment. It soon became apparent, however, that instead of the reserve and reticence I had expected, they were wonderfully forthcoming, refreshingly informative and a great pleasure to meet and speak with.

Some had stayed on in the Royal Air Force after the war and a few of those, very junior in rank during the battle, had achieved very senior positions of authority in the RAF. Others had settled back into civilian life. Almost all began by warning me they would have difficulty recalling events of more than four decades ago. But, with very few exceptions, once we began talking of those days, their memories flooded back, often in vivid detail. I am grateful to them for their welcome, their assistance and their gracious hospitality.

I am grateful in particular to Wing Commander N.P.W. Hancock, secretary of the Battle of Britain Fighter Association, Len Bowman, Group Captain Dennis David and Air Vice Marshal A.V.R. Johnstone for their help, courtesy and friendliness. I am also much obliged to Eric Monday of the Air Historical Branch of the Ministry of Defence in London and to the personnel of the British Public Records Office at Kew, the Imperial War Museum and the Royal Air Force Museum, who helped make the time I devoted to research almost as agreeable as my meetings with the people who fought the Battle of Britain. I am grateful most of all to my wife, Barbara, for reliving the battle with me.

Norman Gelb

The ranks by which military personnel are identified in the following pages are, with a few exceptions, those they held at the commencement of the Battle of Britain, though many were promoted to higher ranks during the course of the battle.

PRELUDE

On 13 May 1940, four days after invading Holland, Belgium and Luxembourg, the German army punched a hole through French defences at the town of Sedan on the River Meuse and poured through to fan out across France. In the process, the Germans set the stage for the Battle of Britain, an episode which was foreseen neither by them nor by the British, and which transformed the dimensions of the conflict that was soon to become the Second World War.

The war had begun with the lightning conquest of Poland the previous September. Subsequently, Denmark and Norway had also succumbed to the ferocity of Hitler's military machine. But there had been no major battlefield clashes, nothing like the murderous confrontations of mass armies in the First World War. Except for those who had fallen under Nazi rule, it was almost as if the peace had remained undisturbed. In Paris, officials had continued to boast that the Germans would never be able to crack the fortifications which made up their Maginot Line, never imagining that the enemy would outflank it. Sophisticates in London had begun calling the conflict 'the bore war'. Journalists dubbed it 'the phoney war'. But with German armoured divisions blasting their way across northwestern Europe, the war could be called phoney and boring no longer.

As the German blitzkrieg thundered forward, as the panzers roared across France and Belgium, British leaders, who had been almost as complacent as the French, realized to their horror that the unthinkable was happening. Suddenly they faced the prospect of having to abandon the comparative convenience of British troops – deployed in France during the uneventful winter of 1939/40 – confronting the enemy only on foreign soil, well away from England's green and pleasant land. Each day, word from the front conjured up the distinct possibility that the British homeland might itself soon be directly threatened with invasion by the cunningly commanded, superbly armed, ruthless, unpredictable and seemingly invincible military forces which were having no trouble whatsoever scattering and demolishing the once much respected French army on its home ground.

Even more ominous, the British Expeditionary Force in France

1

(BEF), which consisted of practically all the combat ready troops at the disposal of the British High Command, including most of its trained field officers and NCOs, was being forced to retreat, retreat and retreat again. Panic was not the British style, but there was growing alarm about the ordeal in store for the country.

Winston Churchill had succeeded Neville Chamberlain as Prime Minister the day the German offensive began, it having by then become apparent to Parliament that circumstances demanded the presence of a dynamic, aggressive bulldog of a national leader in London, one not easily cowed by Hitler's bluster and belligerence. But, like his military advisers, Churchill was astounded by German field successes. He was prepared to concede that the enemy had inflicted a serious blow – the news could not be kept from the British public. But he was not prepared to signal gloom or despair. He would not abandon his belief that proud France could still be counted on not to capitulate, nor his conviction that the forces of Britain and France combined could not merely be brushed aside by the onrushing Germans. Nevertheless, he issued a ringing call to arms.

Winston Churchill

It would be foolish ... to disguise the gravity of the hour. It would be still more foolish to lose heart and courage or to suppose that well-trained, well-equipped armies numbering three or four millions of men can be overcome in the space of a few weeks, or even months, by a scoop, or raid of mechanized vehicles, however formidable. We may look with confidence to the stabilization of the front in France, and to the general engagement of the masses, which will enable the qualities of the French and British soldiers to be matched squarely against those of their adversaries ... Centuries ago, words were written to be a call and a spur to the faithful servants of truth and justice: 'Arm yourselves, and be ye men of valour, and be in readiness for the conflict; for it is better for us to perish in battle than to look upon the outrage of our nation and our altar. As the Will of God is in Heaven, even so let it be.'

* * *

But the front in France did not stabilize. Nor did it stabilize anywhere else where the Germans were attacking. Whatever obstacles appeared in their path were systematically obliterated or swept aside. Where the German big guns could not be brought into play, dive bombers – their terror-generating sirens screaming as they zoomed down towards their targets – performed as airborne artillery with devastating efficiency. German infantry units, ferried in by gliders, leapfrogged Allied defensive positions, making nonsense of traditional French and British troop deployment tactics. German paratroopers descended en masse to seize installations which, because they were virtually unapproachable by military units on the ground, were thought to be invulnerable. German bombers took out Allied airfields, rail depots and other strategic targets. The skies were dark with German aircraft – almost four thousand of them deployed for the various roles to which they had been assigned.

It took the Germans a mere five days to batter the Netherlands – which would have preferred neutrality – into submission, seizing key positions and making the obliteration of the heart of historic Rotterdam by the Luftwaffe horrifyingly needless. The Belgian border fortress of Eban Emaael, touted as impregnable, fell to German gliderborne commandos in a matter of hours. The French air force crumbled. The Luftwaffe seized and held mastery of the skies over Western Europe, while the Wehrmacht proved unstoppable on the ground.

Six Royal Air Force fighter squadrons were based in France when the Germans launched their offensive. Four more were sent over in the days which followed and, while remaining based in south-eastern England, other British aircraft shuttled over to fly from fields in France during the day, or swept across the English Channel to undertake specific patrol or interception missions.

But the RAF was able to make little impact on the enemy. There were occasional successes and many individual acts of great heroism, but the British couldn't even come close to matching in numbers the vast German air armada. Furthermore, many of the German pilots had greater combat experience than their British adversaries, from exposure to combat earlier in the war and from participation in the Spanish Civil War, which had come to an end only the previous year. British fighter pilots, virtually none of whom had ever before fired their guns in action, soon found they had to expend the better part of their energies defending themselves and their airfields, rather than providing cover for the badly mauled Allied ground forces.

The situation bred confusion. Communications, where they existed at all, quickly broke down. As the German ground forces crashed forward, RAF squadrons were forced to withdraw to bases further back, and then to pull back again. They took savage losses.

Modern Hurricane fighter planes were the best of the British aircraft sent to confront the Germans, but they were neither as fast nor as manoeuverable as the Messerschmitt 109. Various other, less modern British aircraft deployed in France were even more at a disadvantage when they came up against the 109 and the Messerschmitt 110 fighter-bomber, and when they had to cope with deadly German ground fire.

Of thirty-two Fairey Battle light bombers which attacked German panzers advancing through Luxembourg on the first day of the offensive, thirteen were shot down and all the others were damaged. Of seventy-one light bombers sent to wipe out the German bridgehead across the Meuse in France four days later, forty never made it back to base – and the bridgehead remained intact. A flight of six twin-engined Blenheim fighter-bombers sent to intercept a German raid near Rotterdam was pounced upon by Messerschmitt 110s and only one was able to make it safely back to England. British fighter pilots in combat in Europe gained experience very quickly, but many of them did not live long enough to put it to use. Their adventures bordered on the sacrificial. 'After just a few days of combat,' Pilot Officer David Looker recalled, 'most of us were living on our nerves.'

Pilot Officer Roland Beamont

We were scrambled from the little grass field to which we had been moved when our main base at Lille was bombed and sent south of Brussels because of reports of a German advance there. It was a lovely day – good visibility. We climbed through broken cloud to about 15,000 feet. I was flying Number Two to my flight commander, Voase Jeff. I had never been in combat before. Suddenly we saw some planes flying right to left in front of us, twenty or thirty of them – Dornier bombers. What I didn't see was that they had an escort of Messerschmitt 110s above them. We went in to attack the Dorniers. I got so excited, I opened fire well out of range. My flight commander tore me off a strip afterwards. He said he was in front of me and still out of range and there I was firing behind him and nearly hitting him.

We closed in on the Dorniers. I hit one pretty hard. While I was wondering what was happening to everybody else, I suddenly noticed some stuff coming down past me, like bright rain. It was tracer bullets. There was a Messerschmitt 110 very close, doing a very tight attack on me from above. I ducked out of that and from then on it became entirely defensive on my part. My reactions were those of a chap trained up to a point but not trained in any detail on what to do once that point was reached. I didn't know what I was doing. I hadn't the slightest idea, except I thought if I'm under fire from a fighter, the thing to do was pull that aeroplane of mine into the tightest possible turn, which I did. I got a view of that 110 diving away out of sight.

I was now very conscious of the fact that there was probably another bunch of German planes sitting up above, waiting to jump on me. I was down to very little ammunition. I was on my own in a very unhealthy situation. I finally got back to our base, after touring around France looking for it, and found we'd lost two of our twelve chaps that day.

We could expect to be outnumbered almost every time we flew. But one day, we flew a three squadron formation to patrol along the Luxembourg frontier. It was tremendous. I'd never flown with thirty-six planes before. Suddenly I saw four aeroplanes appear over the back of the formation and another four behind them. Messerschmitt 109s. That was my first experience of the total inflexibility of big formations. The 109s came in on our bottom squadron. I could see their guns firing. Two Hurricanes streamed smoke and a third went out of formation and turned away. Before anyone could do anything about it, the 109s pulled sharply up, full power, straight up into the cloud, totally out of reach. They'd beaten this mass formation of ours. We lost those three Hurricanes. One chap baled out. The other two were killed. We had a few more battles, but ten days after the Germans began their push, we were evacuated back to England. By that time we had only four Hurricanes left out of our normal complement of sixteen, which wasn't enough to carry on the flight.

In France, it suddenly dawned on you – as your colleagues disappeared one by one – that you might not last out the day. During the height of the battle over there, replacement Hurricanes were being flown in by RAF pilots from England. These were ferry pilots assigned to deliver new aircraft to us and then to be flown back in an Anson [twin-engined light transport] or something like that. But if the Anson didn't arrive and the squadron commander was hardpressed like our squadron commander was – it was Johnnie Dewar at the time – he'd say to these ferry pilots, 'You may think you're going back to England, chum, but you've had it. There's your Hurricane over there. We'll find you a billet for tonight.' They then flew with our squadron as replacements, sometimes without documentation.

Some of those poor fellows then got shot down and there was no record of their having been with us. They were just missing in action.

Flight Lieutenant Peter Brothers

I was at Biggin Hill when things were hotting up in France. We went out there a half-hour before first light, landed in France, operated there and went back for the night to Biggin Hill. The object of the exercise was to try to help stem the German advance. But the organization was so chaotic that we really were operating almost independently. We went over to Merville, refuelled – which we had to do ourselves, from cans – started our own aircraft with handles – we started each other's aircraft, left them ticking over and went down the line to the next one – and then took off and just roamed around looking for German aircraft. One of our first actions was strafing the airfield at Ypenburg near Rotterdam, which had just been captured by the Germans. When we strafed the German planes on the ground, it turned out they'd already been burnt out, apart from one I found tucked in between the corners of the hangars. I set that one afire. We discovered months later that some Dutch people had been saving it to escape to England.

Pilot Officer Birdie Bird-Wilson

Just after the German offensive began, my squadron was ordered to carry out a patrol over the Hook of Holland. Of the twelve Hurricanes that went out, we lost five – the squadron commander, Squadron Leader Tomlinson; a flight commander, Flight Lieutenant Donne; two sergeant pilots; plus Pilot Officer Halton-Harrop. I had tossed up with Halton-Harrop for the twelfth man position on that patrol. He won. He was shot down and spent the rest of the war as a prisoner of the Germans.

It was pretty bad. The wives of the men who were missing came to the mess every day to see if there was news of their husbands. But we didn't get any news. It was a lesson for the rest of us to delay marriage and to try to keep our families out of such things.

Flying Officer Christopher Foxley-Norris

I went to France with a squadron of Lysanders, an Army Co-operation squadron. We lost the lot – twelve out of twelve. Some of the men were killed and others baled out and were rescued. But we finished up over there with no aircraft.

Flight Lieutenant Sir Archibald Hope

The second or third day we were in France, for some reason all the other aircraft in our squadron were unserviceable. For two hours I patrolled our base, sitting above it in case a German raid appeared. One aircraft! What could one aircraft have possibly done if there had been a raid? Our radio facilities were extremely primitive over there. There was no radar. Quite honestly, there was no way of knowing what was going on. When we were sent up to patrol Brussels, which the Germans hadn't yet taken, we were shot at by our own troops.

Assistant Section Officer Molly Wilkinson

There were two Blenheim squadrons at Wattisham in Suffolk where I was at this time and these aircraft were sent across the Channel to provide cover for the British Expeditionary Force. Whenever the planes went out, we'd lose somebody. The losses were dreadful. Friends were being killed. The squadrons would come back and there'd be three aircraft gone. A lot of the pilots later turned out to have been captured and held as prisoners of war. But we didn't know that at the time.

It was shattering. I was nineteen years old. You can imagine what it was like to a young girl. You got very fond of these boys who weren't much older than I was. You knew they'd gone out in the morning and you waited to count the aircraft coming back. We'd go to see who might not be there. We didn't connect it to the bigger battle. We were more involved with the people than with the war. It was our own little world. The awful part was losing a friend. You'd be expecting to do something in the evening with one of your friends and he just wasn't there. He hadn't come back.

Pilot Officer Donald Stones

On one mission, our squadron of Hurricanes was ordered up to escort some Blenheims over Arras. But the Blenheims didn't appear. Our orders were then to look for German aircraft. If we didn't find any of them, we were to attack the spearhead of the German tanks coming up the Cambrai road. Finding no Blenheims or German aircraft, we had no option but to do that. We lost three aircraft to ground fire and I'm sure our .303 ammunition just bounced straight off the tanks below.

Squadron Leader Jack Satchell

I was sent to France to be Fighter Controller at Merville. I'd never controlled a bloody fighter in my life. We started up shop there. We set up an operations room in a requisitioned part of a farmhouse – with no equipment. They fixed us up with telephones all over the place. Every one of them had exactly the same ring so that when one rang you had to pick them all up to discover which was the right one. It was hopeless. It couldn't be done. Anyway, the Huns came along too quickly for us to get started. Somebody said there were some motorbikes coming up the road. It was the bloody Krauts. So we left mills bombs inside the house, primed to go off when anyone touched a telephone. Then we climbed through the loo window in the back and took to the fields.

Squadron Leader Ted Donaldson

Replacements came for the planes we lost in France and we lost them too, and more replacements came and we lost them as well. I think we must have lost dozens of planes in our squadron alone in France – burnt out, bombed or shot down. We were in an awful shape by the time we finally got pulled back to England.

Flight Lieutenant Frederick Rosier

From the Royal Air Force point of view, the battle for France was a complete and utter shambles. There was no intelligence. Communications were poor. Everything appeared to be ad hoc. Things were laid on at very short notice. The roads were crammed with refugees. I arrived there the evening of May 16th with eleven other Hurricanes. A chap came running up to me and said, 'If you have any fuel left, keep your engines running. There are forty plus coming this way.' So we kept our engines running till they started overheating. We then discovered that the RAF ground staff had left the airfield without a word to us. We'd been left completely on our own. I think the confusion was a measure of the strain they'd been under for days.

General Sir Edmund Ironside, Chief of the Imperial General Staff
Diary, 17 May

I wonder if we have told the people in the country how serious things are. It won't do to have them suddenly waking up to a disaster.

Pilot Officer Denis Wissler
Diary, 18 May

This was a bad day as we lost seven out of nine planes and four out of nine pilots, if not more. Derek Allen [who had crash landed after being shot down three days earlier] is missing again. There are rumours of a quick move [from their base in France] and if this is so, I shall lose nearly all my kit ... John Lecky was killed and Flight Lieutenant Boothby injured in a car crash. What a waste.

Sir Alexander Cadogan, Permanent Under Secretary at the Foreign Office
Diary, 19 May

News pretty bad – Germans now driving N.W. to cut through to Channel ports between us and French. French army not fighting ... We must fight on, whatever happens. I should count it a privilege to be dead if Hitler rules England. I had not thought I should have to live through such awful days.

Flying Officer Richard Gayner

Terror and exhaustion dominate my recollections of that period over France and Belgium – terror because of all the bloody Huns. There were many more of them than of us, they had better aeroplanes, they were trying to kill us, and they were better at it than we were. They liked war and most of us didn't like war at all.

I was exhausted because I was getting up at half-past three or four in the morning and flying three or four sorties a day. Communications and orders from headquarters and our wing were practically non-existent. Our job was to stop German aircraft attacking our ground forces and gain air superiority over the battlefield. We weren't even able to start that job. There weren't enough of us. The sky was swarming with Messerschmitt 109s, and we lost over a third of our pilots in twelve days' fighting.

Investigation of Psychological Disorder in Flying Personnel of Fighter Command by Air Vice Marshal Sir Charles P. Symonds and Wing Commander Denis J. Williams (both eminent neurologists), 1942

One officer told how in the Battle of France, he knew quite well when he had had enough – he was so frightened that he sweated every time he got into an aeroplane and couldn't sleep. He had to carry on as there were no reliefs. After a period of rest he did brilliant work, gaining the DFC [Distinguished Flying Cross] and bar and since he was interviewed has won the DSO [Distinguished Service Order].

* * *

As Royal Air Force losses in Europe mounted, with no effect on the relentless German advance, it became an increasingly anguished concern for Air Chief Marshal Sir Hugh Dowding, Air Officer Commanding-in-Chief, RAF Fighter Command. Having carefully monitored enemy air activity in the war, Dowding was certain the Germans were aiming to seize air supremacy over England, as they had elsewhere, when the time came. He was further convinced that if the Germans managed to succeed in that endeavour, Britain was doomed to defeat. He warned that the defence of Britain could not be properly maintained if his fighter squadrons were squandered in Europe in a struggle which increasingly appeared lost. He insisted he needed fifty-two fighter squadrons at home – he had been promised that many by the Air Ministry – to fight off massive German air attacks which he knew were in the offing. But within days of the launching of the German offensive on the continent, Dowding was faced with the fact that Fighter Command was far under strength, so many of his planes having been sent to the slaughter in Europe, and still more apparently destined for the same fate.

A dour, stiff, humourless man, Dowding, appropriately nick-named 'Stuffy' and known by all his colleagues to be overdue for retirement, had become a nuisance to the British War Cabinet and Chiefs of Staff. He was undisguisedly outraged when his squadrons were taken from him and dispatched to France and Belgium. He warned that Britain was leaving itself defenceless by sending off his precious fighter planes and his even more precious pilots, so many of whom had already fallen in combat.

Dowding was not alone among British war leaders in recognizing the need to keep home air defences strong. He was not alone in realizing the implications for Britain of the ferocity of the German air and airborne attacks on France, Belgium and The Netherlands. But the War Cabinet was mesmerized by the sudden irrepressible cascade of German forces across Europe and by the terrifying prospect of catastrophe – of actually losing the entire British Expeditionary Force! British leaders responded with almost reflexive acquiescence to plans for each desperate 'supreme effort' to save the BEF and keep France from collapse – and that meant more air power at the front, more fighters sent forward across the Channel, and more anguished warnings from Dowding that doom was around the corner. The situation in France had become so desperate so quickly that pleas from the front for help to relieve pressure on the bulk of the British Army there would, in any case, not have been easy to resist by the Chiefs of Staff. So much was at stake and so much was happening that a decision to cut and run barely got a hearing.

General Sir Frederick Pile, Commanding General, Anti-Aircraft

The rest of us were so engrossed in the drama of the retreating British army, of the heroic defence of Calais, and of the slender hope there seemed to be of getting anyone back, that the future in which an invasion of this country was likely hardly worried us ... [But] Dowding had only one thought – how he could retain sufficient fighter squadrons and anti-aircraft guns to fight the battle which he so clearly foresaw was inevitable.

Air Marshal Sir Victor Goddard, Deputy Director of Air Intelligence during the Battle of Britain

Dowding's concern was not to win battles in France but to be able to ensure, at all costs elsewhere, the integrity and efficiency of the air defence of Great Britain. It was to provide that deterrent and safeguard that his Fighter Command had been created, and for which he had long trained it, equipped it and was still perfecting it.

* * *

Churchill was particularly receptive to the frantic insistence of the disintegrating French government that one big Allied push could be organized to stop the Germans, throw them back and save the BEF. Churchill's personality had never been geared to sanctioning despair or retreat, certainly not within a few days of taking office. Though the push the French feverishly conjured up in their plans required the dispatch of still more British fighter squadrons to France, he was prepared to go along. Foreseeing the loss of those squadrons as well, and with them the chance to save Britain from disaster, Dowding composed a letter to the Air Ministry in London, putting on record in unmistakeable detail the perils of the situation and the possible consequences. By that act, he may have determined the outcome of the Battle of Britain:

Sir,

I have the honour to refer to the very serious calls which have recently been made upon the Home Defence Fighter Units in an attempt to stem the German invasion of the Continent.

2. I hope and believe that our Armies may yet be victorious in France and Belgium, but we have to face the possibility that they may be defeated.

3. In this case I presume there is no one who will deny that England should fight on, even though the remainder of the Continent of Europe is dominated by the Germans.

4. For this purpose it is necessary to retain some minimum fighter strength in this country and I must request that the Air Council will inform me what they consider this minimum strength to be, in order that I may take my dispositions accordingly.

5. I would remind the Air Council that the last estimate which they made as to the force necessary to defend this country was 52 Squadrons, and my strength has now been reduced to the equivalent of 36 Squadrons.

6. Once a decision has been reached as to the limit on which the Air Council and the Cabinet are prepared to stake the existence of the country, it should be made clear to the Allied Commanders on the Continent that not a single aeroplane from Fighter Command beyond the limit will be sent across the Channel, no matter how desperate the situation may become.

7. It will, of course, be remembered that the estimate of 52 Squadrons was based on the assumption that the attack would come from the eastwards except in so far as the defences might be outflanked in flight. We have now to face the possibility that attacks may come from Spain or even from the north coast of France. The result is that our line is very much extended at the same time as our resources are reduced.

8. I must point out that within the last few days the equivalent of 10 Squadrons have been sent to France, that Hurricane Squadrons

remaining in this country are seriously depleted, and that the more squadrons which are sent to France the higher will be the wastage and the more insistent the demand for reinforcements.

9. I must therefore request that as a matter of paramount urgency, the Air Ministry will consider and decide what level of strength is to be left to Fighter Command for the defence of this country, and will assure me that when this level has been reached, not one fighter will be sent across the Channel however urgent and insistent the appeals for help may be.

10. I believe that, if an adequate fighter force is kept in the country, if the fleet remains in being, and if Home Forces are suitably organised to resist invasion, we should be able to carry on the war single-handed for some time, if not indefinitely. But, if the Home Defence Force is drained away in desperate attempts to remedy the situation in France, defeat in France will involve the final, complete and irremediable defeat of this country.

> H. C. T. Dowding
> Air Chief Marshal
> Air Officer Commanding-in-Chief
> Fighter Command, Royal Air Force

Despite the mesmerizing impact of the catastrophe closing in across the Channel, the danger to Britain if fighter planes continued to be consigned to the bottomless pit over there was finally grasped. After Dowding's letter was circulated in the Air Ministry, among the Chiefs of Staff and in the War Cabinet, Churchill regretfully ruled that 'no more squadrons of fighters will leave the country whatever the need of France', though they would be employed to cover an evacuation of the BEF from France if such an evacuation became necessary – and possible. At the same time, serious thought was being given by the British Cabinet and Chiefs of Staff to the even greater peril facing the country.

Cabinet Paper – Secret

1. In view of the imminent danger of invasion of this country, the Chiefs of Staff Committee have suggested that steps should be taken at once to warn and to rouse the public.

2. Although the mass of the people are not wholly aware of the danger, the idea is beginning to take shape to the public mind. People now want to be *told* how to prepare themselves for the emergency.

The time for exhortation is passing. There is no longer need to persuade people to volunteer for service; they want to be told what to do and where they should offer themselves for service in the national cause.

3. At the moment, however, public feeling about a possible invasion cannot be dissociated from the news of the withdrawal of the BEF from Northern France. Up to the time that this news comes out, we can only prepare the ground, but as soon as the news is announced, the nation should be immediately roused to the danger of invasion and to the need of resistance.

General Sir Hastings Ismay, Secretary to the War Cabinet

Prime Minister,

It has hitherto been thought that a seaborne invasion of this country was an enterprise which the Germans could not hope to launch with any prospect of success for some considerable time. Moreover it has been assumed that the sequence of events would be first a sustained attack to destroy our air force, then an airborne invasion to seize a port, after which the seaborne invasion would take place. Hence our Home Defence preparations at the present time are mainly directed towards dealing with the problems of parachute troops and with the protection of the ports from the landward side. I think the events of the last few days and the grim possibilities of the next must cause us to modify our views.

In view of past experience in Norway, Holland and France, it can be taken for granted that the Germans have the plan for the invasion of this country worked out to the last detail, and have provided all necessary special equipment, such as motor landing craft, &c ... We can be sure that Hitler would be prepared to sacrifice ninety percent of the whole expedition if he could gain a firm bridgehead on British soil with the remaining ten percent. The German numerical superiority in the air is still very formidable. By using a mass of bombers escorted by strong forces of fighters, the Germans might calculate on maintaining a local air superiority sufficient for the launching of a seaborne expedition very early in their campaign against us. Besides landing troops from the air to seize a port, they might make their landings on the open beach with forces which included tanks and artillery.

Recent events have shown the terrible results which can be achieved by armoured forces operating through a country which has not been prepared to oppose them ... No real progress can be made [to build defences] unless the powers over persons and property which it is intended that the Government should assume in a grave emergency are taken at once. Otherwise, the military authorities will be hampered in the preparation of defences, the making of obstacles, &c, by having to go through the normal procedure of acquisition and compensation ... I feel very strongly that the grave emergency is already upon us. I suggest ... that full powers should be given forthwith to the military authorities to enable them to carry out defensive measures of all kinds without reference to any other authority and without hampering forms of procedure ...

Edward R. Murrow, CBS Radio News

London, 21 May – During most of the winter and spring, this seemed an almost casual war as viewed from London. The British exhausted their vocabulary of condemnation, asserted that right was on their side, and seemed to feel that Germany could be strangled at long range without too much trouble. All that has changed. The change doesn't show itself in hysteria or patriotic outbursts. In fact, it would be hard to put into words this change that has taken place. To me it seems that this country is younger than it was ten days ago. There is more bitterness not only against the Germans, but against the men in this country who failed to realize the nature of the German threat, who failed to prepare to meet it, those who failed to drive the aircraft production at top speed in the days following Munich, those who starved the British Secret Service for funds. There is no more talk of peace aims, only talk of holding on, avoiding defeat, and then trying for victory.

* * *

As plans to prepare for the expected invasion attempt by the Germans began to unfold, steps were taken to call back what remained of the RAF squadrons in France, to save them from further destruction and to bolster the country's home defences. Some flew back from base to base through France, until they hopped over the Channel and were finally home. Others scrambled homeward just in time as advancing German ground forces neared.

Flying Officer Peter Matthews

The Germans were just ten miles north of us when we got airborne to fly home. We took back all the planes we could. We put our French interpreter in a plane and he flew it back. One or two Czechs and Poles who were there said they could fly so we stuck them in planes too and pushed them off towards England. They mostly got there. We destroyed the planes we couldn't take along.

Pilot Officer Roland Beamont

When we were out of France, I found myself in a DC2 of KLM being evacuated. We had eight pilots left but only four planes. The squadron commander spun a coin and I was among the losers and was told to get into the DC2 for the flight home. I didn't think much of that because I wondered if that airliner would be able to get out of France without being shot down. Most of the chaps with me in the plane had been wounded, some badly. I was in dirty flying overalls. I'd left all my kit behind. I sat there looking out of the window for enemy fighters as we flew home. We knew the Germans would be coming after us to England and that it would be our job to stop them.

* * *

The cold, cruel facts of their losses in combat and their undignified scramble homeward were bad enough. But the British experienced situations and circumstances in their retreat through France which compounded their anguish. The seemingly indiscriminate terror tactics which were part of the German blitzkrieg strategy gave war, and the threat to Britain, a far more terrifying aspect than any of the young pilots had ever imagined it would contain.

Pilot Officer Dennis David

I saw refugees walking down streets with prams full of their belongings. And I saw the Germans strafing them. It was hideous. The Germans would strafe the roads full of refugees on purpose to cause congestion. Their tanks would then scoot around it. It stopped our troops from coming forward to meet them. It was a carefully organized plan, brilliant in concept. It was something we weren't used to. It put a new dimension into war. They bombed helpless people and used the shambles to move their forces forward. We knew it could happen in Britain.

Once, six of us ran into forty Ju 87s dive-bombing a stream of refugees. We shot down fourteen of them and broke up that raid. As we were going back to our base, another 150 German aircraft came in, but we were out of ammunition. It was hopeless.

Flight Lieutenant Gerry Edge

People were pushing wheelbarrows. Horses were pulling carts. There were trucks loaded with stuff and carrying children. And there was a Stuka above them with its rear gunner machine-gunning those refugees. Just hosing them down. That was the only time I remember deliberately firing at somebody rather than at an object.

I thought it might be a trap for me. I looked around carefully and closed in quickly, ready to break if someone got on my tail. I was not far behind that Stuka when he saw me and started to swing his guns around. I pressed the trigger and he went straight down in flames. I felt a savage delight in killing the two bastards in that plane who'd been murdering the refugees.

P. J. Philip, New York Times

About the effects of these bombing raids on the nerves, no soldier or civilian who has ever suffered one has any doubt. They are hellish. Every soldier agrees that shelling and machine-gunning, as they were done in [the First World War], had nothing of the terror of these 300-mile-an-hour dives to a height of about 200 feet and the scream and pound, pound, pound of the bombs that are neatly released by a little automatic switch.

* * *

The British were also often outraged, and profoundly disappointed, by the performance of their Allies. Despite the pre-war swagger of the French, and though French troops fought heroically in some places, France was woefully unprepared for modern combat and their military forces were led with breathtaking incompetence. The rapid pace of the collapse of the French on their home ground was astounding and even obscene to young Englishmen who had no doubt that they and their countrymen would fight like demons for every inch of British soil. As they fell back in retreat across northern France, many were also appalled by the treatment they received at the hands of many French people.

Squadron Leader Jack Satchell

People have said the French peasants were very good to the British when we were being forced out of France. My experience was: like hell they were! After getting out of Merville as the Germans were coming in, I had to walk to Boulogne, about forty miles – hiding during the day. We were about one field in from the road along which the German armoured divisions were travelling. Ask the French peasants for food and they'd send a boy on a pushbike to fetch the nearest Hun. I pinched things out of the field to eat. Once I knocked off a chicken from somebody's farmyard. We had to eat it raw. We found it was better eaten warm than when it got cold. Pretty revolting either way.

Pilot Officer Roland Beamont

We thought if we're going to rely on the French, God help us. We didn't see any French fighter planes once the battle began. They may have been fighting their arses off further down the line, but we didn't see them.

Pilot Officer Pat Hancock

I was scared because of the way the Germans had crashed through the 'invulnerable' French army. When we pulled out of France, we finally ended up in Nantes, near St Nazaire. Four of our squadrons ended up there. The local French colonel, in charge of ground defences of the field, seriously suggested that we should surrender to him, to be handed over to the Germans when Paris fell. It was appalling. We had gone off the French to such a degree at that stage that our main feeling on leaving France was total gratitude that we'd left the damned place and the perfidious French. We were fighting the Germans, but they were the enemy. The French were a different matter.

* * *

When the air cleared sufficiently for a reckoning to be made and calculations to register, it was finally realized how serious British air losses in Europe had been. The Royal Air Force had lost 320 of its most experienced pilots, killed in combat. More than one hundred others were prisoners of the Germans. Many of the aircrew of British bombers were also killed or captured. The RAF had lost almost one thousand aircraft, including 386 Hurricanes, many of which had been destroyed on the ground either in German air attacks or to keep them from falling into German hands. That was one-quarter the number of Fighter Command's modern aircraft, the planes Dowding had been counting on to fight off the expected German bid for mastery of the English skies. They had been lost with nothing to show for it. Nor could Fighter Command yet begin the process of recuperating, regrouping and recovering.

On 20 May, German forces reached the English Channel near the town of Abbeville in Picardy in northern France to lock virtually the entire British Expeditionary Force and the remains of three French armies against a small stretch of Channel coast. Spirited rearguard action kept them from immediately springing their trap, but they relentlessly forced the battered Allied troops back on the city of Dunkirk. By nightfall four days later, the Germans were fifteen miles from the city and within sight of their most spectacular victory so far. In London, Churchill warned Parliament to brace itself for 'hard and heavy tidings'. But before the German forces could move in to extract an ignominious surrender from the Allied armies, Hitler, who had been growing nervous and superstitious because of the remarkable success of his forces, ordered his generals, to their astonishment and fury, to halt their advance.

Whether Hitler believed he was pushing his luck too far in trying to take almost the entire British army out of the war just a few weeks after launching his offensive, or whether he was convinced that Reichsmarshal Hermann Göring's Luftwaffe could better be relied upon to batter the British into submission on the beaches, the panzers which had spearheaded the blitzkrieg were stopped in their tracks for a full three days.

For the British, who were becoming increasingly reconciled to the possibility of having to leave virtually all of their men on the beaches at Dunkirk, it was a totally unexpected and much welcomed reprieve. They quickly patched together a strong perimeter defence around their positions to slow the German advance when it got moving again and organized the most massive evacuation in history. Over a period of ten days, a flotilla of large and small vessels – destroyers and tugs, minesweepers and ferries, corvettes and yachts, trawlers and motor boats – ferried back and forth across the Channel, lifting men from the beaches and carrying them home to England while the German ground forces, trying to resume their forward momentum after their unwanted respite, battered away at them, and the Luftwaffe, bombing and strafing, sought to do the job Hitler's armoured divisions would have been able to accomplish had they not been held back. Instead of the 35,000 troops the British War Cabinet hoped to be able to evacuate from France when the realities of the situation had become starkly clear, 225,000 British troops were brought back to England.

A. D. Divine

The picture will always remain sharp-etched in my memory – the lines of men wearily and sleepily staggering across the beach from the dunes to the shallows, falling into little boats; great columns of men thrust out into the water among bomb and shell splashes. The foremost ranks were shoulder deep, moving forward under the command of young subalterns, themselves with their heads just above the little waves that rode in to the sand. As the front ranks were dragged aboard the boats, the rear ranks moved up, from ankle deep to knee deep, from knee deep to waist deep, until they, too, came to shoulder depth and their turn.

Some of the big boats pushed in until they were almost aground, taking appalling risks with the falling tide. The men thankfully scrambled up the sides on rope nets, or climbed the hundreds of ladders, made God knows where out of new, raw wood and hurried aboard the ships in England.

The little boats that ferried from the beach to the big ships in deep water listed drunkenly with the weight of men. The big ships slowly took on lists of their own with the enormous numbers crowded aboard. And always down the dunes and across the beach came new hordes of men, new columns, new lines.

On the beach was the skeleton of a destroyer, bombed and burnt. At the water's edge were ambulances, abandoned when their last load had been discharged.

There was always the red background, the red of Dunkirk burning. There was no water to check the fires and there were no men to be spared to fight them. Red, too, were the shell bursts, the flash of guns, the fountains of tracer bullets.

The din was infernal. The batteries shelled ceaselessly and brilliantly. To the whistle of shells overhead was added the scream of falling bombs. Even the sky was full of noise – anti-aircraft shells, machine-gun fire, the snarl of falling planes, the angry hornet noise of dive bombers. One could not speak normally at any time against the roar of it and the noise of our own engines. We all developed 'Dunkirk throat', a sore hoarseness that was a hallmark of those who had been there.

Sub-Lieutenant John Crosby, on the minesweeper Oriole

Everybody went aft to raise the bows as much as possible, and we went lickity-split for the shore and kept her full ahead until we jarred and came to a full stop. As we went in, we dropped two seven-hundredweight anchors from the stern, to kedge off with. The men waded and swam out and many of them had to be hauled over the rails. The snag was that when a rope was thrown to a man, about six grabbed it and just hung on looking up blankly with the water breaking over their shoulders, and it was a hell of a job getting any of them to let go so that the rest could get pulled aboard.

Allan Barrell, Master of the coastal pleasure boat Shamrock

We stared and stared at what looked like thousands of sticks on the beach and were amazed to see them turn into moving masses of humanity. I thought quickly of going in, picking up seventy to eighty and clearing off. With the sun behind me I calculated I should find some east coast town. We got our freight . . . when I realized it would be selfish to clear off when several destroyers and large vessels were waiting in deep water to be fed by small craft, so I decided what our job was to be. We could seat sixty men and with those standing we had about eighty weary and starving British troops, some without boots, some only in their pants, but enough life left in them to clamber on board the destroyers with the kind hand of every available seaman. Again and again we brought our cargo to this ship until she was full.

Navigation was extremely difficult owing to the various wreckage, up-turned boats, floating torpedoes, and soldiers in the water trying to be sailors for the first time. They paddled their collapsible little boats out to me with the butts of their rifles, and many shouted that they were sinking. We could not help them. I was inshore as close as I dared. 'Stop shouting and save your breath, and bail out with your steel helmets,' was the only command suitable for the occasion. Scores offered me cash and personal belongings which I refused, saying, 'My name is Barrell, Canvey Island. Send me a postcard if you get home all right.'

*　*　*

Flying from bases in southeastern England, British fighter planes covered the Dunkirk evacuation – outnumbered, as they had been earlier in France and Belgium, but with a sense of purpose the earlier confusion had done so much to undermine. On the first day of the operation, the Air Ministry in London instructed Fighter Command to, 'ensure the protection of Dunkirk beaches ... from first light until darkness by continuous fighter patrols in strength'. It was asking a lot, but Dowding did in fact hope to maintain continuous protective patrols over the evacuation area during daylight hours to deny the Luftwaffe a free field of fire over the men on the beaches. However, RAF losses earlier, the exhaustion of many of the pilots just back from France and his determination to maintain unimpaired reserves for the defence of Britain should the worst happen meant there were times when only a single squadron was in the skies near Dunkirk to take on and try to disperse the German attackers, and there were often intervals between patrols when there was no protective screen at all.

But the view of the men on the beaches that the 'Brylcreem boys' of the RAF had let them down (there were later incidents in which soldiers saved from Dunkirk and brought back to England beat up airmen they came across in pubs because of it) was misconceived. No doubt aerial protection for the troops would have been more thorough had Dowding been able and willing to spare more of his diminished number of fighter planes for Dunkirk patrols. But the men on the ground had no idea what was happening in the skies over and near Dunkirk, or why the German bombers were able to get through to bomb them, or why Fighter Command often seemed to be nowhere in evidence.

Sergeant Bernard Jennings

What we tried to do was intercept the Germans inland, before they could get to the beaches. That's why the soldiers thought we let them down. We didn't. It was no use flying over the beaches at Dunkirk. By that time, the Germans would have been there to drop their bombs on the men below.

Pilot Officer Steve Stephen

Our function was to get in the way of the German aircraft. It was no good patrolling over the evacuation beach if you were hoping to save the people underneath you. You had to be twenty miles further off to get in the way of the attackers before they reached the beaches. One of the first planes I shot down was, I think, a Henschel 126, used by the Germans for reconnaissance near Dunkirk. He was spying out the defences our army set up, to radio back his news to the panzers on the ground so they could move in. We caught up with this German around seven in the morning just behind Calais airport. There were three of us. I was the junior pilot. We saw him and went down to see what he was about. The first of us went screaming in and overshot him. Number two hit him with a cloud of bullets. It was then easy for me to go in to finish him off and he just went up in flames. It wasn't a pleasant sight to see but our squadron lost nine or ten pilots in the Dunkirk operation.

* * *

Despite the hard feelings of the men on the beaches, the damage the Luftwaffe was able to inflict on them during the evacuation was substantially limited by RAF squadrons shuttling back and forth across the Channel to take on the enemy. By that time, the German air force, pushed hard by the tactical demands of Hitler's generals, was also badly in need of a respite. But its planes were flying from captured fields in northern France, Belgium and the Netherlands, close to their targets on the beaches.

As was the case earlier in France, many of the British pilots were getting their first taste of combat. But had they not been there, the beaches of Dunkirk would be remembered as places of slaughter, rather than for the most monumental evacuation of military forces ever to have taken place.

Pilot Officer Steve Stephen

When Dunkirk started, we thought all air fighting would be below 10,000 feet. The first time we went over, we went over at 1,000-

8,000 feet. But we got attacked from above by German fighters. We looked up and there they were. They came down at us and we got beaten up. The following day, our squadron leader said, 'We got jumped yesterday. We're not going to put up with that again. We're going in at 12,000.' So we went in at 12,000 and met some Germans at 12,000 and got into a bit of a fracas. When we talked about it when we got back to base, we said, 'You know, it's odd. Twelve thousand was only just high enough.' So the following day, we went in at 14,000. By the end of the week, air fighting had gone from 7,000 feet to over 20,000 – in just seven days. The Germans did this and we did that. We did that and the Germans did this. Air fighting moved from a low level right up, high into the sky.

Sergeant Jim Hallowes

We had no idea how big would be the German formations we were going to meet over Dunkirk. The first one we came up against was eighty to a hundred 109s. We just got stuck in, compared notes later and wondered how the devil our small formation got away with attacking so many of the enemy.

Pilot Officer Peter Brown

All of a sudden the sky was full of aircraft with black crosses on them. It was frightening. I realized for the first time that there was somebody up there really trying to kill me. It was a moment of truth. It was the first time we'd come up against the enemy. I had a tough time with one of those 109s. I dived away and went through the smoke coming up from below. When I came through on the other side, he'd gone. I'd also lost the rest of my squadron by then. I climbed up again. I climbed up to about 15,000 feet on my own which was really a stupid thing to do. It was asking for trouble. But I had to do it. It was a personal act. I was proving something to myself. I stayed up there for ten or fifteen minutes by which time I was getting short of fuel so I flew back to England. When I landed, I counted twenty-nine bullet holes in my plane.

Flight Lieutenant Brian Kingcome

It was funny weather over Dunkirk. A lot of the time there you saw nothing but aircraft because you were sandwiched between layers of cloud. An aircraft would suddenly appear and disappear. When there were breaks in the cloud or you were below it, you'd see this great stretch of sand. You saw thousands of troops on it, marshalled and waiting to be taken off. You saw a flotilla of small boats coming in and out.

The evacuation of Dunkirk seemed inevitable. We were being thrown out of France. We'd made a mistake. We weren't ready. The Maginot Line had collapsed. The military plans had gone awry. We hadn't been prepared for the war.

It was very busy over Dunkirk. You didn't have time to follow up an attack. You fired at something which disappeared, perhaps with some smoke coming out of it, into a cloud layer below you. But you knew when you'd hit a Heinkel because instead of pointing at you, the rear gunner's gun suddenly went vertical. He had fallen over it.

You weren't long over Dunkirk. The average flight was an hour and a quarter. By the time your squadron had taken off, rendez-voused with another squadron and flown over, you had maybe ten or fifteen minutes of fighting time before you had to hightail it home again. When you got back to base, you refuelled and stood by to be sent off again. We were over two or three times a day during that period.

At one stage, Fighter Command thought the Defiant was the answer to the Messerschmitt 109. It had a turret in the back with four · 303 machine guns. It was quite lethal if you got in the way of it. They sent a Defiant squadron out over Dunkirk. When the Me 109s saw them, they thought they were Hurricanes and attacked them from the rear. The Defiants blew the 109s right out of the sky. When they came back, Fighter Command was delighted and sent the Defiants back. On the second trip, the 109s had learnt their lesson. They came up from underneath and the Defiants, which couldn't fire down-wards, were blown out of the sky.

Pilot Officer Wally Wallens

The thousands of troops on the beaches were a fantastic sight. It seemed a colossally unco-ordinated operation which I suppose it was at first. The blokes were hiding in the sand dunes from the German bombs. A lot were lying dead on the beach or floating in the water.

When we went back, before a relief squadron could take over from us, that's when the German bombers would move in. The Jerries were listening to our radio talk. We finally realized what was going on. So we pre-arranged a simulated return to base with the controller at Dover. We said over the radio that we were returning early for various reasons and he said he'd try to get a relief squadron in as soon as possible. It was a set-up. We'd been running our planes on a very lean mixture, conserving our petrol. We swept inland instead of back out to sea. Thinking we'd gone, the Jerries came roaring in. They believed another squadron wasn't likely to arrive for fifteen minutes or so. But we came right back and gave them a hell of a clattering. That was a good day's work.

Pilot Officer David Crook

Everybody's idea was to go all out for the first Hun that appeared. This policy does not pay when you are fighting a cunning and crafty foe. The Germans frequently used to send over a decoy aircraft with a number of fighters hovering in the sun some thousands of feet above, who would come down like a ton of bricks on anybody attacking the decoy. This ruse almost certainly accounted for one pilot, Presser [Flight Lieutenant 'Presser' Persse-Joynt], and possible one or two others – the last anybody saw of Presser was when he was diving down to attack a Junkers 88, and there were definitely some Messerschmitts above.

Flight Lieutenant R. D. G. Wight
Letter to his Mother during the Dunkirk operation

Well another day is gone, and with it a lot of grand blokes. Got another brace of 109s today but the whole Luftwaffe seems to leap on us – we are hopelessly outnumbered. I was caught napping by a 109 in the middle of a dogfight and got a couple of holes in the aircraft, one of them filled the office with smoke, but the Jerry overshot and *he's* dead. If anyone says anything to you in the future about the inefficiency of the RAF – I believe the BEF troops were booing the RAF in Dover the other day – tell them from me we only wish we could do more. But without aircraft we can do no more than we have done – that is, our best, and that's fifty times better than the German best, though they are fighting under the most advantageous conditions. I know of no RAF pilot who has refused combat yet – and that sometimes means combat with odds of more than fifty to one. Three of us the other day had been having a fight and were practically out of ammunition and juice when we saw more than eighty 109s with twelve Ju 87s. All the same, we gave them combat, so much so that they left us alone in the end – on their side of the Channel too. This is just the work that we all do. One of my sergeants shot down three fighters and a bomber before they got him – and then he got back in a paddle steamer. So don't worry. We are going to win this war even if we have only one aeroplane and one pilot left. The Boche could produce the whole Luftwaffe and you would see the one pilot and the one aeroplane go into combat . . . The spirit of the average pilot has to be seen to be believed.

Flight Lieutenant Wight was killed in action leading three Hurricanes against sixty Messerschmitt 110s at the height of the Battle of Britain two months later.

Squadron Leader Ted Donaldson
Combat Report, 29 May

Whilst carrying out high escort duties at 21,000 feet sighted five Me 110s in formation flying east towards Dunkirk (escort for some bombers being dealt with by another unit). Ordered attack and chose left-hand fighter. Dived down at 45° on to rear gun and fired 10 sec. burst ending astern. No visible effect. Broke away sharply left and climbed to cover green section. Something went wrong with 56 Squadron. They went off in a different direction (I believe oxygen failed in leader's aircraft) and found myself alone with 4 Me 110s. I fought for about five minutes as hard I knew. Me 110 out-climbed and out-turned my Hurricane at that height (18,000–24,000 feet). Eventually one Me came up either side and above me and two stayed on my tail. There were no clouds whatsoever in the sky. I threw my aircraft all over the place and got in several bursts (inaccurately). There was no way out so I turned onto my back and allowed engine to stop with black smoke pouring out of the exhausts and petrol, glycol etc. pouring out of the vents. Then I pulled the stick back and dived 23,000 feet to the sea. The Me thought I was hit and fortunately did not follow. The belly of the Hurricane split but no other damage. Landed with five galls. of petrol left.

Flying Officer Barrie Heath

We went in pretty high – something like 25,000 feet. Smoke was going right up into the sky from the oil tanks burning down below. There were a lot of bombs going down on the beach and on the mass of men and ships down there. It was an awesome sight. Up in the sky, the Germans tried to shoot our tails off and we tried to shoot theirs. We patrolled up and down in open formation. At one point I moved off to bring back one of our men, Sergeant Sadler, the right-hand man of the back section of the squadron, who'd got a bit lost in a turn. He must have been looking the other way when the squadron turned left. I went out to shepherd him back into the formation. I couldn't contact him on the R/T because we were supposed to be on radio silence. One of the chaps told me that when I went off after him a 110 took my place in that formation almost immediately. If I hadn't turned off, I guess he would have shot my backside off. After that, it was all fighting. I dived down with one or two others on a big formation of Stukas, shot one chap up and was so excited I kept on firing my guns till I ran out of ammunition. There was no point in hanging around after that. I dived down and beetled off at low height for home.

They sent us off again in the afternoon. It was all very exciting and a bit unnerving. It was our baptism of fire. We'd been pretty well trained, but Dunkirk seemed a long way from home and it was a bit shaking to see the British being booted out of Europe.

Flying Officer John Bisdee

The Spitfire hadn't got back armour for the pilot at the time. Some of our pilots were probably shot dead whereas they might have been untouched or only wounded if the armour, which was then put in, had been there. Every day, a few less of our men came back from over Dunkirk. We didn't know the final count for a while because when a man didn't return, lots of things might have happened to him. He might have got shot down and taken prisoner. He might have got shot down and landed on the beaches or in the sea and might be coming back with the troops. He might have gone down in the sea – one of our pilots, Sergeant Bennett, did precisely that – and been picked up by a ship that didn't immediately report the fact. He could have got to one of our advance aerodomes, like Manston. It wasn't till the end of the Dunkirk thing that somebody did the sums and we realized how many people we'd lost.

Flight Lieutenant Bob Stanford-Tuck

We started over Dunkirk with very bad tactics. We were flying over the beaches in formations which were much too tight. Manoeuvering was cumbersome. You had to concentrate on keeping position in the formation. You couldn't look around. The Germans were flying much looser formations. They bounced us in our very first encounter over Dunkirk. We lost a pilot – a young fellow called Pat Learmond. He went down in flames. The next patrol that same day we lost our squadron leader, a flight commander and one or two others. The squadron leader was Roger Bushell, who crash landed, was captured and then was shot four years later by the Gestapo when he organized the Great Escape from Stalagluft 3. I found myself squadron commander. I said to myself and all the boys, 'This is enough. Tomorrow we're flying open formation, in pairs.' But in two days of fighting, the squadron lost five pilots and five Spitfires, too, which was as dicey as losing pilots because we were starting to run short of planes.

Squadron Leader James Leathart

While we were covering the Dunkirk evacuation, I saw a Spitfire that had been hit. White glycol was streaming from behind it. I knew it would never get back across the Channel to England. I watched it go down and saw it land at Calais Marck, a small airfield outside Calais.

When I got back to England, I learned that Squadron Leader Drogo White was missing over France and realized it was his Spitfire I had seen go down. White was CO of 74 Squadron which was based at Hornchurch, as was 54 Squadron, which I commanded. We were the only squadron which had a new Miles Master trainer. It was a wooden two-seater resembling a Spitfire or Hurricane in that it had a Rolls-Royce engine and a fairly high performance.

I went to the Hornchurch station commander and said, 'I saw Drogo White go down at Calais Marck.' I asked him if I could take along my two flight commanders – Al Deere and Johnny Allen – to escort me in their Spitfires while I tried to pick up White in the Miles Master and bring him back. The station master said OK and off we went.

We got to Calais Marck and I landed there but White was nowhere in sight. I thought he'd pop out of somewhere, but he didn't so I took off again. When I got to about 1,000 feet, I heard Al Deere shout, 'Messerschmitts!' At that moment, I saw tracers go right past me. Al Deere and Johnny Allen went after the Messerschmitts, but I'd had a hell of a fright and instead of heading home, as Al and Johnny did when they'd used up all their ammunition and were low on fuel, I landed at Calais Marck again and switched off.

By that time, a real battle had broken out above between other Messerschmitts and Spitfires. I was afraid one of the Germans would come down and shoot up my aircraft and me as well. I ran to a ditch, jumped in and damn near landed on top of the missing Drogo White. He said, 'What the devil are you doing here?' He hadn't seen me when I'd landed the first time. He'd been hiding from the German army. There was a main road at the side of the airfield and German tanks and motorcycles and things were roaring along it. How the hell they didn't see my bright orange aircraft on the ground, I'll never know. We were stuck in that ditch for a half-hour or so, watching the battle going on above us and watching aircraft coming down in flames, including some of ours.

When things calmed down a bit, we thought we'd try to make our getaway. It wasn't easy. We didn't have an electric starter for the aircraft, as they did back at Hornchurch. We had to use cranks which were stored in the aircraft. We had a handle each and were cranking away, with the Germans going by on the road at the side of the field. We cranked and cranked, eventually got it started, both jumped in, took off and flew back across the Channel. We headed back home at about six feet over the water.

Edward R. Murrow, CBS Radio News

London, 2 June – Yesterday I spent several hours at what may be tonight or next week Britain's first line of defence, an airfield on the southeast coast ... I talked with pilots as they came back from Dunkirk. They stripped off their light jackets, glanced at a few bullet holes in wings or fuselage, and as the ground crews swarmed over the aircraft, refuelling motors and guns, we sat on the ground and talked. Out in the middle of the field, the wreckage of a plane was being cleared up. It had crashed the night before. The pilot had been shot in the head but managed to get back to his field ...

I can tell you what those boys told me. They were the cream of the youth of Britain. As we sat there, they were waiting to take off again. They talked of their own work; discussed the German air force with the casualness of Sunday morning halfbacks discussing yesterday's football. There were no nerves, no profanity, and no heroics. There was no swagger about those boys in wrinkled and stained uniforms. The movies do that sort of thing much more dramatically than it is in real life ...

When the squadron took off, one of them remarked quite casually that he'd be back in time for tea. About that time, a boy of twenty drove up in a station wagon. He weighed about one hundred and fifteen pounds. He asked the squadron leader if he could have someone fly him back to his own field. His voice was loud and flat; his uniform was torn, had obviously been wet. He wore a pair of brown tennis shoes, three sizes too big. After he'd gone, I asked one of the men ... what was the matter with him. 'Oh,' he replied, 'he was shot down over at Dunkirk on the first patrol this morning. Landed in the sea, swam to the beach, was bombed for a couple of hours, came home in a paddle steamer. His voice sounds like that because he can't hear himself. You get that way after you've been bombed a few hours.'

* * *

During the Dunkirk operation, the RAF lost eighty pilots and one hundred aircraft, including Spitfires. Dowding had earlier refused to send his most advanced fighting planes over France for fear that one of them might be captured intact by the Germans. Spitfire pilots were, therefore, ordered to patrol only over the sea at Dunkirk, but some pilots, caught up in the heat of battle, went in hot pursuit over land.

The severe RAF losses in the operation were another serious blow to British defences. But it was claimed that, at the same time, 262 German aircraft were shot down by British fighters near or over Dunkirk, more than two for every British plane lost. German records later showed that, in reality, only about half the numbers claimed by RAF pilots were brought down. But for the first time, Fighter Command was believed by the British, and believed itself, capable of facing the Luftwaffe and giving better than it received.

It was a sorely needed morale booster, though dwarfed at the time by the almost delirious relief that most of the British troops had been lifted from the beaches of Dunkirk and brought home, instead of the comparative few the Chiefs of Staff in London had dared to hope for. General Alan Brooke, soon to be Commander-in-Chief of British

Home Forces, said, 'Had the BEF not returned, it is hard to see how the army could have recovered from this blow. The reconstitution of our land forces would have been so delayed as to endanger the whole course of the war.' Also brought back to England from Dunkirk were 112,000 French troops, who were to form the core of the Free French forces that were to fight alongside the British and the Americans later in the war.

As for France itself, it was on the verge of surrender to the Germans. Its capitulation was to be formalized when a new government, rapidly patched together, accepted draconian armistice terms from the Germans on 22 June. But after the dismal experiences of their forces in Europe since the launching of the German offensive less than a month earlier, many British leaders and most British fighting men were not at all troubled by that development.

Pilot Officer Christopher Currant

When France withdraw from the war, my feeling was of sheer and utter relief. At last we were totally on our own. We didn't have to depend on anybody. We felt that now we could really tackle this thing without any hassle, without any political nonsense. We could really get to grips with the thing. There had been a great disadvantage in having our strength frittered away in France, in Europe. We were losing a lot of pilots and aeroplanes. It was denuding Fighter Command of very badly needed men and material at a crucial stage when we were going to be facing the Germans on our own. The French didn't seem to have the determination to fight to keep their freedom. There was too much shilly-shallying. There was great relief when we were finally on our own. I remember people saying, 'Now we can get on with it without any nonsense.'

Air Chief Marshal Sir Hugh Dowding

Thank God we are now alone.

King George VI
Letter to his Mother

Personally I feel happier now that we have no allies to be polite to and to pamper.

PRELUDE

Winston Churchill

The Battle of France is over. I expect that the Battle of Britain is about to begin. The whole fury and might of the enemy must very soon be turned on us. Hitler knows that he will have to break us in this island or lose the war. If we can stand up to him, all Europe may be free and the life of the world may move forward into broad sunlit uplands. But if we fail, then the whole world, including the United States, including all that we have known and cared for, will sink into the abyss of a new Dark Age, made more sinister and perhaps more protracted by the lights of perverted science. Let us therefore brace ourselves to our duties, and bear ourselves that, if the British Empire and its Commonwealth last for a thousand years, men will say, 'This was their finest hour.'

BRITAIN AT BAY

Remarkable though it was, the evacuation at Dunkirk and the events leading up to it had to be put in a proper perspective. As Winston Churchill told the House of Commons, 'We must be careful not to assign to this deliverance the attributes of a victory. Wars are not won by evacuations.'

The fact was that the British had been thrown out of Europe and had paid a steep price for their abortive efforts to stop the Germans in France. In less than a month, they had lost 68,000 troops – killed, missing, captured or wounded. On the beaches of Dunkirk and scattered elsewhere along their line of retreat, they had left most of their military vehicles. Only twenty-two of the 704 tanks sent to France were brought back. They had sent 840 of the 1,000 anti-tank guns in their armoury to France to stop the German panzers; none of those had been brought back. They had also been forced to abandon most of their artillery and a half-million ton of stores and ammunition; anti-tank gun ammunition was so scarce that it was now forbidden to use any for firing practice. The Royal Navy had sustained serious losses as well – six destroyers had been sunk and nineteen more damaged.

Many of the RAF fighter squadrons were now dangerously under strength, and many of the fighter pilots, upon whose capabilities and endurance the defence of the realm now rested, were exhausted and badly in need of rest and recuperation. Those who had become battle tested veterans in four turbulent weeks, and who remained on frontline duty, had to maintain combat readiness, while new pilots, brought in to fill the gaps left by those lost in Europe and over the Channel, had to be trained to do battle in the air.

Sergeant Bernard Jennings

We did a lot of practice. Day and night. Air testing. Testing guns. Everything. You couldn't get too much training. We had two new boys. I'd take them up to a high altitude in a Vic formation and suddenly cut my throttle. Nothing would happen for a while because the air was so thin up there. Then slowly they'd begin creeping up on me. I'd call out over the radio, 'Where do you think you're going?' Then, as they wagged their tails to try to kill off their speed, I'd open my throttle again and they'd suddenly be miles back. They learnt you've got to be careful when you're at high altitude. It's not the same when you're at 1,000 feet. You've got to anticipate a lot earlier, and the Germans were always high above us. Low down you could yank the thing around and pull the throttle back and stay in formation. High up there, you couldn't.

Pilot Officer John Bisdee

We were sent a new CO, George Darley, and he really pulled the squadron together after the beating we had taken at Dunkirk. And we got a whole lot of new pilots. Darley insisted on an enormous amount of squadron and individual training. He used to act as a target. He'd fly along and everybody practised attacks on him – quarter attacks, head-on attacks and every other kind of attack.

Squadron Leader George Darley

I realized when I took command of the squadron that I had to do something with these people. The men ranged in age from thirty down to nineteen. Aside from being past their prime as fighter pilots, the older chaps were depressed from having lost close friends over Dunkirk. There was a danger the morale of the younger ones, who'd just joined the squadron as replacements, might be affected. Time was not on my side so I got them all together – the airmen as well, because lack of morale at the top doesn't take long to filter down – and I gave them all a good talking to. I didn't hold back. I told them exactly what was wrong with them. I told them I knew about their personal and flying problems. But we had a job to do and they would have to change their ways. There was a bit of a deadly hush and some of the men sucked their teeth. They didn't like it at all. But things did improve. I tried to analyse for them what had been responsible for their high rate of casualties at Dunkirk. I asked them what they had done, and what they had done next, and what they should have done. The remarkable thing was, they'd never sat down and analysed what had happened.

And we trained. I had the new boys go up with their flight commanders, and sometimes with myself. I'd see if the chap could stay in formation. We'd practise dogfights to see if he could handle his aircraft and look after himself. We did rolls and turns to see if he could stay on your tail to shoot you down.

Miss Edith Starling, Epsom, Surrey
Letter to her Mother, 6 June

Dear Mother

...We sometimes hear the dull thud of gunfire off the coast of France and yesterday afternoon I saw two Spitfires darting like dragonflies in the blue of the sky, engaged in a mock battle. It was quite fascinating to watch them twisting and turning, weaving in and out in an intricate pattern, but not so pleasant if their guns had been spitting fire in a death duel.

Uncle has a book on identifying British and German planes and after seeing a formation of bombers flying overhead, we hurry in to try to identify them but it will be a long time before I get them correctly named ...

Uncle has been sticking strips of cellophane over the windows and we have had many arguments as to the best place to stand for shelter. Aunty says that if the Germans did invade our land, if she could do nothing else, she would spit at them. Now what do you think of your sister!

Your loving daughter,
Edith

Flying Officer Alan Deere

Our squadron was so badly depleted after Dunkirk, we were sent up north to reform with new pilots coming out of operational training units. Some of them were pushed through in rather a hurry. We were short of pilots. Some of these chaps got five, ten hours on a Spitfire, and their total flying experience wasn't very great. Part of our job was to take them up and train them and get them britched up for our return south to prepare for what turned out to be the Battle of Britain. It was a hairy task, as I learned to my cost. I was teaching one of the newcomers dogfight manoeuvres and how to follow the chap in front when he flew right into me and cut my tail off. It was at about 10,000 feet. I baled out at about a thousand in a bit of a mess with a parachute that was partially torn from me. I was unable to pull the ripcord, but for some miraculous reason it opened on one side and broke my fall. I landed in a horizontal position in a cesspool, which saved my life. The pilot who ran into me got out all right. He was later shot down and taken prisoner by the Germans.

Squadron Leader Peter Devitt

When we were up north at Acklington in Northumberland, there was one young chap in my squadron itching to get into the battle. He even asked at the very beginning if he could be posted to another squadron so he could get into the Dunkirk business. I told him, 'No. There's going to be plenty of time to get into the fight.' When we did get into the fight, he was one of the first of my pilots to get shot down.

Flight Lieutenant Brian Kingcome

The period after the evacuation from Dunkirk was the most dangerous period in my life. They sent us down to South Wales for the defence of the industrial area there. We had a bit of activity. We saw and shot down the odd daylight raider. Then they moved my flight to a field behind a pub called 'The Swan' at Bibury, which is in the middle of the Cotswolds – a beautiful part of the world.

They gave us the most absurd, tiny farmer's field, a couple of bell tents and no facilities at all and we were told we were responsible for the night defence of Wales. We flew from this tiny strip – the sort of thing you'd never dream of doing in peacetime, ever – with no aids at all to get back, except four half blacked-out glim lamps, and one chance light which was switched on for a second or two. We took off and groped our way around the night sky. It was black as sin. We couldn't see a thing. We were landing all over England because we couldn't find our way back. We were lucky no one was killed.

In those days, you believed Operations and tended to do what you were told. We tried to convince Operations what we were doing was an absolute waste of time and there was no way we would be able to find a German bomber on a pitch dark night without aids. You couldn't see them, but you could hear those buggers. It was quite alarming. You'd hear the German R/T getting louder and louder and louder and you'd think, 'Christ, I'm going to be in a collision.'

We finally convinced Operations that this was daft and dangerous and getting us nowhere. Then one chap, Alan Wright, was airborne and happened to look up and there in front of him were four glowing exhaust pipes. He lifted his nose and pressed his tit and shot down a German bomber. He came back all triumphant and he was almost lynched by the rest of us. We were furious. We'd been working hard to get released from this absurd job. He'd destroyed it all with this one total fluke.

Pilot Officer Geoffrey Howitt

We were sent up to Aldegrove in Northern Ireland for convoy patrol mostly. But when things began hotting up in the south of England, our pilots were gradually posted away to replace casualties, as I was later on. They used to post other people in to Aldegrove from all sorts of different squadrons, men who had flown all sorts of different planes – Wellingtons, Lysanders, Battles. They came to us to learn to fly Hurricanes. We'd take them up and teach them formation flying and whiz around with them and practise dogfighting to get them used to the aircraft. Then they'd be posted away again. They'd be all sorts of people, from sergeants to squadron leaders. There was one chap, a squadron leader, a nice chap we converted on to Hurricanes. He went off and became commanding officer of a squadron down south and was killed soon afterwards.

Pilot Officer Jan Zumbach

We were to form a one hundred percent Polish squadron, mechanics included. The greatest difficulty was the language. We would say 'yes' and 'no' without really knowing whether it was the right answer or not, sometimes with surprising results. A friend of mine had answered 'yes' to the questions, 'Are you a pilot?' and, 'Are you in good health?' But he went on saying 'yes' when asked if he had VD! He emerged from a nearby room, after a violent massage of the prostate gland, absolutely livid with rage. A few weeks later, he was dead. Not because of the massage, of course, but because of a Messerschmitt close on his tail.

Finally, everyone passed A1, the grading required to become a fighter pilot. At the time, I thought that even hunchbacks would have been certified A1 if only they knew how to hold a joystick and, like us, had picked up a little fighting experience here and there in Poland and France.

Squadron Leader Jack Satchell

I was posted to Leconfield to form a Polish fighter squadron. Many Polish pilots had escaped from Poland and had made their way to England. They had been operational pilots in their own country. They'd all fought and many of them had shot down enemy aircraft. They didn't speak a word of English. They didn't even know the word 'whisky'. We put them in link trainers and taught them the meaning of our codewords – bandits, angels, pancake, etc. They flew by instrument in those dummy aircraft, but didn't move out of the building.

We had an English and a Polish interpreter. The Polish interpreter was hopeless. The English interpreter was good but he understood far too much for the Poles' liking. He overheard and understood too much of what they said among themselves about us.

To start with, the Poles had no faith in us. They thought they knew it all. They'd fought against the Hun. They had doubts about whether we could. Each section of three in the squadron of twelve had to be English led; those were our rules. But we had to prove ourselves to them. I had a stroke of luck. The very day we were made operational, the section I was leading was scrambled. We took off and played hide-and-seek in the clouds with a Junkers 88. At one point in this game, he went into the cloud and I zoomed over the top, hoping to meet him coming out. I saw him coming out and gave him a full deflection shot and he disappeared into the next cloud. I thought we'd lost him. We couldn't find him any more. We were told on the R/T to come down and when we landed, we found the whole station out on the tarmac waiting to receive us. My one burst had killed the German pilot and he had crashed. I'd shot down our first enemy aircraft. After that the Poles thought I was Dead-Eye Dick. It was sheer luck. I'd never seen a damned Hun in the air before.

We were all very struck, right from the beginning, with the exceptional courtesy of the Poles. They were unnecessarily punc-tilious about saluting – in fact, they saluted me every time they saw me, and practically every time they were spoken to! They also invariably addressed me as *mon commandant*, and the three British flight lieutenants they addressed as *mon capitaine*. If cigarettes were produced, they always hastened to light mine for me – even if they had given me the said cigarette, and, at the beginning, they always said as they did this, 'Excuse, sir.' They were really very nice in very many respects and quite a few of them were first class fellows.

But there were all sorts of discipline problems. They were very inclined to have ladies in their quarters, which was a bit frowned on in the officers' mess. They held boozy parties. Sometimes I would tell them to do one thing and the most senior Pole would tell them to do another. He was a colonel in the Polish Army Air Corps and was made deputy CO of the squadron, as an acting squadron leader, under me. It wasn't a very happy relationship. I'd tell them to do so-and-so, and he'd tell them to take no notice – to do something else. They usually did as I told them but I had to be sharpish at times. It was a bit irritating.

He also caused a lot of difficulties over the question of discipline with the Polish airmen, giving out punishments, most of them highly illegal from an RAF point of view. He gave one man seven days detention in the guardroom with a rigid diet of water for breakfast, one slice of bread for lunch, water for tea, and another slice of bread for supper – every day! At night, a Polish NCO was detailed to go in to the wretched man every hour and wake him up and make him lie down alternately on the floor and on a wooden work bench without any form of bedding, other than a blanket. Of course this sort of punishment would never do in an RAF station. It had to be stopped.

Flight Lieutenant Gordon Sinclair

A flight commander was required in the newly forming 310 Squadron and I was given the job. I was told it was going to be a squadron of foreigners. People wondered who they would be – Frenchmen? Norwegians? We hadn't really heard of the Czech flyers. They were far fewer in numbers than the Poles. Far fewer had managed to get out when the Germans overran their country. This particular lot had made their way to Palestine individually and had come via the Mediterranean and up through France, where they hadn't been treated awfully well.

They varied in age. Their senior officer, who doubled up with Douglas Blackwood as commanding officer, was much older than any of us – about forty-five. He was a very experienced pilot, but I don't think he'd seen any combat. The younger ones were nineteen and twenty. They were very smartly attired in their own dark blue uniforms with quite a lot of gold braiding.

At first they were an unknown quantity to us. We took them up in two-seater training aircraft to see if they could fly. We realized at once that they were very good pilots, except for one man. He'd been swept along with everyone else. Because of the language problem, he didn't understand what was happening. Someone took him up to see what sort of pilot he was. He thought he was just going for a ride. It turned out he couldn't fly at all. He'd been a navigator.

The Czechs were totally disciplined. They did what was expected of them, though not necessarily what they were told to do, because they knew sort of instinctively what they were supposed to do. One of them, a man named Zima, was a marvellous pilot. He'd been a flying instructor before. And Prchal had been a pilot for the Bata Shoe Company before the war, flying shoes from Czechoslovakia to England. He was a very steady pilot.

The young ones were very frightened of their commanding officer. One day, early on, one of these lads crashed a Hurricane in landing. The undercarriage buckled up. They quickly had a court martial among themselves and they were going to shoot him behind the hangar. Douglas Blackwood and I discovered what was going on and said, 'You can't do that sort of thing. We run the show, not you.'

* * *

Foreigners, like the Poles and Czechs who constituted four ferocious RAF squadrons of their own before the battle was over, made up only a small proportion of Fighter Command's manpower. The Royal Canadian Air Force provided another squadron and there was a sprinkling of other foreigners – Free French, Belgians and seven Americans who joined the RAF despite American neutrality.

The British pilots themselves came from a variety of backgrounds. Regular RAF pilots, graduates of the RAF College at Cranwell, the true professionals, included several colonials, like Flight Lieutenant Deere who had come over from New Zealand in 1937 to join the RAF. They considered themselves, and were considered by the other pilots, to be as British as native-born Britons and fought with equal, and sometimes greater, ferocity. There were also 'short service commission' regulars who had been pre-war RAF pilots as well, but who were not really part of the RAF establishment, not having been to Cranwell and unlikely to be seeking a lifelong career in the service, which in no way diluted the central role they too played in the Battle.

Auxiliary squadrons consisted mostly of reasonably well-off young men who had flown pre-war as a hobby at weekends. Theirs had been exclusive clubs. Squadron Leader Sandy Johnstone recalls that before he was permitted to join 602 ('City of Glasgow') Auxiliary

Squadron before the war, he was put through a series of discreet tests to determine his social acceptability, the last one of which was a 'dining in' night during which, 'to this day, I have never had as much booze poured inside me. They wanted to know how I behaved when I was drunk.' A few of the auxiliaries were very wealthy, scions of some of the richest families in the land, owning their own planes and expensive sports cars and regularly seen in the company of glamorous young women. These dashing young men gave many people the impression that all auxiliaries were playboys when, in fact, this was not true. When the war began, the auxiliary squadrons, playboys and all, were formally absorbed into Fighter Command. They provided strength and numbers (fourteen squadrons in all) the RAF could not have done without. They soon lost their exclusive nature as their casualties mounted and non-auxiliary personnel had to be brought into their squadrons as replacements.

Volunteer Reserve (VR) pilots had also been weekend flyers before the war, but of an inferior social rank. They were mostly middle class young men who had worked in banks or offices or ran small businesses. Slotted into existing squadrons when the fighting started, they, like the auxiliaries, brought to battle the experience they had gathered on their weekend flying diversions, as well as the determination to defend their country against the would-be invader.

Men who were RAF sergeant pilots at the beginning of the war tended to be flyers of considerable competence. Many had been RAF groundcrew who had volunteered for flying training. The best of them had been permitted to stay on as pilots. At the height of the battle, when losses were great, there were times in combat when a sergeant led a squadron or part of a squadron which included new recruits who outranked him. It was understood, however, that he would surrender command as soon as an officer in the squadron seemed capable of assuming it, or when one was sent in from another squadron to take over.

There was class distinction in the RAF, as there was and still is in British society as a whole. It was said, for example, that a regular officer was an officer trying to be a gentleman, an auxiliary was a gentleman trying to be an officer and a VR was neither trying to be both. Regular officers and VRs were often cautious about going drinking with auxiliaries, because it was believed to be potentially a very expensive outing, many of the more affluent auxiliaries being known to insist on champagne rather than beer when out carousing with the lads. Several men who were sergeant pilots recall that social

BRITAIN AT BAY

distinctions tended to fall away as the battle progressed. But that wasn't the experience of all of them.

Sergeant David Cox

Some of the officers were very snobbish to sergeant pilots. Most couldn't care less, but even with them the difference was there. You would be in a heck of a scrap up in the sky with everybody equal. But when you landed, the officers went one way and the sergeants went the other. When I was commissioned the next year, I was very quickly told off for spending time with my old friends in the sergeants' mess.

Sergeant Dick Kilner

I was leading the section – I think it was Blue Section – when Paddy Finucane came to the squadron as a pilot officer. I was fairly experienced, having started flying four years before. When the war broke out, I'd had about three hundred hours in all sorts of aircraft. There were other sergeant pilots leading sections as well.

Finucane had no experience when he was put in my section. He flew number two or three to me. When he was promoted to flying officer later in the battle, he was put in charge of the section. The flight commander told me he was putting Finucane in charge – would I fly as his number two and keep an eye on him? I don't think they liked having a flying officer flying behind a sergeant.

Sergeant Mike Croskell

We called them 'Sir' while they usually called each other by Christian names. It never occurred to me at the time that there was anything peculiar about them being officers and me being a sergeant. It was an accepted thing. I guess the authorities couldn't help believing there had to be a 'them' and 'us' situation. But it had no bearing whatsoever on performance on duty or in combat. After we'd lost a lot of men, I led a flight until new officers became sufficiently experienced to take over. I didn't care that they didn't make me an officer, but I sometimes felt, 'Why can't the most experienced people be leading the sections?'

* * *

On the eve of the Battle of Britain, the Luftwaffe boasted almost 2,500 attack planes ready for combat operations in Western Europe – 980 modern fighters and 1,500 bombers. To meet them, the RAF could put aloft 620 Spitfires and Hurricanes, plus eighty-four Blenheims and Defiants, which were, however, no match for Messerschmitt 109s and 110s. For strategic and reserve maintenance reasons, only half of Fighter Command's squadrons were assigned to duty in that part of England which was to bear the brunt of German attacks. This gave the Luftwaffe's superiority in numbers even greater significance. There was no mystery to the fact that swarms of enemy aircraft coming in to attack would regularly be met only by small formations of British fighters sent up to intercept them.

In addition to outnumbering the British in the air, the Germans were able to choose where and when to attack. One of the British pilots described it as, 'something like a tennis match in which you never got to serve. You were always playing back what the other man was doing to you.' But the British had the advantage of a technological innovation about which the Germans knew, but which they didn't yet fully appreciate.

British scientists had been experimenting with Radio Direction Finders, or 'radar' as it was later called, right through the 1930s. By the summer of 1940, a reasonably tight chain of radar stations had been planted along the eastern and southern coasts of England, facing Europe. Radar was able to pick up radio impulses from German aircraft as they climbed from their bases in Western Europe, joined in formation and made their way towards England. Had that radar chain not been in place along the English shore, the outcome of the battle might well have been different. The alternative for Fighter Command would have been the maintenance of permanent patrols over the Channel and the North Sea during daylight hours. Some patrols were maintained as back-up for radar but, with RAF resources so meagre, standing patrols without radar could never have provided wide enough or fast enough early warning. They would also have exposed British aircraft and pilots to further risk away from their primary defence positions. The consequences for Britain could have been calamitous.

* * *

To meet the German threat, Britain was divided by Fighter Command into four 'Groups'. Southeast England was designated 11 Group territory. 12 Group covered the Midlands, while 10 Group, not officially formed until mid-July, covered the southwest. Northern England and Scotland came under the protection of 13 Group.

Fighter aircraft hungrily consumed fuel in combat. They took great risks when venturing far afield in search of action. Accordingly, 11 Group, whose bailiwick was closest to the airfields on the far side of the Channel which the Germans had seized in France and the Low Countries, received the heaviest and most persistent raids as the Luftwaffe sought to control the skies over England. Though the squadrons in 10 Group further west were, with a few exceptions, not as severely put to the test, bases and installations within their zone of cover were also prime targets for the Germans as the battle progressed and they were often also kept fully stretched.

Pilots in 12 and 13 Groups to the north faced nothing like the same intensity of combat, though they were regularly on patrol, sometimes intercepting enemy aircraft, shooting them down, seeing them off or being shot down by them. Their Group areas had to be protected in case German raids came their way. This happened rarely, so their most important contribution turned out to be their active duty in the south when they were sent in as back-up, as was the case for 12 Group pilots; or, as was the case for personnel in both Groups to the north, to fill gaps caused by losses in the south or to relieve squadrons there exhausted or decimated in combat.

Group areas were divided into 'Sectors', each of which consisted of a main airfield (Sector Station) and usually at least one satellite base as well. In 11 Group, such satellite fields as Manston and Hawkinge were very near the coast. Planes were generally based there only during the day for fear of surprise dawn or dusk raids by German aircraft, based only minutes away across the Channel.

Control of Fighter Command operations was centred at Bentley Priory in Middlesex, a handsome, venerable structure which had earlier been a girls' school. There, Dowding set up a 'filter' room to receive radar reports and determine which tracked aircraft were hostile and which were not. These filtered radar reports on which planes required sustained monitoring were then fed to the main 'Ops' (Operations) Room at Bentley Priory, as well as to the Ops Rooms at the appropriate Groups and Sectors. These Group and Sector Ops Rooms were also fed reports from Observer Corps posts in their designated areas, which took over plane spotting once the enemy aircraft had passed over the sea-facing radar stations on the coast en route to their targets. The Groups relayed these Observer Corps reports back to Command Headquarters at Bentley Priory, so it would at all times have as complete a picture of developments as possible.

The Observer Corps was a small army of volunteers equipped with binoculars, sextant-like devices, plane identification manuals and telephones. They reported on the direction, height and number of incoming planes, calculating to the best of their abilities, given the instruments at their disposal. It was a primitive system, but it was all that was available for the purpose at the time.

The heart of each Ops Room was the plotting table. Plotters, mostly young WAAF (Women's Auxiliary Air Force) personnel armed with long wooden rods and linked by earphone to their sources of information, moved markers across the table to trace the movement of the attackers. Overlooking them on a raised platform were Controllers, who made decisions on how to cope with each enemy incursion.

Having received details of an incoming raid from Fighter Command Headquarters and the Observer Corps, Group Ops would decide which of its Sectors would deal with it. Group Controllers would scan big wall boards which listed the state of play of each of the squadrons in the Group – released, available, ordered to readiness, at readiness, ordered to standby, at standby, ordered aloft, in assigned position above, sighted enemy, ordered to land, landed and refuelled. With this overall picture of what was at their disposal, and in what condition, and with markers on the plotting table revealing the challenge that had to be met, the Group Controllers would decide how many fighters, which squadrons or parts of squadrons, should be sent up after the enemy, bearing in mind that other enemy raids might be in the making and might soon materialize. Sector Control would convey instructions from Group, alerting or scrambling the designated squadrons and remaining in radio contact with the pilots as they climbed to intercept, giving directions and height instructions and some idea of the size of the incoming enemy formation. They remained in radio communication until a pilot called 'Tally-ho', to signal he was going in to attack.

Air Chief Marshal Sir Hugh Dowding

Orders were given to pilots in their aircraft by means of a very simple code which could be easily memorized. For instance, 'Scramble' meant take off. 'Orbit' meant circle. 'Vector 230' meant fly on a course of 230 degrees. As a matter of fact, the enemy did pick up and interpret the signals in some cases, but not much harm was done, except when they were able to discover the height at which a formation was ordered to operate and the time when it was ordered to leave its patrol line and land.

'Pancake' was the signal for the latter operation and I therefore introduced several synonyms [for it], the significance of which was not obvious to the enemy.

The codeword for height was 'Angels', followed by the number of thousands of feet. When it appeared probable that the enemy were taking advantage of this information, I introduced a false quantity into the code signal. Thus (for example) 'Angels eighteen' really meant fly at 21,000, not 18,000. On more than one occasion, German fighter formations arriving to dive on one of our patrols were themselves attacked from above.

Wing Commander David Roberts

In early June, I managed to escape from Fighter Command Head-quarters, where I'd been a staff officer, and was assigned to be commander at Middle Wallop. The base there was still under construction. It was a shambles, in the hands of the construction contractors. It was temporarily occupied also by a flying training school. That made things difficult for me personally, because I was only a wing commander and I had to ask the group captain commanding the training school to leave. He was very cross and didn't want to go. But he had to. It had been decided higher up that Middle Wallop would open as a major fighter base when our gallant French allies packed it in and the south of England was suddenly exposed to German aerial attack. Middle Wallop was to be a Sector Head-quarters in 10 Group, which was to be formally established in July. When I got there, there was still a lot of work to be done. An Operations Room had to be set up. Station Headquarters and some of the main buildings had been built, but the hangars were still under construction. Typically, the married quarters, which we didn't need, were ready. The only real problem we had setting up the Sector Headquarters was the damned contractors and their workmen who were all over the site.

Assistant Section Officer Felicity Hanbury

My first husband – he was a fighter pilot – was killed before the Battle of Britain began, right at the end of 1939. So when I became an officer – I was twenty-four years old then – I had already been made a widow by the war. It was quite a shock, coming at the beginning of everything. I had experienced what might happen to other people which, I suppose, wasn't really a bad thing when I was put in charge of the airwomen, about 250 of them, employed at Biggin Hill – plotters, drivers, cooks, people in the armoury, equipment assistants, everything. One of my code and cipher officers married a pilot on the base. He was shot down and she didn't know whether he'd reappear. But he did, thank goodness.

The girls came from all walks of life. Some were well educated; others were not. There were so many wanting to join that you could sort them out as suitable for this or suitable for that. We had no difficulty recruiting. We had some difficulty absorbing them all at short notice.

Corporal Claire Legge

I was in a repertory company on Hastings Pier before the war began. I was twenty-one years old and supposed to be the costume designer, but in a repertory company you did all sorts of things. I played all the maids on stage, all the nannies, all those things.

I had shared a dressing room with Dulcie Langham. She disappeared just before the war started. She said she was going to join the WAAF and that if I ever wanted any help or anything, I was to contact her. So when the war started, I did just that and Dulcie told me what to do. She told me I ought to become a plotter in the WAAF. I hadn't the slightest idea what a plotter was. But that's what I became. I went to school and was taught how to use these great long rods with arrows on the end for plotting. We were given a rough idea of what it was all about. We were – myself and seven other girls – the first ones to arrive at Tangmere [an 11 Group Sector Station]. It was February. We had practically no uniforms. We were given bloomers – they were called 'passion-killers' in those days. We were given a shirt and a tie and a macintosh and a beret. But we wore our own skirts. All we had really been taught was to manipulate those enormous rods. They had a battery at one end and a magnet at the other. We were supposed to pick up small metal arrows with them and place them where they had to be put on the plotting table. That was the basic business of plotting aircraft. You'd get a grid reference and you'd plot one arrow after the other across the board.

But, of course, when we got to Tangmere, they hadn't got any of those sophisticated rods. All they had was a bit of wood with a thumb stall on the end – that rubber thing bank clerks put on their fingers to count paper money. So you were throwing the arrows on the table and sort of pushing them into place. And we had a croupier thing for pulling the arrows off. It was very primitive. The table was arranged in such a way that you could really reach to put most of the arrows in the proper grid references by hand.

We were connected by headphones to two sources, to various Observer Corps posts and to what was known in those days as RDF – Radio Direction Finding. We know it as radar today. The plots were passed to us in a four figure grid reference. The table would be 1-2-3-4-5-6-7-8-9 across and 1-2-3-4-5-6-7-8-9 up. If you got 1-5-0-5, you'd go across one and a half squares and up half a square. That would signify the position of the enemy aircraft coming in.

In front of the plotting table was a raised dais where sat the Controller, who was the boss man; an Ops A, often an airwoman, who would take down instructions from Group when they came in; an Ops B, who was the controller's assistant; and an Ops B1. Also there on the dais was the army, who passed on the information on the table to warn the anti-aircraft batteries of what was happening. The order for any forms of readiness, scramble, do anything, was not the responsibility of the Controller at Tangmere before anything happened. He was only responsible once the battle was joined in his Sector. Up to that point, it was the Controller at Group Headquarters who was responsible. He had a similar, but much more comprehensive picture of the entire Group area. We just had a picture on our table of our Sector and a little bit outside it. So up at Group, the Controller there would decide when something was happening and it was time to bring a squadron to readiness.

When you think of it, it was so laborious it wasn't funny. Ops A had a pink form in front of her. Until that moment, she'd probably just been sitting around. But as soon as she put her hand to her headphone and braced herself to take a message from Group, everybody was alerted. We knew something was coming down. The message would come through and if it said, 'Tangmere', she would write down Tangmere. Then it would say, 'Such-and-such squadron'. She'd write down the squadron. Then it would say, 'A-flight to readiness' or 'A-flight ten minutes'. She'd write all that down and hand it to the Controller and he would see what was happening. He would hand it to Ops B. Ops B would action it. He would lift his telephone and say 'Squadron A-flight five minutes', or 'Come to readiness', or 'Stand by', or whatever it was. The pink form would then be passed to Ops B1, who would tick it off as actioned. The pink form would then be passed to a teleprinter operator in a little cubby hole, who would make a record that it had happened.

How many of us there were on the plotting table depended on how many Observer Corps posts were manned, usually about six and the two RDFs. If something was happening, it would first of all come through from RDF and it would be plotted and it would be watched. Our Controller would be watching it and 11 Group would be watching it. As soon as it was evident as to where it was actually going, Group would decide which Sector would look after it. Our Controller would be getting instructions from Group while using what we were plotting on the table as a reference to see what it was all about. The raid would come up towards the coast and as it arrived within, say, ten miles of the coast, at a distance where it could be seen from the ground, the plotting of that particular plane would be stopped by the radar, and taken over by Observer Corps, who would then plot it until it went out of their area into the next Observer Corps area. We on the plotting board would each be connected by phone to different Observer Corps posts which reported their observations of the incoming enemy. As the enemy moved from one Observer area to the next, the girl connected by phone to that area would take over plotting its movements on the table. There was sometimes some duplication. A supervisor went around in the Ops Room, seeing what was happening and tidying up.

We did the twenty-four hours between us. We had a weekend every three, and a day off every week. Three days a week we had a three watch shift, but the other four days, two watches were operating and that was pretty rough. Then it was usual for us to do one four hour and one eight hour shift in every twenty-four hours.

Fairly soon after the start of the Battle of Britain, I stopped plotting. I was made a corporal and my job was to do a liaison between RDF and the Observer Corps. As a raid came up, I assessed which Observer Corps area it was going into, got onto the appropriate Observer Corps, gave the warning and arranged the hand-over of the plotting as best I could. I was on duty at Tangmere the day North Weald was bombed. The girl on the table who was on to

North Weald got word over her headphones and said, 'Oh my God, they've been bombed.' The supervisor snapped, 'Shut up and get on with your job.'

But up until the day France fell, everything was free and easy. We didn't wear uniforms, for instance, on the evening shift, because if you were going out you'd just put on your high heeled shoes. I remember a remarkable girl called Sunneva. She appeared on duty in a black dress wearing earrings. That was the order of the day. Nothing was happening. We used to take our knitting and our sewing around the table. We used to play throwing pennies onto the table – the aim was to get them in the middle of squares. We threw paper darts around. This was mainly on the late duty, when senior officers weren't likely to come around. We had a super Controller, Squadron Leader Vick. He went along with all of this.

The day France fell, we went on duty as usual, with all our bits and pieces and the sewing and what have you. And Vick came on duty and stood there and looked sternly at us and cried out, 'Flight Sergeant!' The Flight Sergeant said, 'Yes, sir.' Vick shouted, 'Get these bloody women out of here!' One by one we were all sent out, relieved one by one by men, and we were herded off into a rest room. We sat there a half-hour, three-quarters of an hour, and eventually the Flight Sergeant appeared and said, 'Now, you lot, you listen to me.' We were told in no mean fashion that all this was to stop. There would be no more knitting, no more sewing, no more chatting, no more anything. And that's how it was. From that moment onwards, we were soldiers.

Aircraftswoman Second Class Ursula Robertson

I applied to the newly formed WAAF for entrance as a cook, in which I was trained, only to be turned down on the grounds that I *was* trained. I was accepted instead to be trained in the wonders of Operations Room dogma. After preliminary training, I was assigned to the prestigious Fighter Command Headquarters at Bentley Priory in Stanmore, north of London. The Operations Room and Filter Room at Bentley Priory were in the underground block there. It was rather claustrophobic and a good ten minutes' walk through the tunnel when a complete change of watch took place – airmen, airwomen, officers and all.

The Operations table was a table on which a map of the UK had been drawn on a grid system. Each of us who were plotting was plugged into a particular Sector. From Group Operations Rooms we received through headphones the information, which we then plotted on the table. On receiving the first intimation of a raid through our headphones, we would stand up and say, 'X Raid!' loudly, bringing everyone to alert and a rush of liaison staff from the rest rooms. Up to that moment, the atmosphere was calm and rather boring. There was only a token staff present. But within minutes, the whole atmosphere would be changed to alert expectancy.

The plot would be given us as a raid number, two grid mark letters, the direction and strength of the raid. With a magnetic rod we would position the tip of a coloured arrow to that plot. The time clock above the table was marked off in five-minute coloured sections. We had to watch the clock and change the colour of the arrows on the plotting table accordingly, so that the information would be kept up to date. We took a round disc noting the strength of the raid and placed it beside the arrow with the number of the raid. Plots and strengths were received from coastal radar and Observer Corps stations. When we took over on duty, we put on headphone sets, wiping them well if we were sensible, as there was a lot of throat infection to be gained from close living and working conditions at that time. Also, the fairly new and intense strip lighting, to which no one had been accustomed, caused bad eye strain. We plugged our headphones into a dual socket with the plotter who was going off duty. If it was quiet, this was a simple operation. You had time then to have a word or two and to speak with the operative at the Group Operations Room you were plugged into. Usually, talking was not allowed except for time checks and raid alerts. When the raids came over thick and fast, we could plug in for two or three minutes and review the table, number of raids, etc, before taking the next plots. When the raids came in great numbers, we could have two persons working together on, say, four numbered raids each.

Above the plotting table was a gallery from which the C-in-C and Controllers could see the complete picture and function accordingly. In addition, on the gallery were people from the balloon barrages, ack-ack, air raid warning and liaison offficers from the army, navy and air force, and very often some of their junior staffs as well. There were often early morning visits by dignitaries. I particularly remember the visit of the Duke of Kent shortly before he was tragically killed and, of course, Churchill and army, navy and air force chiefs, of whom we poor mortals stood in fear.

One dull, grey night when action was obviously going to be light, the famous cartoonist Fred May, who was with barrage balloons, answered his phone on the gallery and then started to put something down on paper. That piece of paper was passed not directly to the Controller, but right around the gallery arriving finally at the Controller. A ripple of mirth had followed the paper. The message received was from a barrage balloon position and had been, 'I am a farmer and one of your balloons has caught one of my cows.' Fred May had drawn a cartoon of a fat farmer squeezed into a telephone box in the middle of a field with a cow suspended by a balloon above it.

Early July saw the first dawn 100 plus raids appear up the Thames Estuary. When I put one of those raids on the table, I was told it was not a realistic number and to take it off. We were on the outskirts of the bombing area, but it was a most dreadful feeling to be underground and feel the building shake when bombs exploded, even miles away.

Aircraftswoman Second Class Edith Heap

I was in motor transport at Debden airfield when Dunkirk was being evacuated. People felt, 'Invasion any time now. Our backs are right to the wall.' We thought, 'We've got to be ready for them.'

After Dunkirk, the CO said he wasn't having educated girls messing around in transport when they could be doing something that would put their education to use. He wanted some of us to come into the Ops Room and be plotters. We said, 'No, thanks.' We liked what we were doing. We were having a super time in motor transport, driving all over the country. It was great fun. We would stop for petrol at an army base and they'd say, 'Girls! Come and have a sherry.' Because we were in uniform, we were protected. We didn't want to change jobs.

But the CO said, 'You do as I say or I'll post you.' So we went into the plotting room. There was a little bit of a lull at the time. We were first taught to read the plots on the table, which was divided into squares. It was, 'Along the passage and up the stairs', like reading a map reference. We had lots of dummy runs for practice. They would set up an exercise and we'd be told, 'Such-and-such raid coming in, Angels so much, so many aircraft, etc.' We'd hear it over our earphones and plot it on the board. It was easy. All you needed was practice to be quick.

The squadrons were called to the different levels of readiness by the Controller when he saw raids coming in on the board. He'd ring the squadrons at dispersal or the mess and say, 'I want A-flight at half-an-hour's readiness', or whatever.

Air Commodore Gerald Gibbs, Senior Staff Officer, 11 Group

We had long passed the age when some grey-beard of the past refused to employ women in the defence organization despite a terrible national emergency. He is reported to have said, 'No women. They quarrel incessantly and their shrill voices would frighten the dogs.'

In the beginning, we tried to get the girls to leave those rooms in which R/T was broadcast from the aircraft during air fighting – for the language was terrible. But it wasn't idle blasphemy or obscenity. It was the voice of men in the midst of fighting for their lives – and dying. The girls refused to leave their jobs and said that they didn't mind the language as much as we thought. They added that it was nice of us to think of their being like that, all the same.

Sergeant Tom Naylor

When we first started, we had all male plotters in the Ops Room. The WAAFs came in when the war began. By then I was supervising a crew of plotters, and we had mixed crews. Interestingly, the first lot of WAAFs were all part of the horse-riding set, real upper crust, smashing looking bits. We also had one or two very scruffy airmen, the lowest of the low, the type that couldn't get a job on civvy street in peacetime. They used to do all the lousy jobs – scrubbing the floors, running errands, that sort of thing. One of them, I think, had never had a bath. It used to amuse us that our posh young ladies got on better with those scruffy types than they did with us. When the raids came in, I used to detail a corporal to hand out tin hats to all the plotters, including the WAAFs. It was funny, because on some of them those helmets would sit way down around their noses and others had them perched right on top of their heads. But the girls kept on plotting all the time.

They tended to be more nimble than the men plotters. They were younger than the men plotters, some of whom were old-timers. Also, many of the girls were highly educated. As for conduct under fire, when we were hit in a raid, you couldn't help admiring the way the girls stuck to their guns and went on plotting.

In the early part of the battle, when there weren't many night raids, we still had to be on the ball in the Ops Room round-the-clock. We'd get regular phone calls during the night to test the line, but it wasn't easy staying awake on the 10.00 p.m. to 4.00 a.m. shift when nothing was happening. One night, the Controller and the others on the dais actually went to sleep – the whole lot of them! Bob Mason, one of our originals in the Ops Room, got a big piece of cardboard that night and wrote on it 'THE DEFENCE OF BRITAIN' and walked around the Ops Room with it.

Leading Aircraftsman Peter Burney

At the radar station on the Dover Cliffs, we tracked aircraft in, feeding information to Fighter Command Ops Rooms, which decided when and where to scramble aircraft. The installation was just a series of wooden huts with most of the radar equipment underground. I operated as a radar screen reader, feeding information through. It was a miniature Ops Room. You would report action coming in from a certain angle. You would estimate from experience whether it was going to be a small or large enemy attack. This would be cross-checked with other stations dotted around the area. A picture would be assembled. Since one was only looking at blips, you had to estimate roughly that one kind of blip meant fifty planes were coming and another meant only one plane.

Fighter Command depended entirely on the information fed in through its tentacles. If you had conflicting evidence coming from, say, three radar stations – because of atmospheric or other conditions – with one station reading something on the screen that was highly exaggerated compared with the other two, Fighter Command would question your reading. Then, two or three pairs of eyes would double-check.

Sergeant Tom Naylor

Not many people in the country knew at the time what radar was, even though so much of our information in the Ops Room came from radar stations on the coast. There was a chain of radar pylons there and funny stories went around about them. Lots of people swore that when they'd driven past those pylons in their cars, their engines had stopped. So the rumour got around – it was even in the newspapers – that Britain possessed a death ray. The government didn't bother to refute those rumours.

There's no doubt about it that radar saved our bacon during the Battle of Britain. We used to sit in the Ops Room and we used to hear about the German squadrons boiling up around Abbeville in France or someplace like that, building their formations. They'd mill around and we could see them coming into this vortex and forming up a big gaggle.

The numbers of them really shook you. Before the war, when we plotted, we used to play around with twelve Spitfires and three Heyfords and thought that was a lot. Now you'd say to yourself, 'What the devil are we going to do against three hundred aircraft?' And that was only one raid. Another lot would come up – maybe eighty aircraft. The Germans were doing something the pre-war exercises never envisaged. They were sending over a lot of bombers escorted by even more fighters.

Flying Officer Jeffrey Quill

When the battle heated up, the job of the Spitfire squadron was to climb up, engage the German fighter escort and let the bombers go by. We'd take off and be vectored out. We'd see a bloody great formation of Dorniers coming in at 12,000 feet. We'd be told to ignore them. Up above were their fighter escorts. Our job was to get up and engage those fighters, get a good old dogfight going, get everything milling around, during which time the bombers would be groaning inexorably along. With any luck, by the time they got anywhere near their target, we'd have forced all their fighter escorts out of position and down would come our Hurricanes to get at those bombers. That was the general idea. The Spitfire and the Hurricane complemented each other. They were an ideal couple, provided we could handle the battle that way. The two aircraft together – plus the radar – those were the things that won the Battle of Britain.

Flight-Lieutenant Bob Stanford-Tuck

I flew both Spitfires and Hurricanes. It was like comparing a thoroughbred race horse with a brewer's dray, a great big brute. The Spitfire was faster, of course. Better rate of climb. Very nimble to the controls – responded quickly. A very beautiful aeroplane.

The Hurricane was much larger, more sluggish on the controls. But it had one tremendous advantage over the Spitfire in combat.

When you were in a Spitfire, your gunsights just in front of your face, the plane's nose went right out away from you. You had no downward vision at all, hardly. You'd lose sight of your target when you turned because your nose would get in the way. In the Hurricane, the nose tapered down a bit. That was a tremendous advantage, because when you were firing at your target in a Hurricane, you could pull around, place your deflection to hit him, and still have him in view in a steep turn while you were shooting at him, because your nose sloped away.

But the Hurricane wasn't up to the Messerschmitt 109, while the Spitfire and the 109 were exactly similar. I flew the first 109 we captured down to Farnborough and it was a damned fine aircraft. One advantage it had over the Spitfire was direct fuel injection.

I shot down 109s when flying Hurricanes, but only when I had the advantage of height. I'd stick my nose down and go for them. But a Hurricane couldn't match the 109 on the same level. I spoke to German pilots after the war and they said, 'Hurricanes? We didn't worry about them. It was the Spitfire we worried about.'

Pilot Officer Desmond Hughes

The Defiant had the same engine as the Spitfire and the Hurricane but – being a two-seater – was trying to lug around over a ton of extra weight for its turret and second man. Therefore its climb, in particular, was much inferior to that of the Spitfire and the Hurricane and caused it to have a lot of trouble when it was faced with the Messerschmitt 109. It was a good bomber destroyer, if you could get to the bombers before the 109s got to you. And the people who had flown Defiants at Dunkirk, and had done well there, also felt they could cope pretty well with the twin-engined Messerschmitt 110. One time, we ran into nine Dorniers flying along in tight formation. There was a Spitfire squadron on hand to keep their 109 escort occupied on top. There were only seven of us. When we came within range, our squadron commander said, 'Okay, pick your targets.' Those Dorniers were severely mauled. I saw two of them go down in no time at all. But it was one of the few occasions when that sort of attack was successful for the Defiants; one of the few times we were able to get in before the 109s came at us.

Pilot Officer Derek Smythe

A problem with the Defiant was that you had two people instead of one in that aircraft concentrating on combat – the pilot and the gunner. If the plane was being attacked, the gunner might be taking a bead on the attacker while the pilot, who had no guns, might see something else developing from another direction which required him to take pretty smart evasive action. One moment I might be aiming at an enemy fighter in one place. The next, I'd be loking up at the sky or down at the earth below. In a mêlée, the Defiant pilot couldn't very well just provide a gun platform. He'd be shot down in no time flat. But the gunner might find his target disappearing from his sights because of the pilot's evasive action.

I didn't feel particularly exposed manning the guns in the turret of the Defiant. The thing that really frightened me was the fact that the oxygen bottle was right between your legs back there. If you got hit in the oxygen bottle, it was perfectly obvious what would happen. It would blow up and your family fortunes would go with it.

Flight Lieutenant John Cunningham

There was a serious attempt by Fighter Command to see if the Blenheim fighter bombers could be adapted to drop bombs on incoming formations of German bombers. In practice, we did diving attacks to see if we could drop bombs on towed targets. The idea was to dive and overtake the bombers, drop our bombs on them and then hopefully clear out of the way. The thing was given up when the real Battle of Britain started in July and the day battle took over. By early summer, the Blenheim was seen to be more of a hindrance than anything else. During the day battles, we were generally kept on the ground and out of the way, otherwise we'd only confuse the picture. Our own fighters used to think we were Ju 88s. We looked not unlike them. Our only hope might have been at night. Blenheims were sent up at night in the hope that enemy aircraft would be illuminated by searchlights so they could be attacked. We had no other aircraft to send up at night, so the Blenheims had to go. There wasn't much hope of achieving anything with them. We couldn't see anything at night. But from a public morale point of view, I don't think that could have been admitted.

(RAF Museum)

Operations Room with plotters at the plotting table and
Controllers in the gallery above

Squadron Leader Ted Donaldson *(left)* and Wing Commander Victor Beamish

(RAF Museum)

Flight Lieutenant Bob Stanford-Tuck

(RAF Museum)

(RAF Museum)

Squadron Leader Douglas Bader with some of his squadron.
Bader is in the centre with his overall collar up.

(Air Commodore J.A. Leathart)

Members of 54 Squadron. FRONT ROW, LEFT TO RIGHT: Johnny Allen, Alan
Deere, James Leathart (squadron leader), "Wonky" Way, George Gribble.

Exhausted pilots at dispersal hut waiting to be scrambled again

Pilots relaxing between sorties

(RAF Museum)

(Air Vice Marshal A.V.R. Johnstone)

Squadron Leader Sandy Johnstone

(Claire Quill)

Claire Legge, who was commissioned
after the battle

(John Burgess)

Sergeant John Burgess

(Group Captain H.S. Darley)

Squadron Leader George Darley

(RAF Museum)

Pilot Officer Don Stones

(RAF Museum)

Pilot Officer Steve Stephen

(RAF Museum)

Pilot Officer Brian Considine

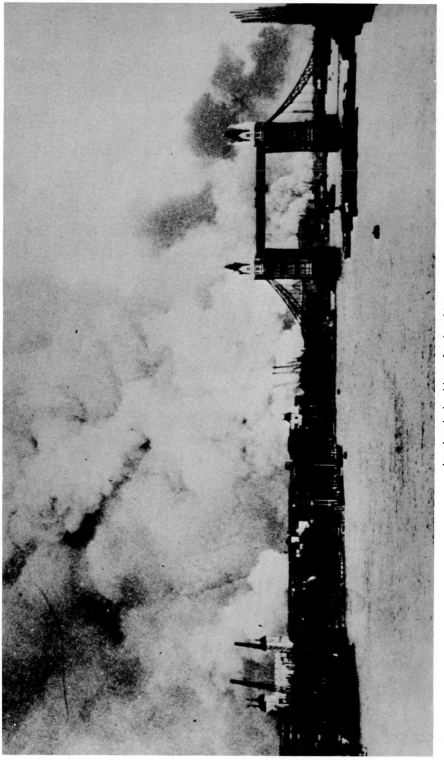

London docks ablaze after bombing

(RAF Museum)

Sergeant Len Bowman, Defiant air gunner

Most of the time, night flying was pretty boring. There was very little you could see. We were vectored onto a bandit one night, found it and were catching up. I had him in my sights and we were closing on him. I made sure my guns were on 'fire' and was just about to press the button when this thing I was aiming at opened up with its guns blazing and shot down a German bomber we hadn't seen at all. It was a Blenheim I'd had in my sights. I'd almost shot down one of our own.

Pilot Officer Andy Anderson

We'd take our Blenheims up at night and fly around the searchlights, trying to see something. If we did see something, we'd nip in. But if you got too close to the searchlights, instead of lighting up German bombers, they'd light you up for the enemy. They were mostly bombers at nights and there was no great danger of getting hurt, but it was possible. Once my air gunner said, 'There goes an aeroplane. We just missed it!' I said, 'Why didn't you shoot at the bloody thing?' He said, 'I couldn't tell whose it was.' Basically it was a very frustrating experience, with an element of waste of time. But we were young and keen and when we went up, we thought we might be lucky. Still, we were envious of the day boys who were getting on with things.

Leading Aircraftsman Francis Pecket

It could get very hectic on the ground, keeping the aircraft serviceable. As a rigger, my job was to look after the control column of the aircraft, and the wiring and all that. The fitter was the flight mechanic. He would look after the engine. There was usually one fitter and one rigger assigned to each plane but sometimes you had to see to others too. A machine had to be inspected before flying. We had to see there was sufficient petrol in, and sufficient glycol to cool the engine, and that the undercarriage and control columns were working properly. We had to check for leaking or faulty petrol pipes and radiator. The working of the engine had to be checked. Bullet holes had to be properly patched up. The armourer looked after the guns and rearmed the aircraft after it had been in combat. We were kept very busy.

SCRAMBLE

Aircraftsman Second Class Albert Hargraves

Bowser drivers not only drove the bowsers; they also refuelled the aircraft from them. The bowsers were small, carrying maybe 850 gallons of 100 octane. At the back was a little auxiliary motor which you started by hand. That drove a pump which drove the petrol into the aircraft tank. If you had trouble with the motor, you had to refuel the aircraft by hand. You'd use square tins, sit on the aircraft and pour the petrol in through a big filter. You used to get doused in petrol every day. All you'd be wearing was boilersuit overalls and a pair of wellies. You'd get petrol all over yourself. You could always tell a bowser driver on the field. There'd be a yellow halo right around his body where the fumes were coming off his overalls. The octane was green. Even when you had a shower, when you sweated, you'd have green streaks coming down your face. You used to stink up the billets with the smell of the octane. Your mates would tease you about it.

* * *

An RAF fighter squadron consisted of twelve planes, though to keep twelve in the air generally required a basic strength of at least eighteen planes. There were always problems which kept aircraft grounded for repairs. One plane might have guns which tended to jam. Another might have oil pressure problems. Others would have bullet holes that had to be patched up or radios which were malfunctioning. They'd be taken out of the line and reserve aircraft would be brought forward. There also had to be replacements on hand for those which were shot down or had been damaged in accidents, which grew more frequent as the men grew more tired and as inexperienced pilots were drawn into the ranks of the active service pilots.

Each squadron was divided into flights of six planes each – A-flight and B-flight. And each flight was divided into sections of three planes each. A flight commander – a flight lieutenant by rank – would lead each section. A-flight would consist of red and yellow sections; B-flight of blue and green sections. This colour coding was by name only, for ease of identification by Controllers and pilots alike.

Generally, the squadron leader would lead the squadron in flight. But he had administrative duties as well and often a flight commander would take command of the squadron in the air. There were, however, countless times during the battle when squadrons had lost their senior flying officers in combat and made do with what was available, sometimes men very junior in rank.

There were three degrees of preparedness for pilots on duty at the airfields: 'Standby' – ready to be aloft within two minutes, with the pilots sometimes sitting in their cockpits on the ground waiting to be dispatched; 'readiness' – ready to go in five minutes, with pilots playing cards or reading or sitting in the sun beside their planes or in huts in the dispersal areas where the planes were parked; and 'available' – on twenty-minute alert, with the pilots getting some sleep or a meal, but remaining on the base.

Group Controllers, eyeing boards in their Ops Room listing the aircraft resources at their disposal at their Group's airfields, would assign squadrons or parts of squadrons to different degrees of preparedness, scrambling them, bringing them forward or standing them down, depending on the needs of the moment. Men who had been on 'standby' and then reduced to 'available' were often yanked away from their meals in the mess a few minutes later and hastily scrambled because a German raid turned out to be more dangerous than had been thought when a squadron at a sister airfield had been scrambled to meet it, or because raiders had sneaked in undetected until spotted by an alert Observer Corps post. Controllers in 11 Group would also, when necessary, call for reinforcements from 10 and 12 Groups on the 11 Group flanks (which led to some controversy within Fighter Command later on).

The standard formation for a squadron in the air was four tight 'Vics' (V-shaped formations) of three planes each, the four Vics making a diamond pattern in the sky, its rear section of three slightly higher than the other three sections. But once the initial attack was made on the enemy raiders, or once the enemy had launched its attack on the British formations, each pilot was on his own, either zooming in to shoot up a bomber or engaged in a frantic dogfight with an enemy fighter. One of the most vivid recollections of almost all the Battle pilots was of one minute being in a sky full of swooping, sweeping, darting fighters trying to shoot each other down, and of being astonishingly, totally alone in a totally empty sky an instant later, their momentum in combat having carried them a great distance from the scene of the fighting.

The Luftwaffe unleashed sporadic bombing attacks on English targets in June and early July. But the Germans had not yet begun their concentrated assault on English targets. Hurrying to build up their post-Dunkirk strength and capabilities, the RAF fighter squadrons thus had time then for some intensive testing and training.

The situation remained ominous. But the reactions of the British varied greatly. Some, notably many of the young pilots and WAAFs, were not at all worried, their youthful exuberance overcoming the premonitions of hardship and worse which some of their countrymen and countrywomen entertained. For some fighter pilots, memories of the losses in France and over Dunkirk weighed heavily. For others, the most pronounced feeling was profound anger, and impatience to be locked in combat with the enemy.

Pilot Officer Pat Hancock

We were under pressure. Tensions were there the whole time. We would drink far more than we should have done at times. We had parties. We'd sing silly songs at times, like all young fighting men do. But 'devil-may-care' – no. It was too serious. I wouldn't say we were straight-faced, po-faced people. Far from it. But we were definitely under no illusions that if the Germans were able they would occupy our country the same way they had already occupied most of Europe. We were on our tod, very much alone. We didn't know at the time that it was the Battle of Britain. The phrase hadn't become commonly used. But we knew it was the battle for Britain.

Pilot Officer Donald Stones

We were angry about France. It was humiliating coming out of there with our tails between our legs. We wanted to get at the Germans.

Pilot Officer Bob Kings

Later in the war, I flew in the Middle East over desert. You'd look down and there was a lot of sand. It meant nothing to me. But flying over Kent and Surrey and the green fields of southern England and the Thames Estuary – that was home. The fact that someone was trying to take it away or break it up made you angry.

Corporal Claire Legge

I don't ever remember being terribly worried. Once, before every-thing started, dear old Trenchard [Air Chief Marshal and 'Father of the Royal Air Force'] – he was retired by then – came down to visit us. We were lined up and he came along and said, 'I don't want you all to worry. You don't have to worry. The chances of anything terrible happening to you are not as bad as you think. For instance,' he said, 'there are all those seagulls flying around over those hangars over there. There's one flying towards us. What do you think the odds are that he will drop something on to one of you?' That was his idea of boosting our morale. It certainly did.

Anthony Weymouth, BBC Commentator
Journal, 2 June

The full force of Nazi brutality, oppression and savagery has been kept for us. What has happened in Germany itself, in Austria, Czechoslovakia, Poland, Norway and Holland will seem trifling compared to what Hitler will do to the hated English once he gets the chance ... I prophesy that Hitler's immediate and future policy will be dictated solely by one factor – what will deliver us most speedily and thoroughly into his hands.

Harold Nicolson, Parliamentary Secretary to the Minister of Information
Diary, 15 June

The events crowd thick and fast and each one seems worse than the other. Yet a curious psychological effect is produced. Fear and sorrow seem to give way to anger and pride. It may be because I know that I shall kill myself and Vita [Sackville-West, his wife] will kill herself if the worst comes. Thus there comes a point where Hitler will cease to trouble either of us and meantime by every means in our power we will continue to worry him. Then there is another state of mind which I notice. I am able almost entirely to dismiss from my thoughts any consideration of the future. I did not even have such pangs about the past as I had when the situation was less catastrophic. My reason tells me that it will be almost impossible to beat the Germans, and that the probability is that we shall be bombed and invaded. I am quite lucidly aware that in three weeks from now, Sissinghurst [his magnificent country mansion with world famous gardens] may be a waste and Vita and I both dead. Yet these probabilities do not fill me with despair. I seem to be impervious both to pleasure and pain. For the moment we are all anaesthetized.

Sir Alexander Cadogan, Permanent Under Secretary, Foreign Office Diary, 29 June

Everything is as gloomy as can be. Probability is that Hitler will attempt invasion in the next fortnight. As far as I can see, we are, after years of leisurely preparation, completely unprepared. We have simply got to die at our posts – a far better fate than capitulating to Hitler as these damned Frogs have done. But uncomfortable.

Pilot Officer Paddy Barthropp

I am absolutely convinced that people my age hadn't the faintest idea, not a bloody clue what was going on. It was just beer, women and Spitfires, a bunch of little John Waynes running about the place. When you were nineteen, you couldn't give a monkey's.

Sergeant Jack Perkin

Looking back, I can't think of anything more exciting than being scrambled. We'd been at readiness, sitting in deck chairs, playing games, always a bit on nerve ends. Then, when that call to scramble came, there was the fun and excitement of actually running to your aircraft – it wasn't good enough to do anything else but run at full speed – perhaps a hundred yards to the plane. Usually there was a fitter already sitting in the aircraft and as soon as he heard the shout to scramble – often accompanied by the shooting of a green Very pistol – he would start the engine immediately. So you'd have an airman on the battery ready to press the button and the fitter inside the cockpit ready to start the engine. He'd jump out and the pilot would jump in. Each squadron aimed at getting into the air in about two minutes. That meant jumping in, doing the straps up and opening the throttle.

I was nineteen years old. We were completely absorbed in this completely new life we were leading. Instead of sitting in offices – I had been an office boy in a timber merchant's office in London and had hated every minute of it – suddenly we had this marvellous life of living with thirty or forty other men, flying aeroplanes all day long. We weren't worried about the war. We had a lot of confidence that it would work out in the end.

At about the time France caved in, I remember some of the men saying, 'That could be the end.' We were very worried that the government would sue for peace. The idea that this very exciting life might suddenly come to an end, and that we might all find ourselves back doing office work, was alarming. We were tremendously relieved when Churchill gave his speeches about never giving in. That was tremendously relieving to all of us who, for purely selfish reasons, didn't want to give in. We wanted to join the fight.

Leonard Marsland Gander, Radio Correspondent of the Daily Telegraph
Diary, 6 July

We were awakened [at home at Angmering-on-Sea, Sussex] just before dawn by a savage fusillade of machine-gun and rifle fire. Was it invasion? Only a hundred yards away Brens were blazing away, the bullets whipping the sea. Hilda nudged me urgently and asked me what we should do. I couldn't think of anything useful to do except to lie where we were and await developments. There was no artillery fire and no sound of aeroplanes so I concluded that it might after all be practice in the grey light.

Keith Park, Air Vice Marshal, Commanding, 11 Group, Royal Air Force

TASKS OF GROUP 11 FIGHTERS
These may be summarized as follows:

1. To avoid being attacked on the ground and when taking off;
2. To destroy bombers and fighters attacking fighter aerodromes;
3. To continue operating from inland aerodromes – sectors and satellites – whilst these are being attacked;
4. To destroy enemy aircraft in the following order of importance;
    (i) Transport aircraft
    (ii) Dive bombers
    (iii) Reconnaissance aircraft and high bombers
    (iv) Fighters which will be attacking our bombers and army co-operation aircraft.

All squadron and flight commanders must impress upon their pilots that to defeat an attempted invasion will demand the utmost physical and mental effort from all flying personnel. An attempted invasion will probably be defeated in twenty-four, or at most forty-eight hours and whilst an invasion is being attempted, all pilots must be prepared to do up to eight short patrols a day. It is anticipated that targets for fighters will be so plentiful that patrols will consist of very short flights, when patrols will be required to land and re-arm, probably not refuelling after every flight.

* * *

There was, of course, never any guarantee that the RAF would be able to beat back the Luftwaffe or that the Germans would wait until Fighter Command had been crippled before trying to invade. It was clear that once the Germans controlled the Channel coast in France, the invasion was conceivable at any time. Consequently, even before the Dunkirk evacuation, plans were being drawn up in London to meet this danger.

Pillars, poles, tank traps, barbed wire barriers and other obstructions were planted and dug to block German landings, either airborne or on the shore – and there were at least 500 miles of English coastline where a seaborne incursion was a real possibility. People were evacuated from coastal regions thought to be particularly vulnerable. Roadblocks were erected. (There were several incidents in which civilians were shot and killed for failing to stop and identify themselves.) Road signs were taken down and people were told that no directions were to be provided to strangers, all of whom were to be considered possible German agents.

Detailed instructions were issued to the populace on how to deal with the enemy should the invasion take place. The duties of the police in such a situation were outlined. Warnings were issued against despair and pessimism. In some cases, individuals heard to utter words of doom and gloom were jailed or fined. There were spy scares aplenty, some of which reached preposterous proportions. A man was reported to the police in Winchester as a suspected enemy agent because of his very un-English and highly suspicious failure to flush the toilet in the house in which he was staying – he was, in fact, a British officer billeted there. Thousands of aliens from Germany, Austria and Italy – which joined the war on Germany's side in June – were interned, including, ironically, many who had fled to England to escape the fascists at home and some of whom later had to share their internment quarters with captured Nazis.

The regular British army at the time consisted of twenty-six divisions. Twelve of those divisions were made up of new recruits being hastily trained. Most of the others were still groggy from the pasting they had received from the Germans in Europe before being snatched back to safety in England. So much equipment had been left at Dunkirk that the army might have been very sorely tried if the Germans had been in a position to attempt to land then, even without mastery of the air. In key places along the coast, there was only a single machine-gun to cover each 5,000 feet of shore.

In such circumstances, a volunteer Home Guard was rapidly recruited. It was composed of men who, because they were too old or otherwise ineligible for regular military service, had remained in civilian life. It was the object of the Home Guard to fill the gaps left by the army, to guard the roads, bridges and coastal locations which the army was too stretched to monitor, and to serve as a reserve force for the army in combat, if needed. Also under-equipped and hardly up to military standards, this 'Dad's Army' trained with patriotic dedication and patrolled with great vigilance, though it is unlikely that its members would have amounted to much of a deterrent if they had ever actually encountered German paratroopers or glider troops on English country roads.

War Office, 15 May

The War Office announces that in order to supplement, from sources as yet untapped, the Home Defences of the country, it has been decided to create a new force to be known as 'Local Defence Volunteers' [this name was soon changed to 'Home Guard' by Winston Churchill who had a better understanding of the impact of words].

This force, which will be voluntary and unpaid, will be open to British subjects between the ages of seventeen and sixty-five years of age. The period of service will be for the duration of the war. Volunteers accepted will be provided with uniforms and will be armed.

Men of reasonable physical fitness and a knowledge of firearms should give in their names at their local police stations. The need is greatest in small towns, villages and less densely populated areas. The duties of the force can be undertaken in a volunteer's spare time. Members of existing civil defence organizations should consult their officers before registering under this scheme.

Assistant Section Leader Molly Wilkinson

After the evacuation of Dunkirk and after France fell, one took a deep breath and thought, 'What happens now?' I was worried, but in a young sort of way – really full of hope. I remember thinking how marvellous that people like my father who had fought in the First World War and were now too old for this war, were in the Home Guard, getting out their shotguns, anything, to train to defend the country against invasion.

Les Linggard, Fire Warden

Some poor perishers who were with the Local Defence Volunteers had only pitchforks for weapons. Our troops were not as well equipped as they ought to have been. We hadn't got as many aircraft as we ought to have had. We'd had the impression that everything was not as rosy as it might have been. But I didn't realize that things were going to get tough until they sacked Chamberlain and Churchill took over. We knew he was a tough one.

Sylvia Yeatman

When my husband was at Detling Aerodrome, I did coding there. I had done coding at the Foreign Office before the war. The CO found it out. They were short of WAAFs at Detling then, so I did night and day duty.

In the hut where I worked there was a row of hockey sticks. I asked the CO what they were doing there. He said, 'That's in case the Germans come. They're for the WAAFs. We haven't got enough revolvers to go round.' I didn't want a hockey stick to hit a German with. I had a friend who worked in the small arms school at Hythe, so I got hold of a revolver. The chaps on the base used to look through the window at my revolver on my desk. I don't think they liked that at all. It made them nervous.

Charles Graves, Home Guard

In the early days, we had orders to stop everybody we saw after dusk on the Downs and ask for their identity cards. I wonder if in any other part of the country so many lovers were disturbed as in that real lovers' paradise. On our first night, we came across a couple in a car – this was before the ban on pleasure motoring – and as they stole furtively away on the approach of our armed party, our leader held them up, demanded their identity cards, and said to the man, 'Do you know that you have been in a prohibited area?' 'No, he hasn't,' snapped the girl.

A big shot from Hailsham came down one day to ginger us up. I was asked to pass on to the troops his somewhat bloodthirsty picture of what was to happen when the Germans came, explaining the roadblocks and tank traps – a sort of 'general idea' of the coming battle. We villagers were to 'contain' the Germans till the arrival of the real soldiers from the rear. 'Of course, none of you chaps will probably be alive when they get here and drive the Huns back into the sea.'

Winston Churchill

Should the invader come to Britain, there will be no placid lying down of the people in submission before him, as we have seen alas in other countries. We shall defend every village, every town and every city. The vast mass of London itself, fought street by street, could easily devour an entire hostile army, and we would rather see London laid in ruins and ashes than that it should be tamely and abjectly enslaved ... All depends now upon the life-strength of the British race ... and of all our associated peoples, and of all our well wishers in every land, doing their utmost night and day, giving all, daring all, enduring all to the utmost, to the end. This is no war of chieftains or of princes, of dynasties or national ambitions. This is a war of peoples and causes ... This is a war of the unknown warrior. But let us strive without failing in faith or in duty, and the dark cause of Hitler will be lifted from our age.

Dr J.H. Leakey

The Local Defence Volunteers were ... at the start ... more of a menace than an asset. I remember one night being called over about 1.00 a.m. to visit the little boys at Benenden as one of them was rather ill. I climbed into the car cursing at the thought of a three mile drive in the middle of the night. As I was turning down Golford corner, an uncouth youth, flourishing some sort of musket of ancient vintage, held me up. As he seemed extremely uncertain how to manipulate his weapon, he filled me with an agony of nervous apprehension. 'For God's sake, put that bloody thing down,' I said. 'I am sure you will do either yourself or me severe damage if you are not careful.' He meekly obliged and laid the musket on the ground. He then asked to see my papers and bent over unarmed, reading them by the light of my side lamps. Then, having given me back my papers, he picked up his blunderbuss and allowed me to go on, obviously feeling very pleased with himself over the whole affair.

Major E.A. Cox Field, A Company, Fourth Buckinghamshire Battalion, Home Guard

We were lucky in that among our earliest volunteers were a high proportion of 'old sweats', ex-NCOs of the regular army and of the army of the last war. They provided us with the nucleus of a grand staff of instructors ... We had one difficulty in our training. In our area, we never had any Field Force troops. But one way or another, we managed to find people to fight ... When we could not get regulars to fight, we fought anybody we could persuade to fight us. We fought two battles against the Thame Home Guard and each time we defeated them against heavy odds ... In one encounter we found [a] substitute for grenades. A man from Lacey Green brought a clutch of addled goose eggs. One of them in your face and you sought the decontamination centre.

Daily Mail, *28 June*

Any motorist who leaves his car unattended even for a minute, at any hour of the day or night, is now compelled to put it out of action, under an order made by the Minister of Home Security. Moreover a car is unattended unless there is someone, aged fourteen or more, either inside or near it and within sight – an important point at night. One person cannot 'attend' more than one car, so do not regard a car park man as 'attending' your car.

This is what you must do to put a motor vehicle out of action: *By day* – (1) Remove the ignition key and lock the car ... If you cannot do both these things you must either (a) remove an essential part of the mechanism – the distributor arm or the main ignition lead, (b) apply a locking device to the mechanism, steering wheel, or a road wheel, or (c) put the car in a locked garage or yard.

By night – You must remove the key and lock the car as before and also remove part of the mechanism. If you cannot do all three things, the car must be locked in a garage or yard.

Air Commodore A. Warrington Morris, Commandant, Observer Corps

TRAINING INSTRUCTIONS
The only weapon available to the parachutist during the jump are a pistol, which is carried in a thigh pocket of the trousers, and several small hand grenades the shape of an egg, which are carried loose in the trouser pockets. If he anticipates resistance by the enemy on landing, he holds a hand grenade in each of his hands, which he holds above his head so that he is in a ready position to throw them. This holding of the hands above the head should not be confused with a desire to surrender.

Assistant Section Officer Molly Wilkinson

I used to have to drive and take secret documents to Huntingdon from Ipswich – eighty miles. I was given a revolver and whenever I did this drive, I had to have it in the pocket of the car in case I met a German parachutist.

Prime Minister to the Home Secretary

The police, and as soon as possible the ARP [Air Raid Precaution] services, are to be divided into combatant and non-combatant, armed and unarmed. The armed will co-operate actively in fighting with the Home Guard and regulars in their neighbourhood, and will withdraw with them if necessary; the unarmed will actively assist in the 'stay put' policy for civilians. Should they fall into an area effectively occupied by the enemy, they may surrender and submit with the rest of the inhabitants, but must not in those circumstances give any aid to the enemy in maintaining order, or in any other way. They may assist the civil population as far as possible.

Gunner Fred Taylor

Every field in the marshes had telephone posts stuck up so no planes could land. And as you went through the villages on the way to the coast, you could see that they'd built concrete bunkers inside village shops at strategic points. Hay ricks in the field were erected around concrete bunkers there so that when the invasion came, there'd be fortified positions to fight from.

Pilot Officer Jas Storrar

They cut the hedges down around our airfield to give better visibility against a German ground attack and we had boxes of grenades at dispersal in case German paratroopers came down on top of us. We really expected them and it was hard to see that we had enough men or machines to stop them.

New York Times

London, 11 June – Working against time to complete preparations before an anticipated German attack, engineers operating massive American-built excavators are tearing huge, jagged scars across the beautiful parklands around London, while camouflage experts are making it difficult or impossible for airmen to recognize former landmarks. For many miles around London now there is not an open space on which a troop-carrying plane could land without crashing into a trench or earthwork. So thoroughly have place names and other marks of identification been removed from garages, stations, post offices and notice boards that a parachutist, even provided with map and compass, would stand a good chance of getting lost ... Cricketers every night push disused trucks onto their playing fields, police block arterial roads, farmers leave implements around and sharpshooters – the 'parashots' – take positions behind hedges and sandbagged emplacements ... Owners of many country houses near London had trees painted over them.

Gunner Robert Angell

I started off in the army in the field artillery. I was eighteen at the time and, being under nineteen, was classed as one of the 'Immatures'. That was the official name for us. The government said we were too young to go and fight abroad. So my battery went off to France at the beginning without me and were all captured by the Germans while I was put on Home Defence. For me, that meant the anti-aircraft. That's what landed me up sitting on the sea-front at Dover, just at the edge of the harbour, nineteen miles from the enemy. On a clear day, you could see them over in France. You could see their cars going up and down and you could see trains puffing smoke.

We soon got used to the fact that the Germans had coastal guns which were firing at Dover. We posted a sentry – sometimes it was me – to watch the coast. He'd watch for a flash, shout a warning when he saw one, and we'd start counting. When we'd counted up to twenty, we'd all get down because we knew bloody well that a shell was about to fall somewhere in the vicinity. The harbour was the target and that's where we were. In fact, a shell did hit the Dover Municipal Swimming Baths right behind us.

Chiefs of Staff Committee, War Cabinet, 14 June 1940

The evacuation [of coastal regions that might be invaded] would be on a semi-compulsory basis in that all evacuees would be told that it was their national duty to move out. All arrangements for the evacuation ... were already made but it would take a little time to sort out those who should go from those who should stay ... It was agreed that on military grounds it was eminently desirable that any evacuation which was to be carried out should be done as early as possible; otherwise it might be too late ... Two or three days' notice was ... necessary before the invasion materialized if the scheme was to be of any value. Some doubt was expressed whether there was any likelihood of our getting this warning of an invasion, but it was pointed out that the Chiefs of Staff had always considered that intensive air attacks on the RAF and the aircraft industries would be a preliminary to any invasion on a large scale. Such attacks might therefore give us the necessary warning.

War Cabinet Minutes, 3 July

The Prime Minister expects all His Majesty's servants in high places to set an example of steadiness and resolution. They should check and rebuke expressions of loose and ill-digested opinion in their circles, or by their subordinates. They should not hesitate to report, or if necessary remove, any officers or officials who are found to be consciously exercising a disturbing or depressing influence, and whose talk is calculated to spread alarm and despondency. Thus alone will they be worthy of the fighting men who, in the air, on the sea and on the land, have already met the enemy without any sense of being outmatched in martial qualities.

General Sir Edmund Ironside
Diary, 13 July

[The Germans] daren't not do something. They will begin with some three or four days' intensive bombing and then air landings with parachutists, followed by sea landings according to the weather. All carried out in different places so as to upset us and get our troops rushing about the country. If our men will attack *à fond*, all is well. But they are so dreadfully untrained that we cannot depend upon them to go in successfully.

*   *   *

There were some 8,000 Americans living in Britain at the time, mostly in London. A group of them formed a Home Guard unit of their own despite the strong disapproval of United States ambassador Joseph Kennedy. Kennedy had advised Americans in Britain to make for home as soon as possible. He was convinced that 'England will go down fighting. Unfortunately I am one who does not believe that it is going to do the slightest bit of good.'

Despite lack of encouragement from the American ambassador, Churchill, the son of an American mother, looked across the Atlantic in his desperate search for arms and perhaps even greater support. The United States had come to the aid of England and France when they had been threatened by Germany two decades earlier. It was clear, however, that this time most Americans preferred to stay aloof from the conflict between foreigners across the sea.

Isolationist sentiments were widely felt and widely articulated, most notably by the 'American First Committee', which was then being formed. Some Americans merely wanted no part of foreign troubles. Others felt that American involvement in any way would just prolong a tragic struggle which they believed could best be settled through negotiations. A comparatively small but vociferous group was tinged with pro-Nazi sentiments. Students at Columbia University in New York and elsewhere demonstrated against American involvement with placards bearing the legend THE YANKS ARE *NOT* COMING. However, a growing number of Americans were coming to believe not only that the Nazis were evil and should be opposed in a concrete fashion on moral grounds, but also that they were a potential threat to America's own security.

As a former Assistant Secretary of the Navy, President Franklin Roosevelt recognized the danger the German fleet could pose to the United States if England was subjugated and the ships of the Royal Navy were seized by the Germans, providing them with truly formidable naval resources. Churchill, who had established a correspondence with Roosevelt many years before when he had been at the Admiralty in London, was not slow to press that point home in private communications to the White House from 'Former Naval Person'.

Roosevelt and others in Washington also saw that a German victory over Britain, and the mood of invincibility it would kindle in Berlin, could be a prelude to a systematic expansion of German influence in South America, where there were already active Nazi movements with close links to Berlin. A Nazi party was, for example, well established in Chile; Uruguay had to beat off an attempted Nazi coup just before the start of the Battle of Britain; and the Brazilian government showed distinct signs of succumbing to fascist doctrines.

Then, as now, the interests of the United States were seen to be directly at stake in Latin America. The British did not overlook this fact when trying to pry armaments and supplies out of America. They sought to convince American leaders that Britain's struggle was their struggle as well, and they were not without success. Secretary of the Interior Harold Ickes was, for example, not alone when he told President Roosevelt, 'It seems to me that we Americans are like the householder who refuses to lend or sell his fire extinguishers to help put out the fire in the house that is right next door although the house is all ablaze and the wind is blowing from that direction.' American diplomats in Berlin also sent warnings about long term German intentions.

Roosevelt was sympathetic, but there were congressional restraints on him; and generally, the American public simply did not want to be enmeshed in a war it could avoid. The President wasn't about to push them into one, certainly not in an election year in which he was running for an unprecedented third term. Aside from that inhibiting quadrennial factor, there was no certainty that Britain would be able to withstand the expected German onslaught, even if it received American aid. Ambassador Kennedy, one of whose sons would later also occupy the White House, had been sending

Roosevelt and the State Department gloomy prognoses even before the Dunkirk evacuation.

The United States Ambassador in the United Kingdom to the Secretary of State
24 May

PERSONAL FOR THE SECRETARY
The situation according to the people who know is very, very grim. The mass of people just never seem to realize that England can be beaten or that the worst can happen to them ... They feel that they will protect themselves well in the daytime and, at night, the efforts of the Germans cannot be anything but indiscriminate, and they expect to return the attack on German locations, and in this way hold on for some time until help can arrive from the United States. Finally, I don't think that, if the French and British Expeditionary Force are licked in their present struggle, things will turn out quite as well as the English hope. I do not underestimate the courage and guts of the people, but from the reports brought back by American newspapermen who were with the forces in Belgium and northern France, it is going to take more than guts to hold off the systematic air attacks of the Germans coupled with their terrific superiority in numbers.

For the President from Former Naval Person
London, 15 June

SECRET AND PERSONAL
Although the present Government [of Britain] and I personally would never fail to send the fleet across the Atlantic if resistance was beaten down here, a point may be reached in the struggle where the present ministers no longer have control of affairs and when very easy terms could be obtained for the British islands by their becoming a vassal state of the Hitler empire. A pro-German government would certainly be called into being to make peace and might present to a shattered or a starving nation an almost irresistible case for entire submission to the Nazi will. The fate of the British fleet ... would be decisive on the future of the United States because if it were joined to the fleets of Japan, France and Italy and the great resources of German industry, overwhelming sea power would be in Hitler's

hands ... This revolution in sea power might happen very quickly and certainly long before the United States would be able to prepare against it. If we go [down] you may have a United States of Europe under the Nazi command far more numerous, far stronger, far better armed than the New [World].

Alexander Kirk, United States Chargé d'Affaires in Germany, to the State Department
Berlin, 17 June

The United States is the only power in the world which can effectively oppose Hitler now and in the future, and he knows it. It is easy to say that it is safe, in so far as Nazi aspirations are concerned, or even that in the post-war plan of the regime, a world is envisaged in which the United States will maintain its established position in co-operation with the German hegemony in its extended spheres of influence, and the utterances of Hitler himself would tend to quiet any fears to the contrary. The development of Nazi aims in the past, however, and the contradictions in fact which have characterized his other assurances, would not justify any belief in those assumptions. It is also easy to assume that even if Hitler intends to launch an offensive against the Western Hemisphere, the United States can oppose and destroy Hitler after he has established his domination of Europe; and finally the assumption may be offered that, as there is a limit to what the power galvanized by one human being can achieve, time and the extension of that power will eventually negative its effectiveness ... The position of America, therefore, is clear. There will be no place in the world envisaged by Hitler, and he will exercise his power with a view to eliminating it as a great power as soon as possible. He will not attack the Americans by force, as he can attain his aims by other methods, once he has established his domination over the countries of Europe. He will strangle the United States economically and financially and even if he does not succeed in breaking down the solidarity of the countries of the Western Hemisphere, which may be precarious at present, he will confront the United States within a brief measure of time with the impossible tasks of adjusting its system to an economy in which it will be excluded from access to all foreign markets. The fight, therefore, which is now being waged in Europe, is a fight for the preservation of the American order, and complete defeat of the Allies in the present battles is the defeat of the United States.

American First Committee

STATEMENT OF PRINCIPLES
1. The United States must build an impregnable defense for America.
2. No foreign power, nor group of powers, can successfully attack a prepared America.
3. American democracy can be preserved only by keeping out of the European war.
4. 'Aid short of war' weakens national defense at home and threatens to involve America in war abroad.

Century Group, Committee to Defend America

If Germany wins control of the North Atlantic, the period prior to the completion of our own two-ocean navy will be a period of acute danger for us. During that period, the United States could be invaded from the Atlantic. In order to remove the risk of invasion, the government should take all possible steps to prevent German control of the North Atlantic. The most certain preventative – until our two-ocean navy is built – is the continued existence of the British Fleet. And the fate of the British Fleet will be settled by the battle for the control of the North Atlantic which is about to begin on the shores of England, Scotland and Ireland.

* * *

Despite his pro-British sympathies, Roosevelt was strictly bound by congressional restrictions not to diminish America's own defensive capabilities by distributing arms to foreigners. But he did manage to find a half-million rifles which could reasonably be considered 'surplus to American requirements' and to let the British cart them off. These were of First World War vintage, but had never been used and had been stored in grease. They were greatly welcomed by Churchill, who was finally able to distribute a fair number of usable weapons to the Home Guard. An American Committee for the Defense of British Homes managed to put together a few cases of shotguns, hunting rifles and other small arms to send to the British, but that was little more than a gesture. Of far greater significance, Roosevelt managed during the course of the Battle of Britain to push a Lend-Lease Agreement through Congress. Fifty old but usable American destroyers were transferred to the British to beef up the

Royal Navy, in return for leases on military bases in British colonies in the West Indies and Newfoundland. It was easy enough to dismiss the protests of isolationists by pointing out that American control of extra bases in the Western Hemisphere enhanced rather than diminished the security of the United States in a troubled world. Besides, a corps of highly professional, London-based American newspaper and radio correspondents daily fed vivid accounts to the American people of the heroic efforts of the hard-pressed British to thwart Nazi attempts to subjugate them and of the daring exploits of the outnumbered RAF fighter pilots. It aroused widespread admiration on the other side of the Atlantic.

THE BATTLE IS JOINED

Short of pilots, short of planes and solemnly pondering the baptism of battle it had just endured, Fighter Command could at least take satisfaction from the realization that everyone now acknowledged the crucial, central role it had to play in the defence of Britain. But though it had begun rebuilding its operational strength during the post-Dunkirk lull in June and early July, there was no real break in the conflict. There was no recurrence of the 'phoney war', no suggestion that the worst was over. While licking and treating their earlier wounds, RAF fighter squadrons continued to tangle with the enemy in furious, spasmodic encounters.

After Dunkirk, they were dispatched to cover smaller scale evacuations of units of British forces driven back helter-skelter to other points along the French Channel coast. At the same time, the Germans, trying out their newly acquired bases in westernmost Europe, began sending planes on reconnaissance missions over the Channel and over parts of Britain. Fighters were sent aloft to intercept them and to intercept German aircraft on sporadic bombing raids against British targets, sometimes in response to British bomber raids on German-occupied Europe.

BRITAIN IS BOMBED
Waves of German Planes Attempt Retaliation for RAF Raids
Air Alarm in Berlin
By James MacDonald
Special cable to the New York Times

London, Saturday 22 June – German bombs thundered over parts of this country early today as the Nazi air force retaliated for new British aerial attacks on targets in many points in Germany, France and the Netherlands. Names of counties where warning sirens went off and anti-aircraft guns blazed were withheld when the raids began at about midnight. But the area affected was large, embracing east and south coast points and even western England ... In some communities, the alarm lasted four hours or more and the people, huddled in shelters, heard terrific explosions ... Bitter aerial fights between raiders and defending planes occurred after a network of searchlights enmeshed the Germans in their beams.

Gunner Fred Taylor

I worked the searchlights on the Romney Marsh just off the coast. We were very primitive in those days, listening for incoming planes with great big earphones – square, six-foot-long, box-shaped things, stretching out to a point. By closing your eyes and listening, you could get an idea of the position of the plane. The position was relayed by the listeners to the men who directed the searchlights. We always had to be twelve degrees in front of the plane because of the sound lag. And, with luck, there was the plane. At the time, there was no ack-ack down where we were. We lit up the incoming planes for our fighters to see. During the daytime, we manned machine-guns in case there was an enemy attack. One day, I was reporting by telephone to a relay point on a plane I saw coming in, heading for the town of Rye. When it was over Rye, I reported I could see one, two, three flat things falling from the plane. I always imagined that if they were bombs, they would be falling point downward. But these were falling flat. The man at the other end of the line asked, 'Are they bombs?' I said, 'I don't think so. But hold on a minute. They've turned and now they're falling point downward.' Then I heard the whumph, whumph, whumph, and I told him, 'They were bombs all right.'

New York Times

London, 25 June – The authorities obviously have done much to co-ordinate defense measures. Thus, instead of one suburban siren following another – and some confusedly and belatedly wailing the alarm while others were sounding the all clear – all seemed to blast out today's warning together. Early commuters to London found only one aftermath of the three hours upset in the city. There were no morning papers and those travelling in the first trains sat idly gazing at advertisements they had perhaps never previously noticed.

Pilot Officer Donald Stones

One day towards the end of June, we were told to stand by for an investiture by King George on the parade ground at Biggin Hill.

That was the day Flight Lieutenant Jimmy Davis and Sergeant McQueen were shot down. Jimmy Davis was an American who had been commissioned in the RAF before the war. He was a first class pilot and a great chap. In the afternoon, Sergeant Cartwright, Sergeant Whitby and myself received our decorations from the King. Jimmy, having been killed, wasn't there to receive his. The King asked about the remaining Distinguished Flying Cross on the table. He was told what had happened to Jimmy. He seemed quite moved.

Mollie Panter-Downes
London War Notes, 28 June

Rural areas have had far more alarms and actual bombings than the cities, and it's ironical that many people who fled to country retreats when war broke out have been in the thick of it, as they wouldn't have been if they'd stayed put in peaceful Chelsea or Hampstead. The German raiders have turned up in all sorts of places where they weren't expected. A boys' school which migrated from a danger area on the east coast to a supposedly quiet spot in the southwest came in for quite a spectacular raid the night the boys arrived – to the delight of the pupils and the consternation of the staff.

Leonard Marsland Gander, Radio Correspondent of the Daily Telegraph
Diary, 10 July

I have been exploring the possibilities of turning the garage ... into an air-raid shelter. Elmer, the builder, says however that there will be difficulty in getting timber to support the roof. There is also the question of what I shall do with the car and the feeling that the passage downstairs is probably just as good anyway.

Daily Express, *10 July*

For an hour early yesterday morning, the people of a southwest coast town sat in their air-raid shelters. They listened to the anti-aircraft guns. Some heard the engines of the German planes. They heard the roar of the British fighters overhead. Then they heard a series of terrific bomb explosions and they pictured their town in ruins. As the all clear sounded, the townsfolk came out to see what damage had been done. Those near the seashore stopped amazed – then they ran home as though the Germans had returned. Back they came with baskets, tin baths, buckets, prams and barrows. They waded into the sea and filled up with fish killed or stunned by the explosion of bombs in the water. They pulled them in in the hundreds – flat fish and fat fish, big fish and small, cod and whiting ... The Germans did not damage the town, but when they dropped all their bombs in the sea and fled, they provided enough fish to supply the town's breakfast, dinner *and* tea.

War Cabinet Minutes, 11 July

War Cabinet had before them a memorandum by the Minister of Information [Alfred Duff Cooper] urging recommendation of the decision reached by the War Cabinet on 3 July that reports of casualties caused by German air raids should in the future be stated in general terms and should not give details of the precise number killed and injured. In favour of the publication of the exact number, it was urged that the withholding of publication of facts known to a large number of people in this country created doubt and disquiet.

The Minister of Information and the Minister of Home Security [Sir John Anderson] said that evidence in this sense was accumulating in reports from the regions. Public opinion in this country could be relied upon to accept bad news, provided they knew that they were being given the full facts. On the other hand, it was argued that the Home Front was now the frontline trench, and that there was no more reason to publish the detailed casualties inflicted on civilians each day than there would have been to publish daily casualties inflicted in particular sectors of the battle front in Flanders. The day-to-day publication of the numbers of civilians killed must have a depressing effect on public opinion here, and must have some value to the enemy.

The Prime Minister suggested that, if it was necessary to publish information as to total civilian casualties sustained, this could be done periodically.

* * *

For the Fighter Command pilots who had tangled with the Luftwaffe over France, Belgium and Holland, the battle had commenced in earnest weeks earlier. But as a distinctive, critical episode in the

Second World War, the Battle of Britain is reckoned to have begun on 10 July 1940. The fixing of that date might be considered arbitrary. During the ten days *prior* to the 'opening' of the battle, no less than twenty-eight British fighter planes were destroyed and eighteen pilots killed. One squadron had been so relentlessly engaged during that period and earlier that it had to be sent north to recuperate (where two of its most experienced pilots immediately crashed in a simple training exercise). Another squadron was down to only eight operational aircraft and others were below strength as well.

But 10 July, as Dowding later noted in his report to the Secretary of State for Air, was the day the Germans employed 'the first really big formations – seventy aircraft – intended primarily to bring our fighter defences to battle on a large scale'. It was a harbinger of things to come. Before the Battle of Britain was brought to a close, such formations, and very much larger ones, regularly darkened the skies over England.

The Battle was divided into phases. During the first phase, which lasted until 12 August, the Germans concentrated most of their attacks on convoys steaming through the Channel and on English coastal targets. Their bombers were sent out with strong formations of fighter escorts. The primary object was to exhaust Fighter Command by luring its fighters, which were obliged to defend British targets from bombing raids, into combat within comfortable reach of the new German airbases in occupied Europe. They would be overwhelmed by the numbers of the enemy and Britain's capacity to resist would be crippled even before the main Luftwaffe onslaught was launched.

In terms of gains and losses, the opening day of this first phase of the battle was a good day for the British. The Germans managed to sink a small ship in a convoy, but they lost sixteen aircraft (shot down or damaged) to six lost by the RAF. British pilots returning to their bases were elated by their performance and the performance of their aircraft. But the events of the day contained a frightening message for Fighter Command. When all reports were in, it was realized that, in notching up its impressive score, RAF fighters had flown more than 600 sorties by the end of the day – an extravagant outlay in view of Fighter Command's strained circumstances.

In the days that followed, this pace was for the most part sustained, and while the British retained a convincing lead in the kill-loss ratio, most of the German aircraft they shot down were bombers which, aside from their bombing assignments, were decoys for Luftwaffe fighters hovering above them, waiting to swoop down; on the other hand, virtually all the British aircraft destroyed or damaged came, as the Germans intended, from Dowding's precious stock of Spitfires and Hurricanes. Furthermore, most of the British pilots killed during this period were experienced flyers, many of whom had been blooded over France and during the Dunkirk episode. They would be impossible to replace at short notice. And many who survived had been flying two or three sorties a day, practically every day, had been kept on readiness when not aloft, and were close to exhaustion. At that rate, questions could be asked about whether Fighter Command would be in any condition to beat off the expected Luftwaffe assault on inland targets.

While assessing the grim prospects, Dowding, still carefully husbanding his reserves, was pressed to shift fighters to bases closer to the coast, the better to be able to meet the German attacks quickly. Such a move presented problems. For one thing, the Germans regularly sent out several attacking formations. Though they were usually picked up by radar as they formed up over France, it was rarely possible to predict which would head for targets deserving priority defensive attention from the limited numbers of forward aircraft. Aside from that, being based so close to the incoming attackers, the British fighters did not have time to climb to altitudes above the enemy and were often sitting ducks for Messerschmitt 109s zooming down on them from above and out of the sun. BEWARE THE HUN IN THE SUN became a maxim for British fighter pilots, but not one they were always able to observe.

ENGLAND FIGHTS OFF BIGGEST AIR ATTACK
By Frank Kelley, New York Herald Tribune

London, 11 July – Day-long sallies by waves of German bombers against coastal objectives in England, Wales and Scotland reached a grand climax yesterday in the greatest and fiercest air battle in ten and a half months of war when seventy-five Nazi bombers, escorted by forty-five or more fighters, roared across the English Channel in two formations and showered bombs on a strongly defended convoy bringing vital food and other supplies to these besieged islands.

For more than an hour, the Germans came over. They churned up the Channel with scores of bombs which touched off thundering echoes along the chalk cliffs of England, dodged a fierce barrage of anti-aircraft fire from merchant ships and warships and whirled about the sky with dozens of Spitfires and Hurricanes on their tails.

Pilot Officer Steve Stephen

For me, the period up to the end of July was the most intense, the most vicious part of the Battle of Britain. The Germans were dive bombing harbours, dive bombing installations, bombing convoys. And large numbers of German fighters came in, trying to shoot us out of the sky. They kept coming over. They were at us all day long. You felt the pressure. We fought back. They had to be stopped, but by 1 August, we had only about eight of the pilots left from the ones we had had earlier.

Flight Lieutenant Frank Howell
Letter home

Bags of excitement here – almost too much. The other day, Red Section was sent up to 18,000 over Portland. It was a mucky day, and we had to go up through two layers of cloud. Control gave us a bearing to fly on and said that we ought to meet a Jerry, possibly two, which were in the vicinity. He had hardly finished speaking when out of the cloud loomed a Ju 88. Whoopee! I told numbers two and three to look out for enemy fighters while I made an almost head on attack at it. I don't think he liked that one little bit because he turned over and went split arse for the sea, releasing four large bombs, and doing over 350 mph. I got in another attack and got his port motor. I was going to do a third when I saw the other chaps screaming down at him. So I let them have a go, being a generous chap! Just then I smelt a nasty smell! An 'orrid smell! I looked at the dials and things and saw that the coolant temperature was right off the clock – about 180°C, and the oil temperature was at 95° and going up. The bugger had shot me in the radiator! White fumes began pouring back into the cockpit, so I thought that was not really good enough. The poor old motor began to seize up. I called up Bandy and said, 'Hello Bandy Control, Red One calling – I am going to bale out four miles off Poole!' The silly C at the end, of course, couldn't hear me and asked me to repeat. Bah. Still, I still had 5,000 feet so I told him again and wished him a very good afternoon, and stepped smartly from the aircraft.

I read something somewhere about pulling a ripcord so had a grope, found same, pulled same, and sat up with a jerk but with no damage to the important parts.

Everything was lovely – quiet as a church, a lovely day, a spot of sun, three ships two miles away who would be bound to see me! Found myself holding the handle so flung it away – chucked my helmet away but kept the goggles! Undid my shoes, blew up my Mae West, and leaned back and admired the scenery. The water quite suddenly came very close – a swish and then I began my final swim of the season. I set out with a lusty crawl for Bournemouth, thinking I might shoot a hell of a line staggering up the beach with beauteous barmaids dashing down the beach with bottles of brandy. Instead, the current was taking me out to sea, and I was unceremoniously hauled on board a twelve-foot motorboat. Still, the navy pushed out a boat and the half tumbler of whisky went down with a rush!

Sergeant Mike Croskell

We were based for a week at Hullavington near Bristol. It was just a field, just a farmer's field. We didn't even have loos. We'd go to the farmer's place next door. They were expecting German bombers over Bristol. We were patrolling the area at night. We never saw anything. We just went up and down for an hour and a half and that was it. One of the fellows managed to bring his car down. We went into the nearest town and paid sixpence for a bath.

My first combat engagement was not long afterwards. It was during a very big raid – a lot of dive bombers with a large fighter escort. They were going to raid the big naval base at Portland Bill, I think. We intercepted them over the sea as they were coming in. I got behind a Ju 88. I didn't seem to shoot for very long before it started to smoke out of the port engine. The crew obligingly got out, slid down the wing and parachuted down. But there were a lot of their friends about, Me 109s, who began paying a good deal of attention to me. I went around and around in circles with about five of these chaps chasing after me, until I eventually got behind the last of the five and shot him down. Suddenly his mates didn't seem to be around anymore. But that was a bad day for us. Our squadron alone lost three aircraft. Two pilots were killed – both very experienced men.

SCRAMBLE

Pilot Officer Birdie Bird-Wilson

Our standard formation was an extremely tight one which would have been ideal for pre-war air shows. Very compact. Very close together. The pilots in the formation were looking at each other so as not to collide. We were not looking around as we should have. The Germans, who had learned many flying lessons during the Spanish Civil War, knew better. They flew in much looser formations and were able to pick us off.

Squadron Leader James Leathart

All our attack practice had been designed for us to meet unescorted bombers. There had been years of a complete waste of bloody time. We had to learn from scratch how to fight the Germans.

Squadron Leader Peter Devitt

We were absolute sitting ducks to start with. We didn't know what to expect. We didn't know anything about dogfighting. All we'd learnt was 'Fighter Command Attack Number One. Go!' That sort of thing. It meant you were flying along and you'd dive down and come up underneath the enemy bomber and shoot him down. That's all there was to it.

Of course, it didn't happen like that in real combat. We had to find our own way. We had to decide what was the best thing to do as the battle developed. We were learning all the time. You could lead the squadron or a flight up high and get it into position. But once you got engaged, it was individual fighting. And the whole thing was over so quickly. You'd have a good old shot at somebody or other and then somebody else would be shooting at you so you'd peel off and dive down to get out of the way and you'd quickly come up again and find the whole lot had gone.

At the beginning, our air–sea rescue was very sparse. Some of our men were being shot down over the Channel, baling out and landing in the water and there weren't very many launches to send out to pick them up. I told Group, 'Look, if this thing is going to go on for any length of time, we must get some more launches out into the water to pick up our pilots.' It improved later on and more of our men were saved after they landed in the water.

We were down at Warmwell, right down on the coast. The trouble with being at Warmwell was the Germans were not very far away in France. We took off but where could we go to gain height? We had to get to about 18,000 feet or so. Do we fly straight up underneath the enemy? Do we head back inland and come back again after we gained height? We could have been based further back, at Middle Wallop, and had time to get above the Germans as they came in. It was no good going up underneath them because their 109 escorts would see you and come straight down at you.

Oberkommando der Luftwaffe
Intelligence Report, 16 July

The Luftwaffe is clearly superior to the RAF as regards strength, equipment, training, command and location of bases. In the event of an intensification of air warfare, the Luftwaffe, unlike the RAF, will be in a position in every respect to achieve a decisive result this year if the time for the start of large scale operations is set early enough to allow advantage to be taken of the months with relatively favourable weather conditions – July to the beginning of October.

Pilot Officer Brian Considine

Some squadrons were better than others on tactics. They actually got together and worked out what they were going to do and developed better combat tactics. We never did. We stuck to the old-fashioned ways. We'd go up in Vics of three and go into line astern when we saw the enemy. Then, one by one, we followed the leader down onto the attack. On two occasions, I never got in on the attack because I was shot up the arse by enemy fighters before I could go down there.

Sergeant Jack Perkin

Somebody said Sailor Malan's squadron is spreading out in formation on patrol. It seemed like a mistake. It seemed highly dangerous. Somebody said, 'They'll all get shot down.' The Germans were flying these loose formations, but we thought it was very untidy. It took us a while to learn better.

Pilot Officer Wally Wallens

In the early days, we were always firing out of range. You thought you were opening up at the right distance but you weren't. You were miles out. That's what our camera guns showed. A fellow would say, 'Oh yes, I was in range.' Then the film from his camera gun would be developed and he'd see that instead of a German bomber up close, all he had in front of him was a little spot in the sky. It got us to move in closer.

Squadron Leader George Darley

The only way to overcome German superiority in numbers was to have superiority in tactics. Our tactics were awful to start with. The basic prescribed formation was a V shape of three aircraft. They had taught us that you fly astern of the bombers and open fire – bang, bang, bang. The curious omission was that they told you nothing about the enemy fighters who might be on your tail. That is where a lot of early losses occurred. You went in at the bombers, looking forward, nobody looking behind, and you were picked off. I adopted a more flexible formation. I made all our aircraft fly in line astern in formations of three, each of us protecting the other's tail.

It was also a mistake to split the squadron up into penny packets when we were coming up against huge German formations, some of us flying from our home base at Middle Wallop and the others down at the satellite base at Warmwell on a different assignment. It was bad tactics. I complained about it very strongly and finally we were permitted to fly as a squadron again.

We had had too many of our people killed in the beginning, with nothing to show for it. We had to kill a sight more Germans than we had men shot down ourselves if we were going to get anything done. The tactics had to be changed. When they did change, our kill–loss ratio went up and up and up.

Pilot Officer Dennis David

Part of our flying uniform had been semi-stiff collars and ties. They looked very nice, but if you fell in the drink, the collar could strangle you and to be able to look behind you and around while flying, you had to get rid of them. So we took to wearing those scarves for which RAF fighter pilots became famous.

Daily Express, 11 July

Tremblers and 'wonder-if-we'll-stand-it-ers' and all those other people who aren't sure how the population of this country would act in air raids should take a look at this busy little east coast town where people have almost forgotten what it's like to get an uninterrupted night's sleep. Worried? Scared? Not on your life. Raids here are the regular routine.

People don't prepare for bed wondering if Jerry will be over. They go to bed *knowing* he'll be over. They adjust their lives accordingly. The great thing is to get sleep and then you do not become nervous and jumpy. So most of the women finish their housework as early as possible and take a nap in the afternoon . . . No heroics, no terrors, no nerves. Just common sense.

Squadron Leader Sandy Johnstone

I was at Drem near Edinburgh during the early part of the Battle. We were really quite busy up north in June and July. The Germans were doing a lot of raiding in Scotland, against Glasgow and on the east coast. I shot my first aircraft down at night there. He had dropped his bombs and was on his way out when I caught him. I had been up there on patrol and was told by radio that there was some enemy activity around. I was watching the searchlight beams when I suddenly saw two of them latch on to an aircraft, so I went to look and saw that it was a Heinkel. I went for it too quickly to begin with and nearly ran into it the first time. But I sorted myself out. The searchlights were marvellous. They stayed with this thing all the time, so I was able to come around again and went in much more carefully, and let fly. The next thing I knew, I couldn't see anything. I had punctured his oil tanks and my windscreen and everything were all covered with oil. I pulled over to the side to see what was happening. I saw that one of his engines was on fire so I followed him along, realizing that we were getting lower and lower. The searchlights still hung onto him. He finally went into the sea. I later discovered that my final burst had taken place right over our airfield. All the chaps on the ground had been watching.

SCRAMBLE

Flying Officer Alan Deere

After shooting a Messerschmitt down over the water, I pulled up to look for another and found one coming head-on at me. There was no way I could have got out of the way, nor he, I suspect. It all happened so quickly. I went straight into him, hitting him underneath. It was a hell of a crash. He went right into the sea. I couldn't bale out; my cockpit hood was jammed closed where we had collided. I couldn't see because the plane was full of smoke, but I was able to keep a reasonable angle of glide and just carried on till I reached land and hit the ground. The first I knew I was down was the bounce. I hit amid some posts that had been put into the ground to stop enemy aircraft from landing. I sawed through those and finished up in a heap, on fire, at one end of a cornfield in Kent. I had to break open the hood, smashing the perspex with my hands, and I clambered out. I was lucky. The plane was burning pretty fiercely by then.

Edward Angly, New York Herald Tribune

London, 15 July – The Royal Air Force is in the market for American flyers as well as American airplanes. Experienced airmen, preferably those with at least 250 flying hours to their credit, would be welcomed by the RAF ... [They] will find a ready welcome into the RAF if they will cross the Canadian border and can pass the physical examination, it was said by the Air Ministry here. For such volunteers, there will be no question about signing or swearing an oath of allegiance to the British crown.

James MacDonald, New York Times

London, 25 July – Hundreds of German planes fought it out with the British, sometimes at altitudes of five or six miles, and countless anti-aircraft guns roared angrily and almost continuously from dawn until late evening today as the Nazis intensified their drive to blockade this country by air attacks on its shipping and various coastal points ... The Germans lost twenty planes, eleven bombers and nine fighters, the British said ... The British loss was placed at five planes.

92

Daily Express, *2 August*

A Messerschmitt 110 twin-engined fighter, diving suddenly from high clouds, bombed and machine-gunned streets in the centre of Norwich this afternoon. Five people were killed and several injured, and buildings were damaged. People in the town saw the raider diving, engines roaring. He flattened out at 400 feet, opened fire with his machine-guns, dropped his bombs, repeated the machine-gun fire, then fled for the coast, chased by British fighters. Windows of shops and offices more than a quarter of a mile away were smashed by the explosions . . . Mr R. Perkins was making for shelter with friends after hearing the first bombs fall when machine-gun bullets spattered the street ahead of them. Two more bombs fell before they reached the shelter. The foreman of a building squad shouted, 'It's a Nazi!' when he saw the Me 110 coming out of the clouds. As he threw himself down flat, he saw three bombs leave the plane. 'Then bullets started whizzing over me,' he said.

Sergeant David Cox

A bandit was reported off the east coast and we went off into broken cloud in a Vic of three to find it – Flying Officer Haines, Flight Sergeant Steere, both very experienced pilots, and myself, very inexperienced and treated with a bit of disdain. I spotted the bandit first. There was suddenly a break in the cloud and off in the distance, a long way off, there was this long, pencil-shaped thing. I cried, 'Bandit!' and shot out into the clear sky over the sea, and there was this Dornier bomber. I opened fire straight away when I got within range. The others came in after me. Then I went at it again. It started to burn and the crew baled out.

After that, I was accepted. Haines changed his attitude towards me. He took me under his wing. He said, 'You fly with me. Just keep behind me. Don't get too ambitious.' It did me a lot of good. A lot of my friends who went through flying school with me were shot down the first or second time they went into combat. I managed to survive up there till the end of September before being shot down.

* * *

Even before the Dunkirk evacuation, it was clear that Britain had far fewer fighter planes than it needed for its first line of defence, and aircraft factory production schedules offered little hope that this dangerous shortfall would soon be overcome. Keenly aware of the implications, within days of being named Prime Minister, Churchill gave Lord Beaverbrook the job of remedying the situation.

The son of a poor, Scotch-born Canadian clergyman, Beaverbrook was notorious for his un-English, thrusting business practices. He had made a fortune in financial wheeling and dealing in Canada before he had arrived in Britain at the age of thirty, to build both a newspaper empire and a political career.

As soon as he took over the Ministry of Aircraft Production, Beaverbrook set about dissolving the thrombosis of bureaucratic red tape which more often than not undermined plans for crash government programmes. Ignoring proper channels, he sent his men to factories and warehouses around the country to determine what resources were available and unceremoniously to claim on the spot what was wanted for fighter construction and repair. His men even raided airfields for damaged aircraft that could be rehabilitated or cannibalized.

There were howls of protest, not least from people at the Air Ministry horrified that Beaverbrook was making a shambles of their long term programmes for the construction of bombers, trainers and other aircraft. Other government departments were equally offended by his eccentric, outlandish approach to government business. Beaverbrook scorned their complaints and declined to change his ways. A cartoon at the time showed him dressed as a buccaneer, lurking around a corner with his band of pirates, prepared to pounce on a bunch of smug, stiff-necked bureaucrats, telling his merry crew of ruffians, 'Skin them for their toolbags, watches and penknives – and don't forget the nails in their boots and the fillings in their teeth.'

Each night during the worst of the battle, Beaverbrook telephoned 11 Group commander Keith Park to ask what the situation was and how many planes were needed. He then proceeded to supply them. When complaints about his contempt for standard bureaucratic procedure reached Churchill, the Prime Minister stiffly noted, 'In the fierce light of the present emergency, the fighter is the need and the output of fighters must be the prime concern until we have broken the back of the enemy's attack.'

Pilot Officer Dennis David

We were losing planes every day, but heard terrible things about replacements for them. We heard that certain Maintenance Units where Hurricanes were being assembled to come to us were closed on Saturdays and Sundays. Beaverbrook stopped all that. He said, 'Twenty-four hours a day solid working, seven days a week.' That was Beaver. He petrified people into working and the aeroplanes started coming to us.

Lord Beaverbrook

This is an appeal to all workers in the aircraft industry. Urgently we ask for the fullest output this week and next ... I want to reach all of you with my words: the work you do this week fortifies and strengthens the front of battle next week. The production which you pour out of your factories this week will be hurled into the desperate struggle next week.

And make no mistake, in meeting this crisis we have none to rely on but our own energy and driving force. Britain stands or falls on her own resources. You have the power to multiply and to magnify them. The young men of the Air Force, the pilots and gunners, are waiting to fly the machines. We must not fail them. We must provide the aircraft, engined, armed, equipped and ready for battle.

A few days later, Beaverbrook announced that aircraft production had increased by sixty-two percent.

Francis Rodwell Banks

The principle that Lord Beaverbrook worked on was to get supplies of everything quickly – leaving long term planning to go ahead on a longer term basis. We proceeded to organize the companies on a twenty-four hour basis, and also expand them as quickly as possible. In addition, we searched all the RAF stores for equipment that was urgently needed by the aircraft and engine manufacturers – even sometimes risking the supplies to the RAF units in the field. Service storekeepers, and others, always think that they are doing their jobs well when the stores are full. But in the early days of the Ministry of Aircraft Production, we on Lord Beaverbrook's staff decided that we must rob the stores and keep the Air Force flying in those critical Battle of Britain days. It was like pulling teeth from an unwilling child, but the stores people finally accepted with good grace. They had to!

Lord Beaverbrook

Women of Britain, give us your aluminium. We want it and we want it now ... We will turn your pots and pans into Spitfires and Hurricanes, Blenheims and Wellingtons. I ask therefore that everyone who has pots and pans, kettles, vacuum cleaners, hatpegs, coat hangers, shoe trees, bathroom fittings and household ornaments, cigarette boxes or any other articles made wholly or in part of aluminium, should hand them in at once to the local headquarters of the Women's Voluntary Services.

Commander R. Fletcher, Member of Parliament

For seventeen hours a day, that man is at his job. If when I say goodnight to him he is angry, I go to bed and sleep peacefully for I know that Lord Beaverbrook's anger means that in the morning there will be some great improvement in our war effort.

Winston Churchill

This was no time for red tape and circumlocution, although these have their place in a well-ordered, placid system. All [Beaverbrook's] remarkable qualities fitted the need. His personal buoyancy and vigour were a tonic. I was glad to be able sometimes to lean on him. He did not fail. This was his hour. His personal force and genius, combined with so much persuasion and contrivance, swept aside many obstacles. New or repaired aeroplanes streamed to the delighted squadrons in numbers they had never known before.

Air Chief Marshal Sir Hugh Dowding

We had the organization, we had the men and we had the spirit which could bring us victory in the air, but we had not the supply of machines necessary to withstand the drain of continuous battle. Lord Beaverbrook gave us those machines and I do not believe that I exaggerate when I say that no other man in England could have done so.

* * *

By the time the first phase of the Battle of Britain drew to a close, the

British, buoyed up by Churchill's Shakespearean rhetoric and exultant newspaper accounts of RAF achievements, believed they had reason not to be despondent. They realized they were still under serious threat, but the Luftwaffe had lost 227 aircraft during that period to the RAF's ninety-six. Spitfires and Hurricanes had proved themselves reliable battle machines and British pilots had proved themselves worthy of the critical role to which they had been assigned at that historic moment. They had roared out from their bases to hurl themselves without hesitation at the swarms of enemy aircraft sent to lure them to disaster.

At the same time, however, the Germans, despite their losses, were convinced they had achieved what they had set out to achieve. In view of their superiority in numbers, they could absorb their losses more easily than the RAF. They were prepared to move on to the next, more intense phase of the Battle of Britain.

Though the air war had been hotting up, right through this first phase and almost till the closing October days of the battle, the prime focus of concern for the British had been the threat of a German invasion. This concern now intensified. The War Cabinet and the Chiefs of Staff examined and re-examined the possibilities and procedures for coping with an invasion attempt when it occurred, with almost everyone in the country convinced it was only a matter of time.

General Staff Headquarters, Southern Command, 13 July

1. The following notes are published so that all personnel may understand the sequence of events that may be expected at aerodromes if the enemy invades this country. An appreciation of what is taking place to a great extent eliminates surprise and this aids the defence.

2. Large scale attacks on aerodromes will probably take the following form:

   (1) Attack made at dawn.
   (2) Me 110s arrive first to draw off our fighters.
   (3) Soon afterwards, very low flying bombers attack. Bombs [are dropped on the] perimeter of aerodrome and aerodrome defences.
   (4) More heavy fighters then attack the defences with front cannon and machine-guns. At the same time:
   (5) Complete companies of parachute troops are dropped at three

or four points around the aerodrome about 1,000 to 1,500 yards away.

(6) Parachute troops form up in 12 to 15 minutes and storm the aerodrome with machine-guns, hand grenades and perhaps 2-inch mortars.

(7) About 10 minutes after this attack has started, Ju 52s and large troop carriers land on aerodrome at about six a minute. These troops have machine-guns and probably 2-inch and 3-inch mortars and guns and also motorcycles.

(8) Fighters then land whilst a fighter umbrella is maintained over the aerodrome until attempted capture is complete.

3. Should any high bombing take place, do not let the whistling bomb scare you. It is no more dangerous than any other bomb.

Fighter Command Diary

Fighter Command [has] published to its Groups the codewords which had been adopted by the navy and the army for making the first reports of Hitler's invasion:

BLACKBIRD: Surface vessels, submarines and motorboats have been sighted but not yet identified.

GALLIPOLI: The enemy are landing from ships, boats or caterpillars.

PARASOLS: The enemy are landing by parachute.

STARLING: Enemy air transports are landing on our aerodromes.

Chiefs of Staff Committee
Report by Joint Intelligence Sub-Committee, 16 July

The principal enemy objective in an invasion of this country is likely to be the capture of London.

To achieve this, it is considered that beaches will be selected on which to land a wave of AFVs [Armoured Fighting Vehicles] carried in small flat-bottomed craft, supported by troops carried in specially equipped merchant ships which can be run ashore to facilitate disembarkation.

Large numbers of small craft of all types are likely to be used in addition, both to assist in any main landings and as feints.

It is considered that the main seaborne invasion is most likely to be made between the Wash and Newhaven, and the areas most likely for beach landings are in the region of Southwold and in East Kent. Simultaneous landings in both areas are to be expected, with the object of a pincer movement on London. Additional subsidiary landings may be expected elsewhere, but there is no reliable evidence as to where they may take place.

We may also expect the Germans, with the assistance of airborne troops, to attempt to seize from the land side, a port such as Harwich, the Humber or Dover in order to facilitate the disembarkation of additional troops and stores ...

Seaborne troops: Up to five divisions might be landed as an initial striking force, assuming that they could avoid detection and interference by our naval force for twenty-four hours, and that they could obtain control of the necessary beaches and landing facilities. The main landing force would probably be carried in transports of substantial size ... There is reason to suppose that Germany possesses special craft for landing tanks on open beaches ... Gliders may be used. It is practicable to carry light tanks by aircraft. The Germans are known to possess 5,000 parachutists and others are believed to be in training.

Captain Euan Wallace, Senior Regional Defence Commission, London
24 June

It's no use kidding ourselves that we are not within the next few weeks or days going to get a taste of German frightfulness. One object of that frightfulness ... will be to intimidate and terrify the civilian population. We can beat that ourselves if we remember what to do when an air-raid alarm comes. Remember that on courage, coolness and resolution depends the defeat of Hitler.

Ministry of Information Poster and Circular

IF THE INVADER COMES

1) If the Germans come, by parachute, aeroplane or ship, you must remain where you are. The order is 'Stay Put' ...
2) Do not believe rumours and do not spread them. When you receive an order, make quite sure that it is a true order and not a

faked order. Most of you know your policeman and your ARP[Air Raid Precautions] wardens by sight, you can trust them. If you keep your heads, you can also tell whether a military officer is really British or only pretending to be so. If in doubt ask the policeman or ARP warden. Use your common sense ...

3) Keep watch. If you see anything suspicious, note it carefully and go at once to the nearest police station or officer, or to the nearest military officer ...

4) Do not give the German anything. Do not tell him anything. Hide your food and bicycles. Hide your maps. See that the enemy gets no petrol ... Remember that transport and petrol will be the invader's main difficulties. Make sure that no invader will be able to get your cars, petrol, maps or bicycles ...

5) Be ready to help the military in any way. But do not block roads until ordered to do so by the military or LDV authorities ...

6) In factories and shops, all managers and workmen should organize some system by which a sudden attack can be resisted.

7) Think before you act. But think always of your country before you think of yourself.

General Raymond E. Lee, United States Military Attaché, London

Went over the land defenses in the morning. The whole coast defense machinery includes minefields, the navy, the RAF, the anti-aircraft, the army and behind all, the Local Defence Volunteers. It looks fairly good, if it can all work smoothly together. It could all, of course, be much stronger, but it is fairly strong now. The main trouble is going to be that Hitler may produce some new surprise weapon like thousands of glider transports, or he may attack at so many distant points that he'll be able to form one bridgehead and get some of his big tanks ashore. Every day that he puts it off is immensely valuable and I should say that in another three weeks the coastline will be nearly impregnable to ordinary attack. But the whole thing is going to depend on the navy and the RAF.

Former Prime Minister Neville Chamberlain
Broadcast, 30 June

If the enemy does try to invade this country, we will fight him in the air and on the sea. We will fight him on the beaches with every weapon we have. He may manage here and there to make a break-through. If he does, we will fight him on every road, in every village, and in every house, until he or we are utterly destroyed.

Sergeant Tom Naylor

Just before the Battle of Britain began, they discovered that among those of us who'd been recruited for Operations Room training, there was one man who'd had over a thousand hours' flying experience. That was Dudley Mason. He was quickly winkled out and given a different job and just before the threat of invasion reached its climax during the battle, old Dudley was given a Tiger Moth [a pre-war biplane] somewhere down in Surrey, where they were busy welding milk crates under the wings to carry bombs with which to bomb the beaches when the Germans landed. He told me, 'The darn thing won't even fly, never mind carry bombs, with all that garbage on it.'

Winston Churchill
War Cabinet Minutes

The land defences and the home army are maintained primarily for the purpose of making the enemy come in such large numbers as to afford a proper target to the sea and air forces . . . and to make hostile preparations and movements noticeable to air and other forms of reconnaissance. However, should the enemy succeed in landing at various points, he should be made to suffer as much as possible by local resistance on the beaches, combined with the aforesaid attacks from the sea and the air. This forces him to use up his ammunition, and confines him to a limited area. The defence of any part of the coast must be measured not by the forces on the coast, but by the number of hours within which strong counter attacks by mobile troops can be brought to bear upon the landing places. Such attacks should be hurled with the utmost speed and fury upon the enemy at his weakest moment, which is not, as is sometimes suggested, when actually getting out of his boats, but when sprawled upon the shore with his communications cut and his supplies running short. It ought to be possible to concentrate 10,000 men fully equipped within six hours and 20,000 men within twelve hours, upon any point where a serious lodgment has been effected. The withholding of reserves until the full gravity of the attack is known is a nice problem for the Home Guard.

* * *

Where and how the Germans would land was a matter of constant worry and speculation. It was feared the Germans might quickly try to follow up their victories on the continent and move against Britain before they lost their momentum, before British forces could recover from the trouncing they had taken in France, and before the RAF could regain its strength and balance. British leaders had been dazzled by the lightning military coups executed by elite German airborne troops in Belgium and Holland. The use of the same tactics against England could not be ruled out.

In fact, Hitler wasn't certain at the time that he would actually proceed with an invasion of England. He still hoped the British, their noses badly bloodied, would seek to extract themselves from the war so that he might devote the energies of his forces to expanding the borders of the Third Reich eastwards into Russia. But so long as the British insisted on continuing to fight, they could not be ignored. British bombers were raiding targets in Nazi-occupied Europe. Fighter Command was rebuilding its operational strength. It was an increasingly inescapable fact that only defeat would remove the British from the conflict and that only an invasion of England could bring that about. A start was made in gathering supplies and equipment for a Channel crossing and landing. Though a date for the invasion was not yet set, German leaders radiated confidence that it would succeed and Britain would be crushed.

Colonel-General Alfred Jodl, Chief of Operations, OKW
(Oberkommando der Wehrmacht)
30 June

The final German victory over England is now only a question of time. Enemy offensive operations on a large scale are no longer possible.

Flight Lieutenant Gerry Edge

I've always thought that had they come straight across and landed all their aircraft and paratroops in Kent before we got the Dunkirk people back or before the army was reformed, we would have been in serious trouble. Troop morale was very low and our squadrons had taken such heavy losses in France.

OKW
2 July

The date of the commencement [of a landing in England] is still undecided. All preparations to be begun immediately ... All preparations must be undertaken on the basis that the invasion is still only a plan and has not yet been decided upon.

Sir Alexander Cadogan, Permanent Under Secretary, Foreign Office Diary, 30 July

Can't make out what the Germans are doing. Various good indications that they *are* going to attack us. But why haven't they done so? And what are they doing with these costly and half-hearted air raids? ... Must be something very deep.

James Reston, New York Times

London, 18 July – Prime Minister Churchill, who has always worked on the theory that anybody who sleeps more than five hours a night is a worthless slacker, announced in the House of Commons today that he has asked his leading Cabinet ministers to move out of their houses and sleep in their offices, where they can be gathered together at a moment's notice. Members of Parliament, who are never surprised by Mr Churchill's requests, decided tonight that this move had three advantages:

First, it will enable the Prime Minister to call his colleagues together in a hurry in the event of a German invasion.
Second, it might improve the attendance at his 'breakfast Cabinet meetings'.
And third, it will enable the Prime Minister to get a quick audience for his latest inspiration at any hour of the day or night.

Mrs H.E. Miles, Surrey
War Journal

Story about Hitler and Michelangelo's great picture of 'Moses', which he is reputed to have looted from the Louvre. The Führer is supposed to have been found on his knees before the great Jew and he was saying: 'Dear Moses, tell me how you got across that strip of water.'

*   *   *

With no firm invasion decision forthcoming from the German High Command, no urgency was felt by the Gestapo and other security authorities in Berlin to produce plans of their own for Britain. Nevertheless, the matter did receive close consideration and, over the next few weeks, a programme for policing occupied Britain did emerge. Professor Dr Franz Six, a colonel in the SS who would later be implicated in the massacre of civilians in Russia, was to head German security services in the country. He was told his task was to combat 'all anti-German organizations, institutions, opposition and opposition groups which can be seized in England'. A list was drawn up of Britons who were to be taken into custody as soon as possible, including parliamentarians, writers, academics and other public figures who were outspoken in their denunciation of Nazi doctrine and practice. Special attention was also to be paid to European refugees who had found sanctuary from the Nazis in Britain. The people of Britain were to be told that 'all thoughtless actions, sabotage of any kind, and any passive or active opposition to the German armed forces will incur the most severe retaliatory measures'. A programme was to be outlined for deporting able-bodied British males between the ages of seventeen and forty-five to Europe to man the industries which fuelled Germany's war machine. 'Action Groups', of the kind that were later notorious for the slaughter of civilians in Nazi-occupied Europe, were to be deployed in various parts of Britain 'as the situation dictates and the necessity arises'.

Though the security services in Berlin were beginning to hatch their plans for occupied Britain, it was not until a full six weeks after the German forces had driven the British out of Europe and into the sea at Dunkirk that Hitler actually gave the order to prepare 'landing operations against England'. Even then, he declined to make this order final, stipulating that the operation was to be carried out only 'if necessary'.

The Führer and Supreme Commander of the Armed Forces
Führer Headquarters, 16 July

DIRECTIVE NO. 16
ON PREPARATIONS FOR A LANDING OPERATION AGAINST
ENGLAND

Since England, in spite of her hopeless military situation, shows no signs of being ready to come to an understanding, I have decided to prepare a landing operation against England and, if necessary, to carry it out. The aim of this operation will be to eliminate the English homeland as a base for the prosecution of the war against Germany and, if necessary, to occupy it completely.

I therefore order as follows:

1. The landing will be in the form of a surprise crossing on a wide front from about Ramsgate to the area west of the Isle of Wight ... Preparations for the entire operation must be completed by the middle of August.

2. These preparations must also create such conditions as will make a landing in England possible, viz:
   (a) The English Air Force must be so reduced morally and physically that it is unable to deliver any significant attack against the German crossing ...

Associated Press

Grenoble, 16 July – The newspaper *Petit Dauphinois*, quoting foreign diplomatic quarters in Switzerland, said today that Germany had 600,000 troops ready for an invasion of the British Isles and that 'zero hour' may come Friday night if weather permits. The expeditionary force, it said, is poised along a 1,200-mile front from Brest, France to Bergen, Norway. Originally the long-threatened assault was scheduled for the night of 9–10 July, the newspaper said, but dissension in the German High Command led to delay. (Unconfirmed elsewhere, the French newspaper report was viewed in some quarters as a possible German-inspired propaganda effort to spur Britain into accepting peace terms.) The newspaper, in a dispatch from Berne, Switzerland, said a group of German generals headed by General Walther von Brauchitsch, Commander-in-Chief, protested that the original plan of attack was 'too dangerous'. The initial plan, it said, called for a fleet of hundreds of German ships and captured French, Belgian and Dutch passenger liners, freighters, fishing smacks and tug-towed barges to swarm across the English Channel in the wake of minesweepers and waves of bombers.

Colonel-General Franz Halder, Chief of the German General Staff
Diaries, 22 July

Führer: No clear picture of what is happening in Britain. Preparations for a decision by arms must be completed as quickly as possible. The Führer will not let the military–political initiative get out of his hand ... Reasons for continuance of war by Britain: (1) Hope for a change in America. (Roosevelt's position uncertain, industry does not want to invest. Britain runs risk of losing its position of first sea power to the United States.) (2) Puts hope in Russia.

Britain's position is hopeless. The war is won by us. A reversal in the prospects of success is impossible.

Home Defence, Chief of Staff Committee, London
Air Staff Memorandum on the role of operational Commands of the
Metropolitan Air Force in the event of the invasion of this country

The first phase of the invasion of this country is likely to be a large scale air offensive against the fighter defence, i.e. fighters in the air, fighter aerodromes and organizations, and the aircraft industry ... The task of the Fighter Force is to meet the attack on its own organization and the aircraft industry and defeat it.

Adolf Hitler
19 July

The struggle, if it continues, can only end with the annihilation of one or the other of the two adversaries. Mr Churchill may believe this will be Germany. I know that it will be Britain. In this hour, I feel it to be my duty to appeal once more to reason and common sense in Britain ... I consider myself in a position to make this appeal since I am not the vanquished begging favours, but the victor speaking in the name of reason. I can see no reason why this war must go on. I am grieved to think of the sacrifices it will claim ... Possibly Mr Churchill again will brush aside this statement of mine by saying it is merely born of fear and of doubt in our final victory. In that case, I shall have relieved my conscience in regard to the things to come.

Associated Press

Berlin, 20 July – Germany unleashed a thunder of words today in an attempt to sway the British people over the head of Prime Minister Winston Churchill and get them to end the war. The alternative, Nazi Germany says, is destruction. Radio transmitters dinned Führer Adolf Hitler's 'last appeal to reason' into British ears until, as authorized sources here put it, every Briton must know exactly what is in store for him unless he gets rid of 'the plutocratic ruling clique' which wants to keep on fighting.

Count Ciano, Foreign Minister of Italy

Hitler is now like the gambler who has made a big win and wants to get up from the table without risking anything more.

Foreign Secretary Lord Halifax
Radio Broadcast to the British People, 22 July

Many of you will have read ... the speech in which Herr Hitler summoned Great Britain to capitulate to his will. I will not waste your time by dealing with his distortions of almost every main event since the war began. He says he has no desire to destroy the British Empire, but there was in his speech no suggestion that peace must be based on justice, no word of recognition that the other nations of Europe had any right to self-determination, the principle which he has so often invoked for Germans. His only appeal was to the base instinct of fear, and his only arguments were threats ...

Hitler has now made it plain that he is preparing to direct the whole weight of German might against this country. That is why in every part of Britain there is only one spirit, a spirit of indomitable resolution. Nor has anyone any doubt that if Hitler were to succeed it would be the end, for many besides ourselves, of all those things which make life worth living. We realize that the struggle may cost us everything, but just because the things we are defending are worth any sacrifice, it is a noble privilege to be the defenders of things so precious. We never wanted the war; certainly no one wants the war to go on for a day longer than is necessary. But we shall not stop fighting till freedom, for ourselves and others, is secure.

George Axelsson, New York Times

Berlin, 28 July – The process of 'softening up' Britain by means of dive bombers, submarines and torpedo-carrying mosquito craft now seems to have begun in earnest and a big landing attempt may be only a matter of days, if not hours.

Anthony Weymouth, BBC Commentator
Personal Journal

An Englishman said this to me today: 'I am high on the Nazi blacklist. I have been attacking them for years. If we are conquered I shall be one of the first to be arrested. I can't stand the thought of being put in a concentration camp. Can you tell me some drug which I could take if they do get here? I would much rather die than submit to what goes on in a Nazi concentration camp.'

* * *

His overtures rebuffed by the pig-headed British, the momentum of his breathtaking European triumphs fizzling out, summertime invasion weather rapidly passing, Hitler finally recognized there had to be an end to shilly-shallying. If the British were to be removed from the war, he had no alternative. He would have to issue unequivocal instructions for invasion preparations to proceed, and to proceed quickly. The Channel would have to be crossed and a landing would have to be made. First the Luftwaffe had to be given the go-ahead for full-scale attacks on the installations and services which kept Fighter Command operational. It was time to seize uncontested control of the skies over England.

The Führer and Supreme Commander of the Armed Forces
Führer Headquarters, 1 August 1940

DIRECTIVE NO. 17
FOR THE CONDUCT OF AIR AND SEA WARFARE AGAINST ENGLAND

In order to establish the necessary conditions for the final conquest of England I intend to intensify air and sea warfare against the English homeland. I therefore order as follows:

1. The German air force is to overpower the English air force with all the forces at its command, in the shortest possible time. The attacks are to be directed primarily against flying units, their ground installations, and their supply organizations, but also against the aircraft industry, including that manufacturing anti-aircraft equipment.

2. After achieving temporary or local air superiority, the air war is to be continued against ports, in particular against stores of food, and also against stores of provisions in the interior of the country ... I reserve to myself the right to decide on terror attacks as measures of reprisal ...

Alexander Kirk, United States Chargé d'Affaires in Germany, to the Secretary of State
Berlin, 2 August

Responsible [German] Government officials continue to stress the view that England should sue for peace and that it is foolhardy for it to attempt to withstand the forces that are about to be directed against Great Britain. Furthermore, private individuals of various neutral nationalities are professing that they are receiving projects for peace in conversations with the highest German authorities but exclusive of Hitler himself and that they are attempting to or have succeeded in conveying those projects directly to prominent persons in England ... In all these efforts, conspicuous emphasis is placed on the opportunity for peace talks ... and all seem to be entirely impervious to the argument that it is difficult to characterize as a peace offer a statement wherein Hitler makes clear that although he professes no wish to destroy the British Empire he will proceed to that destruction unless the British Government accepts a peace which in the Nazi mind is termed reasonable, but which to others tokens the ruin of that Empire as the immediate champion of democracy in the world.

In the meantime, reports of projects of imminent action against the British Isles accumulate and the rumored date is set from one weekend to another.

Anonymous

'What did you do in the war, Daddy?
    How did you help us win?'
'Take-offs and landings and stalls, laddie,
    And how to get out of a spin.'

ATTACK OF THE EAGLES

Fierce though they were, the July encounters over the Channel and the ports of southern England were only the curtain raiser to the Battle of Britain. The main German objective, mastery of the skies over England, was still to be achieved. By early August, the Germans decided the preliminaries – the probings and the threats – had gone on long enough. It was time to proceed to the main event.

The heart of the British defences was now to become the target, while the Channel was still to remain as a no-go area for British vessels. Massive formations of bombers, closely escorted by fighters, were to blast fighter airfields (mostly near the coast at first), radar installations and aircraft factories. This was to be the 'Attack of the Eagles' (*Adlerangriff*), the second phase of the Battle of Britain, the onslaught that was supposed to mark the beginning of the end of British air defences and thus set the stage for the invasion.

Convinced that Fighter Command was reeling from what had already transpired, Reichsmarshal Hermann Göring assured his Air Fleet commanders that it would not take them long to clear the way for a landing on English soil. According to his calculations, British coastal defences would be knocked out within four days and, as the Luftwaffe pressed home its assault, all of Fighter Command would be crippled within four weeks. By then, the invasion troops, equipment, supplies and landing craft would have been assembled for the Channel crossing, and the conquest of the only nation which had so far not succumbed to the German onslaught could take place.

The British had reason to be apprehensive, and not only because of German invasion preparations. Though they were shooting down more German aircraft than they themselves lost, their losses were frighteningly heavy. Some squadrons had been so badly battered that they had already been pulled out of the line and relieved from the reservoir of jealously guarded reserves in the north. All in all, confidence among British leaders that the enemy could be repulsed was tempered by a sense of foreboding.

The Attack of the Eagles began on 13 August, codenamed by the Germans 'Eagle Day'. Though damage to strategic British installations was, in fact, limited that day and though the Germans lost forty-six aircraft to fourteen lost by Fighter Command, the Luft-waffe had flown an unprecedented 1,500 sorties over England by nightfall. Fighter Command was kept fully stretched in the south, trying to intercept wave after wave of raiders.

Though sometimes astounded by the great numbers of German aircraft they were sent to fight off, British pilots were not intimidated by the odds. At this stage, most of them returned from combat exhilarated by their experiences aloft. As they hopped out of their planes, they flocked together on the airfields, excitedly telling each other of their triumphs and narrow escapes, their swooping hands fashioning dogfights, their voices aping the chatter of their Browning machine-guns, oblivious of the omens that there would be excru-ciatingly hard days and weeks ahead for them, as the Germans – convinced victory was around the corner – pressed on with the Attack of the Eagles.

Pilot Officer Roland Beamont

You were young and you were excited as hell. When you came down from a mission, you'd been up against a challenge and you'd got through it. You wanted to talk to your mates. You'd fought battles in the air alongside them. You may have seen one of them shoot a German off your back – you recognized him from the colour of his spinner or his aircraft number. You wanted to talk about what you'd done and what he'd done. And you wanted to discover who was missing. All this happened right on the field with the frustrated intelligence officer trying to get combat reports from us. But we didn't want to waste time talking to him. We wanted to stand around chi-hiking – 'There I was, nought feet and on my back!' – motioning with our hands to show how the dogfights had gone. Meantime, the groundcrew would be turning the aircraft round, refuelling and re-arming them, sticking patches over bullet holes, getting us ready to go up again.

FROM REICHSMARSHAL GÖRING TO ALL UNITS OF AIR FLEETS 2, 3 AND 5. OPERATION EAGLE. WITHIN A SHORT PERIOD YOU WILL WIPE THE BRITISH AIR FORCE FROM THE SKY. HEIL HITLER.

ATTACK OF THE EAGLES

Squadron Leader Ronald Adams, Operations Room Controller at Hornchurch

We all knew how limited our resources were, how few aircraft and trained pilots we had got ready for action and we did not – we could not – understand why the enemy did not come for us at once ... We held our breath ... and then early in August, the radar plots began to show the enemy assembling in the air behind Cape Gris Nez in France. There he was, milling around as one formation after another joined up, and we went to our loudspeakers when our Group Headquarters gave the order telling the squadron to take off ... 'Scramble' we would say and Spitfires would tear into the sky ... We would sit there on the ground and watch the plots ... We would pass information to the pilots, telling them all changes in the enemy's direction, how he was splitting up into different formations, what height he was flying at, and guiding our fighters to the most advantageous position up in the eye of the sun, ready to attack. The Battle of Britain is summarized for me in one snatch on the radio-telephone from a famous New Zealand fighter ... I heard his voice in my ear as he sighted the enemy: 'Christ Almighty, tally-ho! Whole bloody hordes of them.'

Nurse Frances Faviell

We began seeing dogfights overhead and watched our Spitfires chasing Messerschmitts and engaging in exciting battles, and in the still summer air we could hear the gunfire from the combatants and could see parachutists descending and the planes crashing down with a spurt of fire from their tails. It seemed impossible at first to believe that these were actually deadly battles and not mock ones as we had watched at aerial displays at Hendon. It gave one a strange, shaking, sick feeling of excitement to watch their every movement as though we were following with rapt attention a mock battle, but never before had we seen such a thrilling exhibition of aeronautics. Twisting, turning, their guns blazing, the sunlight picking them out in the clear sky, they would dive under, over, round, and then straight at their opponents, until one would fall in a trail of smoke and flame, often with a gleaming parachute like a toy umbrella preceding the final crash to earth. It was horrible – but it had a macabre fascination impossible to resist.

Flight Lieutenant P. B. Robinson
Combat Report

As leader of Red Section 601 Squadron I was ordered to intercept bandits at Colchester. I saw approximately thirty bombers escorted by Me 109s above. While approaching bombers from astern and to one side, I saw a Me 109 below and to my left. I dived down and the Me 109 pulled up and we carried out a head-on attack at each other. The Me 109 broke away at the last moment and I turned and got on his tail. He was smoking from below his engine and after a short burst, he rolled over and dived inverted for the ground. At this time I saw a second Me 109 and got a short burst in from the quarter. He also emitted smoke and white vapour and dived vertically down. I then ran out of ammunition but saw a third Me 109 dive past me. I followed him down to ground level and chased him southwards. He never rose above 100 feet until well south of Maidstone, and then throttled back. I overtook him and formated on him, pointing downward for him to land. He turned away, so I carried out a dummy quarter attack, breaking away very close to him. After this, he landed his Me 109 in a field at about 140 mph. The pilot got out apparently unhurt and held up his hands above his head. I circled around him and waved to him and as he waved back I returned and threw a packet of twenty Players at him and returned to base.

Flight Lieutenant Brian Kingcome

If you did what had been considered the normal thing and came around behind the bombers to bust up their formations, their fighter escorts would get to you before you could get to them. Also, the rear guns of a tightly-packed bomber formation could bring a huge concentration of fire to bear on you. But if you attacked them from the front, it was very frightening for the bomber pilot. He saw a fighter coming straight at him. He didn't have protective armour plate. As you came at him, you'd see him nervously getting ready for you, bouncing around long before you were within firing range. If you were a German pilot sitting at the front of a bomber with your rear gunners and a whole lot of metal behind you, when there was an attack from the rear you couldn't really see what was happening back there. So you went droning on towards your target. But if the attack was coming right at you personally, you were in the front line. You'd see the tracers flashing past and the enemy coming at you. They had to be very, very tough and very, very brave to keep going steadily onward.

Flight Lieutenant Gerry Edge

If you left it till your last hundred yards to break away from a head-on attack, you were in trouble. With practice, you got to judge when to break. But once you knew how, a head-on attack was a piece of cake. When you opened fire, you'd kill or badly wound the pilot and the second pilot. Then you'd rake the line of them as you broke away. On one attack, the first Heinkel I hit crashed into the next Heinkel. There was a lot of crashing among the bombers we attacked head-on.

Pilot Officer Paddy Barthropp

A few brave buggers used to do head-on attacks. Bloody dangerous. There were one or two lunatics who revelled in it. The chance of hitting something going head-on was pretty remote unless you were attacking a big formation of bombers. Then you'd rake them, getting your nose up and down, knowing something was going to connect. That was very effective.

Pilot Officer Dennis David

To split up a bombing raid, we tried to aim at the leaders. There was a good chance that if you shot down the leaders, the other bombers would disperse. It also had the effect of distracting them from their targets. Before the Battle of Britain, the Luftwaffe had things their own way. They had won in Spain, in Poland, in Belgium, in France. Over Britain, for the first time, they came up against something they couldn't beat. It was not easy for them to understand that.

Pilot Officer Dave Glaser

The squadron's CO, Sawyer, was killed on a night take-off just before I got to the squadron. Sammy Saunders, who was a flight lieutenant, took over the lead and led the squadron brilliantly. We used to fly in a snake. He'd bring us up to an altitude above the bombers. Then he'd let Gordon Olive, the flight commander of A-flight, take over and lead while he'd just go straight down vertically, right through the centre of the bomber formation. You'd see the bombers start peeling away as he went down. That was the signal for the rest of us to go in to pick them off. It worked.

Squadron Leader George Darley

It was around teatime when our squadron was scrambled on what the Germans called Eagle Day. We were told there was a big formation of bombers and fighters coming in towards us. We were off in good time. The sun was getting down towards the west and we had time to go around and come at the bombers from behind. There were the usual 109s above and behind some Ju 87s – about thirty of each. I told our two sections on top to keep an eye out for the 109s while the rest of us went down and to sort out the bombers. Then they were to try to disentangle themselves from the 109s and come down and join us in dealing with the bombers.

I managed to get in below the fighters – I don't think they even saw me. I throttled back a little – not too much; otherwise I would have thrown the whole formation out of position – and went through the whole lot of Ju 87s, letting fly with everything I had. The chaps coming in behind me were able to pick their targets. By that time, the 109s saw us and were coming down so we turned to take them on.

On that day we lost no one but claimed thirteen aircraft shot down, of which eight were bombers, the others 109s. Later, we learned it was only five Ju 87s we shot down. But even if you only shot up a German bomber and it got back to its base, with airmen inside maybe wounded or dying, that wasn't good for German morale.

Pilot Officer David Crook

I saw about five Messerschmitt 109s pass just underneath us. I immediately broke away from the formation, dived on to the last 109 and gave him a terrific burst of fire at very close range. He burst into flames and spun down for many thousands of feet into the clouds below, leaving behind him a long trail of black smoke ... He crashed just outside a small village, and I could see everybody streaming out of their houses and rushing to the spot.

I climbed up through the clouds again to rejoin the flight, but there was nothing to be seen, and so I returned to the aerodrome where all the groundcrews were in a great state of excitement as they could hear a terrific fight going on above the clouds, but saw nothing except several German machines falling in flames.

All our machines were now coming in to land and everybody's eyes were fixed on the wings.

Yes – they were all covered with black streaks from the smoke of the guns – everybody had fired.

There was the usual anxious counting – only ten back – where are the others – they should be back by now – I hope to God everybody's OK – good enough, here they come! Thank God, everybody's OK.

We all stood around in small groups talking excitedly and exchanging experiences. It was very amusing to observe the exhilaration and excitement which everybody betrays after a successful action like this ...

Hitherto we had not had many successes, but had suffered rather heavy losses, and this state of affairs always shakes confidence. But now, for the first time, the glorious realization dawned on us that by using clever and careful tactics we could inflict heavy losses on the enemy and get away almost scot-free ourselves.

Sergeant A. G. Girdwood
Combat Report

When the squadron followed a Ju 88 down through cloud, I stayed above, just in case the enemy did not go right through. After waiting for about one minute, I also went down through cloud to about 2,000 feet and saw the e/a in front and below me. I gave it a twenty-degree head-on three-secs burst, turned sharply round the back of it, and came in again at the front to repeat the attack and gave him a similar burst. The e/a was now down to about 500 feet, moving slowly in from the sea to the coast, just west of Selsey. I climbed to about 400 feet above it, dived on it shooting. It shuddered and lost height quickly. Flames were then pouring out of both engines. Someone jumped from the a/c but the parachute only half opened. The a/c reached about the second field from the shore. As it touched ground, it exploded into a mass of flames.

New York Times

London, 14 August – Germany sent over more than 500 planes [yesterday] to attack shipping in the English Channel and Thames Estuary, as well as British airbases and other objectives in Southampton, the Kentish coast, Berkshire, Wiltshire, the Isle of Wight and other points northeast and southwest ... British officials would not say whether the Nazi airmen damaged or destroyed any important military objectives in this country or sank any ships. All they divulged was that some civilians were killed, others injured, houses and business buildings wrecked and bowling greens and other playing fields damaged by German bombs ... The day's bag of German planes shot down over and around Britain was a record, it was declared ... The extent of the big German onslaught gave rise to the question whether the long-awaited Blitzkrieg had finally started or was about to begin in earnest. Competent observers say that the Germans are gradually increasing the number of planes they send over here daily. It is pointed out at the same time that Germany could afford to dispatch as many as 1,000 planes at a time to batter Britain and still have reserves on which to draw.

Pilot Officer Robert Deacon-Elliott

On 15 August, we were sent off from Acklington up in Yorkshire to patrol at Angels 24, east of the Farne Islands, off the coast in the North Sea. We intercepted a raid of at least 150 aircraft coming to bomb the north of England while others were attacking down south. Every type of German plane we knew of was there. We'd never seen anything like it before. During our training, we'd learned to do 'Number One Attack', Number Two Attack', 'Number Three Attack.' You knew exactly what each of those meant. So someone called to our acting squadron commander, Ted Graham, 'Have you seen them?' Ted, who stuttered, replied, 'Of course, I've seen the b-b-bastards. I'm trying to w-w-work out wh-wh-what to do.' But we already were about to reach them. Graham hurtled in through the gap between the bombers and their escort and each of us picked a target. I saw two Huns literally disintegrate. The bombers quickly began jettisoning their loads. The sea below churned up white with bombs as if a colony of whales was spouting. We hacked them about so badly, the formation split apart and they made for home. That was the first and last time formations of Germans came over the North Sea by day.

Pilot Officer Robert Doe

We were shifted in August from Cornwall, where nothing much had happened, to Middle Wallop and were bombed twenty minutes after we had landed. We were being driven in lorries to the mess for lunch at the time. There was nothing we could do but watch. Another squadron was in the air trying to intercept the bombers. It was over so fast. They hit a hangar. They didn't get many planes, but they killed about thirty people.

The following day was my first day of actual combat. It was a chaos of errors, I was petrified because I knew I was probably about the worst pilot in the squadron. Fighter pilots were supposed to be wonderful at acrobatics. I didn't like acrobatics. I was a very experienced flyer – all of us in the squadron at the time were. But we were inexperienced in tactics. When we took off from Middle Wallop, we flew off in four Vics of three in tight formation, which was ridiculous. I was number two to the leader, which was fairly safe because I was towards the front end. We were vectored to intercept 200 aircraft coming in over Swanage to the south. We got there before the Germans and were told to patrol. So we patrolled up and down the sun – a basic stupidity. At one point, we turned up sun and found we only had nine aircraft of the original twelve left. We hadn't seen anything happen. We'd lost three planes without knowing it.

Two minutes later we were in the middle of a mass of German aircraft. We all broke up. I followed the leader because it was my job to protect his tail. I saw him shoot at something but it didn't go down so I shot at it and it did go down. I was so elated that I followed it down and watched it crash into the sea. As I pulled up, another German aircraft passed right in front of me so I followed it and got that one as well, almost reflexively.

Archibald Sinclair, Secretary of State for Air

I have it in command from His Majesty the King to convey the following message:
Please convey my warmest congratulations to fighter squadrons who in recent days have been so heavily engaged in the defence of our

country. I, like all their compatriots, have read with ever increasing admiration the story of their daily victories. I wish them continued success and the best of luck.

Pilot Officer Dennis David

There were six of us and it looked like hundreds of them, coming in to bomb the oil tanks near Weymouth. Just as we were getting properly into the bombers, their fighter escort came alone. Voase Jeff – he was a nephew of J. Arthur Rank – was leading. He was hit and killed. I had bullet holes up the side of my aircraft. Out of the corner of my eye, I saw a parachute. Johnnie Cock was shot up and had baled out at 20,000 feet. On his way down, one of those 109s came round and started shooting at him. His parachute cords went ping! ping! ping! – beginning to separate him from his chute canopy as the bullets flew around him. I managed to get behind that murderous Hun and shot him down. I circled Johnnie till he hit the water, because I wasn't going to let another Hun shoot him down.

I came to know and like some Germans later on. But I hated the enemy then for what they tried to do to Johnnie Cock and what they did to Johnnie Dewar, our squadron leader, later in the Battle. He parachuted out, but when we found his body, it was riddled with bullets. Some of our people say what wonderful men the German pilots were personally. But I still feel that men who could shoot boys in parachutes are not people I want to meet or know.

Sergeant Philip Wareing

Our squadron commander said, 'You've got to shoot down four enemy planes before you're shot down yourself because that's what the odds are. Otherwise you're wasting your time.'

C. B. Allen, New York Herald Tribune

Washington, 16 August – Army Air Corps reaction to Germany's methodical mass air raids on England was summed up today by a spokesman for that service in the words: 'It looks pretty dark for the British.' This officer based his observations and conclusions – which he admitted were only informed guesses as to what was going on in

Europe – both on press reports of the great aerial conflict and on information sent back by Air Corps observers stationed in London ... The Air Corps estimate, he said, was that the Germans had a five-to-three superiority over the British in combat airplanes and that they could keep up indefinitely the pace they had set for the last four days, barring a shortage of fuel or ammunition or an unforeseen counterstroke by the Royal Air Force, seriously crippling Nazi sources of supply.

Edward R. Murrow, CBS News

London, 18 August – During the last three days, I have driven more than 500 miles in the south of England. Many times the sirens sounded and a few times we saw the bombs fall. There is something unreal about this air war over Britain. Much of it you can't see. The aircraft are up in the clouds, out of sight.

Even when the Germans come down to dive bomb an airfield, it's all over in an incredibly short time. You just see a bomber slanting down toward his target; three or four little things that look like marbles fall out, and it seems to take a long time for those bombs to hit the ground.

The other day, we drove for twenty-five miles through rural country while an air-raid alarm was on. Coasting down the smooth white road between tall green hedges, we would slide through a little village tucked away at the bottom of a hill beside a stream. There would be one grey stone church, an arched bridge over the stream, perhaps a couple of dozen little brick cottages with red-tiled roofs, and a public house. That village would be dead, the streets as empty and silent as they were at two in the morning in peacetime. Even the air was quiet and heavy as it is just before a thunderstorm, but standing on the bridge near the church or at the crossroads would be one small middle-aged man, generally with a moustache, generally smoking a pipe, and always wearing a tin hat. He was an air-raid warden, in complete command of the village until the 'all-clear' sounded – the sole protection against the German bombers, except for the boys in Hurricanes and Spitfires high overhead, and the men manning the anti-aircraft batteries.

In some of the cities and larger towns, people stand about in the streets, but the small villages take cover ... From what I could see, the people down along the coast had been badly shaken. Many of them don't like the sound of the siren. It is loud, penetrating, and can't very well be ignored. The sirens seem to be about as disturbing and upsetting as the distant crump of bombs.

Miss Edith Starling, Epsom, Surrey
Letter to her Mother, 22 August 1940

Dear Mother and All,

... At almost the same time on Sunday, Uncle and I looked questioningly at one another across the dinner table for we could hear the distant drone of a considerable force of aircraft drawing nearer. Aunty had left shortly before to visit Gran and I was hoping she would catch her train before anything happened. We were listening to the news when it abruptly switched off and at the same time the sirens started up. We were getting better organized by this time and in two bats of a butterfly's eyelid, Uncle and I had whisked a small table into the hall, whisked a cloth on it and grabbed our plates which got gloriously messed up. I am sure I finished Jeanne's dinner for her and vice versa! It wasn't long before we heard the crump, crump of bombs falling. It was a very clear day and I wished I could see what was happening overhead, but as such things are not allowed we just sat tight. One of our Hurricanes crashed about four minutes' walk from the house in the RAC grounds. The pilot seemed quite cheerful, although he had been shot through the foot. He drove off, whistling, in an RAF car, but perhaps familiarity breeds contempt for this was his third crash in two days.

Love to all,
Edith

Pilot Officer Wally Wallens

We were short of pilots but we were short of aircraft too. They arrived from the maintenance unit, but you couldn't just put some ammo into a plane, jump into it and fly off. There were so many things that had to be done to it after it was delivered. Radios had to be fitted. The guns had to be sighted and made operational. Modifications had to be made by our fitters and armourers and other groundcrewmen, things that hadn't been done as the planes were rushed out of the maintenance units because they were so badly needed by the squadrons. It was non-stop day and night work getting those planes operational and keeping them operational after they'd been in combat. Our Spitfires and Hurricanes were being patched up with fabric and glue after they'd been shot up. People said the First World War practice of just putting on patches of doped fabric to mend bullet holes wouldn't work on a stressed skin modern aircraft. But it did, by God! They patched the buggers up and off we'd go again.

Pilot Officer Roland Beaumont

Few people realized what hard work a dogfight was. You concentrated like mad while it was going on. It was an incredibly energetic thing. You'd be wet with sweat.

Flight Lieutenant Peter Brothers

I enjoyed a dogfight. I had been one of those schoolboy idiots who had started playing with model aeroplanes when I was nine years old. My father had me taught to fly when I was fifteen to cure me of the habit so that I'd settle down and go into the family chemical manufacturing business. But I whizzed off to join the air force when I was seventeen and a half. My heroes were Mannock and McCudden and Ball and Bishop – our First World War air heroes. In a dogfight, I thought this was a great chance to try to live up to those characters. I don't think I did.

In a dogfight, you had to convince yourself that you were better than the other chaps. This I learnt from Taffy Jones, a First World War ace who was our mentor when I first joined the air force. He stuttered. He said there was going to be a war and, 'You ch-ch-chaps are g-g-going to b-b-b-be in it. Ne-ne-never forget that you will b-b-b-be terribly frightened. B-b-but always remember, the ch-chap in the enemy aircraft is t-t-twice as frightened.' I remembered that when I first got into combat. I was terrified. Then I thought, 'I feel sorry for the chap in the 109. He must be in a terrible state.' I figure Taffy Jones saved my life – many times over.

Pilot Officer Steve Stephen

There were times when you couldn't *not* see a German up there. You came skidding up to one and tried to put him out of the sky, set him on fire, or damage him in some way, and then slip away before someone got on your tail.

Pilot Officer Dennis David

There was a lot of nonsense at the time about 'perfect deflection shots'. There was never a time for that in a dogfight. The only way you could shoot down a German fighter was getting very close to its backside and letting it have everything. Then you'd pull the stick right back into your gut for a sharp turn. You were pushed way down into your seat. Your eyeballs were pushed down into your face. It was like swinging a bucket of water around. The bucket goes around but the water stays in the bucket. You didn't keep it up for long, but you were pulling a lot of 'G' while it was happening. There were a lot of aircraft in the sky. If you could, you made your attack on the bombers. But almost immediately, you were in a dogfight with the fighters which had come down to protect them. It seemed to go on forever – minutes at least – though it was only seconds. The fact was that if you kept your finger on the trigger, your ammunition would run out in fifteen seconds. So you fired only short bursts. You'd be fighting and turning, turning and fighting. You'd miss colliding with other aircraft literally by inches. It sounds barmy, but then suddenly, the sky was empty. You were suddenly alone. Your momentum had carried you miles away from the battle. You might see a blur of aircraft in the distance, but the sky around you was suddenly empty.

Flight Lieutenant Tony Miller

In a dogfight, the sky was speckled with aeroplanes. Everybody was manoeuvering for position. People were upside down and going in all directions. I was chasing a Ju 87 one time when my special angel tapped me on my shoulder and whispered, 'My boy, look in your mirror.' I looked into the mirror and it was entirely occupied by another Ju 87. Gull wings. Couldn't mistake it. He was right behind me. I did the smartest diving turn I'd ever done. There was so much 'G' on me that my seat collapsed. I sort of went down into the bottom of the cockpit. I even blacked out for a few seconds. He actually put a bullet through one of my wings. I found out about it afterwards.

Pilot Officer Dennis David

Some Ground Controllers were better than others. You always get good and bad. The system was new, unique, never been used before.

And it was complicated. On the whole, ground control was good and that was one of the reasons we won the Battle of Britain. There were bound to be certain pilots who didn't like certain Controllers and certain Controllers who didn't like certain pilots. Some of the chaps – both pilots and Controllers – were very bossy, a bit God Almightyish.

Wing Commander David Roberts, Sector Commander, Middle Wallop

Aside from my Senior Controller, Gavin Anderson, the other Controllers at the station were very much under training. But the chaps in the air had all the information we could possibly give them to intercept. We had problems with the radio. UHF hadn't yet completely come in so everybody was still on HF. There was a lot of static and interference and distance limitations. It complicated communications.

Air Vice Marshal A.D. Cunningham to Air Vice Marshal Keith Park

RDF [Radar] frequently underestimates the numbers of enemy aircraft in a raid. This is probably due to the practice of the enemy of stacking the a/c above one another. Further experience may enable the RDF operators to recognize the stacked formation. Heights obtained from RDF stations at present are the best that can be obtained with the apparatus at hand.

Squadron Leader James Leathart

Controllers had to cope with poor radar reports, poor communications and mistakes by the Observer Corps. They had to do an awful lot of co-ordinating of information. It was true that they sometimes put lame ducks – who weren't much good at flying and fighting – in the Ops Room. But that didn't necessarily mean they were poor Controllers. The good Controllers were very good indeed. The Controllers we trusted, we trusted implicitly. Ronnie Adam was one of those. There were times when we'd say among ourselves, 'Oh hell, Ronnie isn't on today.'

Flight Lieutenant Peter Brothers

Our squadron had pre-war experience in dealing with control, such as it was, before the war began. We did experimental flying at the time. We would intercept incoming airliners. We weren't allowed to fly close to them. We had to fly straight past and pretend we just happened to be in the air at the same time. But as early as 1937, we were 'intercepting' KLM and Lufthansa airliners. In those days, all the plotting in the Operations Room was done in chalk on a blackboard. When we weren't flying, we acted as plotters in the Operations Room so we watched the system develop and, by the time the war came, we knew a lot about it and understood exactly what the Controllers were doing.

They tried their best, though their information wasn't always as accurate as it should have been. The main complaint was that very often they weren't giving you the height advantage you wanted. And often the scramble signal was given too late, but that was because the last thing we wanted was to be caught by a spoof raid and be back on the ground refuelling when the main raid came in. Until the Controllers were satisfied that it was the real thing and not just another spoof, they didn't launch us and that meant we were sometimes sent up late. We'd complain over the radio and say, 'For Christ's sake, the Germans are way above us.'

Sergeant Jim Hallowes

We always went for the bombers a couple of thousand feet higher than the Controller said. We found it produced results.

Flight Lieutenant Sir Archibald Hope

We were supposed to know the codenames of the convoys going through the Channel. One time, the Controller, who was an ex-member of our squadron, said, 'Patrol Bosom', which was the codename for a particular convoy. But it sounded as if he'd said, 'Patrol Bosham', where there was a pub we used to go to together. Bosom, the convoy, was south of the Isle of Wight. Bosham, the village, was just outside Chichester, and that's where we patrolled. Finally, I told the Controller, 'We're over Bosham but there's nothing to be seen.' He said, 'Are you over Bosom?' I said, 'Yes, we're over Bosham.' He said, 'Where the ships are?' I said, 'Where "The Ship" *is*!' That was the name of the pub. That's when the penny dropped and he said, 'You're in the wrong bloody place.' We finally got to the convoy. Fortunately, nothing was happening there.

By and large, the Controllers were pretty good. The Controller could only use the information he got, and if the information he got was faulty, he couldn't improve on it and so often it *was* faulty. Some of the radar stations were bombed and that affected radar coverage.

The day Tangmere aerodrome was bombed, we were kept at 20,000 feet to deal with the fighter escort. They said, 'There are 109s coming and you've got to tackle them. Don't bother about the bombers.' Another squadron was going to deal with them. We could see all the Ju 87s below coming in to bomb the aerodrome and none of the enemy fighters we were supposed to concentrate on in the sky at all. Not one. We were doing nothing up there. In the end, I said, 'To hell with this. I'm going down after the bombers.' I suppose somebody had misinterpreted the radar information.

Squadron Leader Sandy Johnstone

Some reports took longer to come through to the Controller than others, but they all somehow had to be married together. An enemy formation could climb 2,000 feet between the time it was first seen till the time it was plotted. The Controller sometimes put me in a wonderful position above the enemy with the sun behind me – you couldn't ask for anything better than that. But one or two were a little bit stupid. They tried to get us to do things that were beyond the pale. We found, for instance, that when the Germans started using their advanced model 109s, they could fly very high, up to 35,000 feet. Once the Spitfire got to 30,000 feet, it was beginning to run out of oomph; it was hanging on its prop a bit. And you weren't really doing any good up there. But for some Controllers, it was against their pride to see another lot of Germans and not send us after them. Strictly speaking, we were required to follow their instructions. But I'd call down and say, 'No can do.' Junior chaps leading a flight wouldn't have the authority to say no. I lost one chap because he was sent up too high.

Pilot Officer Roland Beamont

One morning, we were waiting at dispersal and heard a throbbing noise. We looked up and saw a twin-engined aircraft flying towards us at about 4,000 feet, under cloud. I said, 'That's a Ju 88!' My colleagues said, 'It can't be.' So we called the Operations Room and asked, 'Do you have any enemy plots near here?' They said, 'No. The board's clear, old boy. Nothing at all.' I said, 'We've got a Ju 88.' They said, 'You can't have.' It went half circle around our field, unmistakably a Ju 88. Eventually, my flight commander picked up the phone to Operations and said, 'I don't give a damn what you fellows say. I'm taking a section up after him,' which he had no authority to do. We scrambled a section, but couldn't find him any more. He had pulled up into cloud and we'd lost him.

* * *

Right through the summer, well before the start of the night blitz on London in September, the Luftwaffe engaged in sporadic night-time attacks on Britain. Sometimes they hit such specific targets as the strategic port areas of Plymouth and Bristol. But often the night attacks during the summer were just harassing raids, with bombs dropped wherever they might fall, part of a German campaign to snipe at British defences in off-hours and to encourage the people of Britain to force their obstinate leaders to sue for peace.

The raids were not big. Often it was just a solitary bomber coming over after dark to do its damage. But British air defenders, whether on a standard nocturnal patrol or dispatched to intercept specific attackers, had little success in coping with them. With only very primitive radar apparatus in their aircraft, they could rarely see anything in the night sky. They went up, looked futilely around till their fuel ran low and then came down again. Virtually no attackers were brought down at night and a number of British aircraft were lost in landing accidents on fogged-in and badly illuminated fields. But for public morale purposes, Fighter Command felt obliged during the Battle of Britain to dispatch interceptors against the German night-time raiders, while pressing ahead with efforts to develop suitable equipment for effective night fighting.

Wing Commander Peter Chamberlain

Dowding was becoming more and more confident that his fighters could probably head off the bombers the Germans sent over by day. But he feared that their bombers would get through at night. That was why he set up the Fighter Interception Unit.

On Blenheims, with which most of the night fighter squadrons were equipped, the AI [Air Interception radar] was pretty ineffective. What we were trying to do at the Fighter Interception Unit was place a properly equipped fighter into position to secure an interception at night. Until the Blenheims could be provided with efficient AI, it was close to a waste of time to try to intercept in the dark. Crews were lost in bad weather at night. It simply didn't serve any useful purpose. My orders from Dowding were to develop the night fighter into a useful aircraft.

My team consisted of clerks, pilots, gunners, riggers, fitters, Uncle Tom Cobbleigh and all, and of course there were the boffins and the odd gremlin. The boffins were the scientific folk – professors, inventors, mathematicians. Gremlins, on the other hand, bore no scientific examination. They were a crafty, pestilential race, grotesque in their habits and thoroughly blameworthy. You could plead that they guzzled your glycol. You might allege that they muddled your maps. It wouldn't do any good.

Flight Lieutenant Tony Miller

I had got very interested in airborne radar. But I was posted instead to the Operations Room at 11 Group headquarters at Uxbridge, which disappointed me very much. One of my duties was to appear in the Ops Room at 6.00 each morning to go through signals that had come in during the night and hand them out to senior people. One morning, I saw a signal which said Fighter Command was going to form a special unit for experimenting with airborne radar. Names were asked for posting to it. I seized that signal and ran all the way up the stairs to the senior staff officer's room and said, 'Please, sir, me!' He said, 'No. I'm afraid somebody else has been posted.' I rang up somebody I'd worked with earlier at Fighter Command headquarters, Walter Pretty – he later became Air Chief Marshal – and I said to him, 'Walter, who's got the job?' He said, 'I'm not going to tell you. That's against the rules.' I said, 'OK, but is he in such-and-such squadron?' He said, 'No.' I said, 'Then is he in such-and-such squadron.' He said, 'Not there either.' I said, 'Right. Then he hasn't flown a Blenheim at night as much as I have and I ought to have the job.' And I got it.

We flew by day or by night, as was appropriate, carrying out our experiments. The apparatus didn't work all the time. It was difficult to interpret the signals. We'd take off in Blenheims in a pair. One would settle in. The other would come up behind and check signals on its own radar system and try to interpret them. We were trying to work out some procedure for falling in behind a target and getting within shooting range. When we tried it by day, the intention was, of course, that all this would eventually happen at night.

But there was a serious snag about airborne radar at the time. The maximum range of the apparatus was its height above the ground, because it was broadcasting electronic pulses which came back from the ground as if it was picking up a target. So we needed direction from ground control to get into position behind a target. He would tell you when he'd done his best and for you to switch on your AI set. Willie the Wasp [as Wing Commander Peter Chamberlain was called by his men in the Fighter Interception Unit] invented a code signal for switching on the radar in the aircraft – 'flash your weapon'. When the Controller saw you were within your range of a target, he'd say, 'Flash your weapon', which of course means something else in a modern context.

Willie the Wasp was a cheerful chap with enormous energy. He was always prodding us on – 'Do this. Do that. Come on, get on with it!' – which was why he was called Willie the Wasp. He was the guiding spirit of the Fighter Interception Unit.

Flight Lieutenant John Cunningham

There wasn't much hope of the Blenheim achieving anything at night, but from a public morale point of view, I don't think that could be admitted. They were sent up at night in the hopes that incoming enemy aircraft would be illuminated by searchlights and because we had no other aircraft to send up at night until the advent of the Beaufighter late during the summer.

The Beaufighter was a very toughly built, rather brutal looking aircraft. It was a jolly good war machine, but its airborne radar was extremely unreliable in the early days. We had to rely on external aerials on the aircraft and we had endless trouble with 'squint'. Because these planes lived out in the open, when they got wet, water got into the radar system and the signal that came in from the wing aerials could not be balanced up. We learned early on to send the planes up in pairs during daylight to test their radar. Your target would sit in front of you and your radar operator would sit in the back of the Beaufighter looking towards the tail. As you came up to your 'target aircraft', you'd ask him to sing out its range and elevation. You'd position the target dead ahead and ask him, 'Where is it now?' He'd look at the radar and say, 'It's about thirty degrees left and above you.' So you'd tell him to come off his seat and look forward and he'd see that the aircraft which he thought was in one place was somewhere else. That was 'squint'. We tried and we tried during that summer, but we didn't achieve any success with that problem until after the Battle of Britain.

Another problem with the early Beaufighter was that when you loaded it up with ammunition, it became unstable in pitch. The aeroplane would either tend to go into a dive or climb more steeply than it should have. It didn't have the basic stability that all aircraft must have. It could only be brought under control with great concentration of effort. That was why a lot of people were killed in Beaufighters early on, flying unstable aircraft at night or in cloud or when they had no visual horizon. It was very demanding. A lot of pilots failed on that.

I spoke to Fighter Command almost immediately and said, 'Hey, this isn't right!' They told me to take the aeroplane back to the manufacturers in Bristol to get their chief pilot to fly it, which I did. At Bristol, they were horrified. They hadn't tested the aircraft loaded with cannon ammunition and all the junk that we'd got. As a result, the later editions of the Beaufighter which were produced after the Battle of Britain came out with a much bigger tail. But before that happened, there were pilots who crashed, worn out by the struggle to keep themselves in the air in Beaufighters.

* * *

Grossly inflated 'kill' claims on both sides in the Battle of Britain were inevitable. A pilot shot at an enemy aircraft, saw smoke come out of it or pieces of it drop off, saw it go into a spin or into a seemingly uncontrollable dive, and believed he had shot it down. He reported as much to the squadron's intelligence officer when he landed, and, unless challenged, his kill was added to the accumulating scores of one side or the other. In a sky full of swooping, twisting, diving enemy aircraft, a pilot couldn't always be expected to follow his victim down to make sure of his fate. Even when the sky was clear, it wasn't wise to linger about when something might come swooping down at him at any moment.

Often a pilot would shoot up a plane, see it begin to smoke and believe it was his kill. Another pilot would then come along to finish off the smoking aircraft and claim it as well. It was common for more than one pilot to claim the same kill and for it to be counted twice.

For the Germans, these exaggerated claims proved damaging. It lifted morale among their pilots but, at the same time, contributed to the assumption by Luftwaffe commanders that the British were in a far worse condition than they really were. It influenced their strategy and their tactics. When the Luftwaffe launched the Attack of the Eagles, German intelligence, basing its figures on the reports of Luftwaffe pilots, reported that Fighter Command had only about 300 serviceable aircraft left to withstand the German attacks; in fact, with the extra planes being churned out by the aircraft factories, it had about twice that number.

Reconciled to never being able actually to wipe out the Luftwaffe, the British suffered no such euphoric consequences of their exaggerated kill claims. They were badly needed morale boosters for the pilots, the military commanders and the general public. Nevertheless, an effort was made to draw up guidelines for accurate kill claims, though figures found in German records after the war showed that even then, British claims had also remained inflated.

Pilot Officer Dennis David

The Germans destroyed us three times over on paper. By the time Eagle Day came around, they thought we had nothing left.

Pilot Officer Birdie Bird-Wilson

We were given a very good press write up. Our scores were listed like in a cricket match – how many Germans we'd shot down and how few we'd lost.

Squadron Leader Sandy Johnstone

When we were up in Scotland, we used to get most of our information from the barmaid at the local pub. She was better informed than any of us. One night, she said she'd heard rumours that our squadron was moving south. When I rang up Group that night, they said, 'Oh yes. We were going to tell you. You're going south the day after tomorrow.' We were pleased to be heading into the heavy combat area. We had heard that the squadrons down there were knocking up big scores on enemy aircraft. That was the great thing and we wanted to get in on it.

Air Chief Marshal Sir Hugh Dowding

I must disclaim any exact accuracy in the estimates of enemy losses. All that I can say is that the utmost care was taken to arrive at the closest possible approximation ... The German claims were, of course, ludicrous. They may have been deceived about our casualties, but they knew they were lying about their own. I remember being cross-examined by the Secretary of State for Air about the discrepancy. He was anxious about the effect on the American people of the wide divergence between the claims of the two sides. I replied that the Americans would soon find out the truth – if the German figures were accurate, they would be in London in a week. Otherwise, they would not.

Winston Churchill

The important thing is to bring the German aircraft down and to win the battle and the rate at which American correspondents and the American public are convinced that we are winning, and that our figures are true, stands in a much lower plane ... There is something rather obnoxious in bringing correspondents down to air squadrons in order that they may assure the American public that the fighter pilots are not bragging and lying about their figures.

Flight Lieutenant Peter Brothers

We had this business of half an aircraft, when two of you had shot at it and it went down. They said, 'That's half for each of you.' But I didn't bother with that. I said to my number two, who was a young pilot officer, 'That's all yours,' so he could have his first swastika painted on his aircraft.

For confirmation of an enemy plane shot down, there was preferably cinegun proof. And there were witnesses, other pilots, where available. Your intelligence officer would want to know details of place, height, time, type of aircraft, weather conditions, how the action had taken place, that sort of thing.

I don't think there was much deliberate overclaiming. There were certain people who got a name for it, who always happened to be on their own when they shot something down. But in general, the problem was that a lot of you would be mixed up together in one fight and somebody would shoot at something, it would start smoking, then somebody else would have a bash at it, and two people would claim it, separately. If they were from different stations and landed back at different places, there was no co-ordination in scoring.

Sergeant Bernard Jennings

When suddenly there were no Germans in the sky, when there'd been a lot of them there a minute before, we knew they usually flew down the Thames Estuary on their way home. So when this happened one time, I belted down after them. I soon caught up with a 110 with a Spitfire on its tail. I flew alongside the Spitfire and saw the pilot was Sailor Blake, a sub-lieutenant in the navy, flying with us, all the carriers having been sunk.

I said to him, 'What are you doing?' He said, 'I'm going to ram that so-and-so.' I said, 'Don't be a fool. We're only about three hundred feet over the sea. You'll go straight into the drink.' He said his cannon were jammed and he wasn't going to let that German get away. I told him I had one cannon still working and to move over so I could take him. He said, 'Only if you give me half.' I said all right and he moved over to my port side. I said, 'Get over to my starboard side. I've only got my port cannon working and as soon as it fires, I'm going to swing into you.' So he moved there.

I aimed at the German's wing tip, pressed the button, knocked the top off his starboard engine, and then my remaining cannon jammed too. So Sailor and I flew up alongside that 110. The German pilot was just sitting there, absolutely rigid, as though he was drugged, not looking at either of us. The strange thing was he had no tail gunner, otherwise we never could have done that. Sailor said, 'I'm going to ram him.' I said, 'All right, if that's what you want to do. Cheerio. I'm off back.' I landed at base and five minutes later, in comes Sailor. Of course, he didn't ram the German.

Pilot Officer Dennis David

More often than not, I didn't find it possible to confirm aircraft shot down. We shot at a lot. We destroyed a lot. We damaged a lot. But there was too much going on in the sky to see the results. You'd tell the squadron intelligence officer when you landed. You'd fill out a report listing date, time, weather factor, your aircraft number. Then he'd ask, 'What did you see? What did you do?' Gradually from the report would emerge a confirmed score, or perhaps not. The system wasn't always accurate. It couldn't be. A list was published throughout Fighter Command once a month. It would list high scores. I was given seventeen on that list once. It was really only to boost morale.

Pilot Officer David Crook

The squadron ... caught two Dorniers that had dropped behind the rest of the enemy formation ... The two wretched Dorniers were overwhelmed by the twelve Spitfires and were literally shot to pieces in mid-air. Everybody in B-flight was absolutely determined to have a squirt at the Hun and as a result there was a mad scramble in which people cut across in front of each other and fired wildly in the direction of the Dorniers, regardless of the fact that the air was full of Spitfires. Fortunately, nobody collected any of the bullets that were flying about, and their energy was duly rewarded as each pilot was able to claim one-sixth of one Dornier very definitely destroyed!

Squadron Leader Jack Satchell

One of my Polish sergeant pilots shot up a Hun and saw him start to go down with smoke coming out. He assumed that he was going to crash, so broke off his attack to attack another German plane. When he got back to base, he was told he was only credited with a Hun 'damaged' because he had not seen it crash and not unquestionably on fire.

He was very angry and said he *knew* it would crash and that there was no point in his following it all the way down when there were other Huns waiting to be shot down. But it was to no avail and he got credited with it only as a 'damaged'. But he was determined to be credited with a Hun definitely destroyed. So that afternoon, when he was scrambled, he attacked a Dornier, first set its starboard engine on fire, then he went to the other side and set the port engine afire. Not content with this, he began firing at the fuselage to make certain. The Huns within started to bale out and one of them, to show how close that pilot got to the wretched German aircraft, jumped straight into his prop! Needless to say, the prop smashed to bits and the radiator was also smashed off, but he managed to crash land the aircraft near North Weald without further damage. When he got out, he saw that his whole aircraft was smothered with blood and bits of flesh. There was no question this time. He was credited with that Hun as 'confirmed destroyed'.

Chichester Observer, *17 August*

People who reside anywhere near the coast of the southeastern counties ... are not likely to complain of want of excitement during the past week. From all directions come stories of battles in the air of a severity compared with which previous raids sink into insignificance. The war is indeed 'on', and it is difficult to run against anybody who has not got some little tit-bit of unconfirmed information to add to the sum total of rumours abroad. It is doubtless an inevitable state of things, condemn the chatterbugs as much as we like, but ... this week's gossip is mostly of a nature to cheer people. Tales multiply, of course, about the skill and gallantry of our RAF, and now many have seen it for themselves who had hitherto only heard about it ... Who can resist the temptation, when it offers itself, of watching those thrilling chases up in the mist, even though the rattle of an aerial dogfight seems ominously near? If we believed all the stories of enemy planes brought to grief, the countryside would be littered with smashed-up bombers. But there are quite a number of well authenticated instances.

Air Ministry

DEFINING ENEMY CASUALTIES

DESTROYED

   (a) Aircraft must be seen on the ground or in the air destroyed by a member of the crew or formation, or confirmed from other sources, e.g. ships at sea, local authorities, etc.
   (b) Aircraft must be seen to descend with flames issuing. It is not sufficient if only smoke is seen.

(c) Aircraft must be seen to break up in the air.

PROBABLES
(a) When the pilot of a single-engined aircraft is seen to bale out.
(b) The aircraft must be seen to break off the combat in circumstances which lead our pilots to believe it will be a loss.

DAMAGED
Aircraft must be seen to be considerably damaged as the result of attack, e.g. undercarriage dropped, engine dropped, aircraft parts shot away, or volume of smoke issuing.

Sergeant Philip Wareing

Churchill visited Kenley Aerodrome five days after we got there from the north. We were scrambled soon after he arrived. I thought it was put on just for his benefit, but we intercepted some Germans near Canterbury, fighters on top, bombers underneath. A-flight went for the bombers. We went for the fighters which had formed a defensive ring. We just barged in. It was an unholy mêlée. The sky was full of aircraft, all very close, going in all directions. I saw four Germans in a long line astern going off towards France and went after them. I pressed the emergency boost to get double power, caught up with them over the Channel, and fired at each one in turn. I thought, 'This is easy.' I could see my tracer bullets hitting or appear to be hitting them. Down they went with smoke coming out and I thought, 'I'm going to be an ace. Four already, all at once.' Not till later did I learn that the German way of getting out of a jam was to turn upside down and put full boost on. A lot of smoke comes out of them as they dive away – and that may be all that happened, though I've always thought I really got at least one of those for sure and probably damaged the others.

But my aircraft must have been hit in the radiator during the earlier mêlée, because after I intercepted the four Germans over the Channel, it started getting hot. The oil pressure and temperature went right off the clock. I didn't realize it, but I was now over France; it took only three minutes to fly across the Channel. I was beginning to slow down and another lot of Germans appeared and went for me. I was going slower and slower and then my engine caught fire. I sideslipped and it went out. I was almost gliding by then. The Germans were using me for target practice. Their machine-gun bullets on my armour plating sounded like one of those old alarm clocks going off.

My aircraft was very badly hit. I did a very steep turn to get away and spun down a couple of thousand feet. That shook them off for a minute or so, though it may have been only seconds. I had no idea of time. I thought the whole thing lasted an hour, but it probably was only ten minutes.

I looked at my poor Spitfire. It was a new one. I'd only had it a few days. Now there were holes all over it. I knew I'd have to get out. There was a lot of smoke. It seemed to get quiet again for a moment. I opened the cockpit lid, undid my straps and took off my helmet. I thought I'd remembered everything that I had to do and was going to turn upside down to fall out, when I was hit again, a cannon shell I think, and then everything happened at once. The petrol tanks just in front of me went up in flames. I felt the heat coming up my legs. At the same time, they blew my tail off and I was thrown clear of the plane. I'd heard stories that the Germans might shoot at you when you were parachuting down, so I delayed pulling the ripcord. I was thrown out of the plane at 6,000 feet but didn't open my parachute till I was down to about 1,000 feet. I was tumbling over and over, waiting until the Messerschmitts got smaller and smaller in the distance so they wouldn't get at me. The ground came up very quickly. When I opened my parachute, it was only a matter of seconds before I landed, but it was an easy landing anyway.

I came down in a field near the Channel coast in France. A German motorcycle with a sidecar came riding right up. The driver drew his pistol and pointed at me and said, '*Haben sie pistol.*' I said, 'Don't be silly.' He spoke a little English. He said, 'For you, the war is over.' I think they all said things like that. He put his pistol away, put me in the sidecar and, with another chap riding behind him, he took me to an airfield close by.

I was very impressed with that field. The planes and everything there were very well camouflaged, far better than ours were. It was haymaking time and the aircraft were literally under the hay, well hidden. The Germans were very friendly. Of course, they were winning, or thought they were. One chap said to me, 'Cheer up. We'll be in London next week and you will soon be home.' They had quite a party for me. They said they were sorry they'd finished all the English whisky that had been captured at Dunkirk and they only had French brandy and beer. It was good fun, really. Some of them showed me family photographs. Two asked for my home address and one of them was shot down over England a few days later, either with my address in his pocket or he said during interrogation that he'd seen me. That was the first news anyone at home had that I was still alive. They took off early the next morning. I watched them form up above. It was impressive – several hundred aircraft going round and round, getting into their massive formations. I was then taken away and spent a day in the office of an adjutant. He was writing letters of condolence to families of Germans who were being shot down. He told me, 'Not only you. We lose a lot, too.'

I ended up in a prison camp in Germany where I was interrogated. They asked a lot of innocuous questions, pretending it was routine, for the Red Cross – my mother's name; that sort of thing – and then more detailed questions – about my squadron – till I finally said no. Strangely, they didn't ask anything about radar. They knew about it, but didn't realize how much it meant to us. One German asked me, 'How is it you're always there when we come.' I said, 'We have powerful binoculars and watch all the time.' They didn't query that at all.

Wareing was later transferred to a prisoner-of-war camp in Poland from which he escaped two-and-a-half years later and got home after stowing away aboard a Swedish ship.

* * *

Tales of the heroism, pluck and skill of the RAF fighter pilots spread quickly throughout Britain. But little was reported of the difficulties Fighter Command was increasingly facing. Of course, no effort was made to minimize the continuing German threat. There were repeated military and civilian counter-invasion drills. Air-raid precautions became part of everyday life. Exhortation for people to watch out for fifth columnists and saboteurs was incessant. However, details of growing RAF losses as the German onslaught intensified were carefully withheld. Few people in the country knew the extent of the damage inflicted by the Luftwaffe raids. Not many knew that some airfields in the south of England were so badly hit that they were temporarily knocked out of action.

Subject to censorship restraints, spoonfed with Ministry of Information propaganda, shielded from the real dimensions of the struggle, London newspapers were jubilant. Their front pages screamed tales of glory. HUNS LOSE 113, RAF 6. AGAIN! SIXTY SHOT DOWN. 140 RAIDERS OUT OF 600 DESTROYED. AT LEAST 115 MORE! JERRIES DRIVEN OFF, MASS RAID FOILED. The fact was, however, never before had Fighter Command been under such sustained pressure.

Increasingly short of men, it began sending recruits who had barely begun their flying training to make up the falling numbers at hard-pressed operational squadrons, where they were sometimes permitted no time at all to settle in before being rushed into combat. In one case, two young pilots showed up for duty with one of the frontline squadrons, were assigned aircraft and were sent up before they had time to unpack. One was immediately shot down and killed; the other ended up in hospital that very afternoon. By nightfall, all that remained at the airfield to tell of their arrival that day was their car, their luggage still inside.

Men began paying increased attention to tactics. Even experienced flyers, like chief Spitfire test pilot Jeffrey Quill, a volunteer newly arrived at a frontline squadron, was briefed in detail on combat dangers by veterans who were often only twenty-one or twenty-two years old. 'Get in as close as you can; you're usually further away from the plane you're attacking than you think you are.' 'If you hit a 109, don't follow him down to see him crash; another will get you while you're doing it.' 'Scan the skies constantly; it's essential you see them before they see you.' 'Never get separated if you can help it; and don't hang about on your own.'

Air Vice Marshal Keith Park to Group and Sector Controllers
19 August

The German air force has begun a new phase in air attacks which have been switched from coastal shipping and ports to inland objectives. The bombing attacks have for several days been concentrated against aerodromes, and especially fighter aerodromes, on the coast and inland. The following instructions are issued to meet the changed conditions:

(a) Dispatch fighters to engage large enemy formations over land or within gliding distance of the coast. During the next two or three weeks, we cannot afford to lose pilots through forced landings in the sea;

(b) Avoid sending fighters out over the sea to chase reconnaissance aircraft or small formations of enemy fighters;

(c) Dispatch a pair of fighters to intercept single reconnaissance aircraft that come inland. If clouds are favourable, put a patrol of one or two fighters over an aerodrome which enemy aircraft are approaching in clouds;

140

(d)   Against mass attacks coming inland, dispatch a minimum number of squadrons to engage enemy fighters. Our main objective is to engage enemy bombers, particularly those approaching under the lowest cloud layer.

Pilot Officer Peter Parrott

The 109s were always above you. You tried to get up there but it took time. It was very frustrating. They usually took the initiative. They'd come down and try to bounce you. Because of their limited range, they didn't have long over England. They had to get into action quickly if they were going to achieve anything. You would be going up to get at them and wondering when they'd be coming down to get at you.

Pilot Officer Bobby Oxspring

I was on a forty-eight-hour pass when the squadron moved south. We hadn't seen much action up to then but even before I could rejoin the squadron at Kenley, six of our pilots had been killed. We lost so many men that within ten or twelve days, though I was only a pilot officer, I was made B-flight commander.

Flight Lieutenant Brian Kingcome

In those days, people were promoted in fighter squadrons on seniority, which was the normal peacetime thing. But it wasn't working because you needed somebody who actually had operational experience. The mere fact that you had a lot of flying hours under your belt, all of which had been done in peacetime or in training command, didn't qualify you to lead a fighter squadron right in the middle of the Battle of Britain. We had an awful lot of experienced pilots, but not many experienced *fighter* pilots.

There was a very nice chap who came to take over our squadron. One of the first mornings he came down to dispersal, he had some oil on the sleeve of his tunic. He got a rag, dipped it in some hundred-octane fuel and rubbed it on the sleeve of his tunic to get the oil off. He then lit a cigarette and, of course, burst into flames. He had to be carried off to hospital, so I became acting CO of the squadron, though only a flight lieutenant.

I led the squadron for two or three weeks and then we got another

CO, a squadron leader who had a decoration for activity on the Northwest Frontier in India. His operational experience was chasing Pathan tribesmen in that part of the world. He'd dropped notes on villages where people had misbehaved, saying, 'We're going to bomb you rotters at twelve o'clock on Tuesday. So get the hell out.' And then at twelve o'clock on Tuesday, they'd drop a couple of bombs and afterwards the people would go back and carry on as before. That was the operational experience of our new CO. He decided to fly on my wing for a few days for experience. On the second flight, he was shot down. Not killed – the bullet came up through the floor of his cockpit, took skin off his ankles, the inside of his knees, and the tip of his tool, the tip of his nose and went out through the top. So I continued as CO.

Two or three weeks later, we got another CO, a very nice chap who had lots of flying hours under his belt but only as a flying instructor. He also flew as my number two to get the hang of it. He was shot down too, off my wing tip, his third or fourth flight. So I continued as CO until I was shot down.

Pilot Officer Bob Kings

I was at an operational training unit in August when Fighter Command was having a very rough time and replacements were needed. We were very keen to get into the fighting and very annoyed at being held back when we thought we were well enough trained. We were strained to get assigned to squadrons. Our instructor kept saying, 'Don't be in such a hurry. When you leave here, your life is worth no more than half-a-dollar.' In fact, of the dozen or so of us who were soon farmed out to various squadrons, some of the names were soon on the 'missing, believed killed in action' lists.

I was only a very junior pilot officer when I finally joined my squadron. We had a flight lieutenant with a DFC, somebody you looked up to. He and two others just vanished one day – missing, believed killed. I thought, 'By golly, if somebody experienced like that could be lost there isn't much hope for somebody like me.' I really didn't expect to survive. But it didn't worry me. I remember thinking, 'I must get home on leave (where my widowed mother was) to tidy up a few things,' so I could get the chop without leaving anything too untidy.

At dispersal at the aerodrome, we'd be sitting in the Nissen hut, waiting. There'd be an airman near the telephone in the corner. We'd be reading, writing letters, playing cards, playing shove ha'penny, playing chess. And the phone would ring. If it was 'Scramble!' everybody would leap up. Tables would go over, the cards and chess boards would be knocked aside. In two minutes or so you'd be in your plane and climbing like mad and thinking, 'I wonder if I put my queen's bishop's pawn in the right place.' Once I was playing shove ha'penny with a Czech sergeant. We were scrambled and he didn't come back. We'd been playing shove ha'penny only twenty minutes before.

Flight Lieutenant Sir Archibald Hope

Unquestionably Billy Fiske was the best pilot I've ever known. He was an American, one of the first to join the RAF. It was unbelievable how good he was. He picked it up so fast, it wasn't true. He'd flown a bit before, but he was a natural as a fighter pilot. He was also terribly nice and extraordinarily modest. He fitted into the squadron very well. The day Tangmere was bombed, Billy Fiske was airborne with the rest of us. We were up at 20,000 feet and came down to chase the Ju 87s, which had dropped their bombs and were going out to sea. We went after them. When we'd exhausted our ammunition and were low on petrol, we returned to the aerodrome and landed. As I came down, I saw one of our aircraft on its belly, belching smoke. It must have got a bullet in its engine.

I taxied up to it and got out. There were two ambulancemen there. They had got Billy Fiske out of the cockpit. He was lying on the ground there. The ambulancemen didn't know how to take his parachute off, so I showed them. Billy was burnt about the hands and ankles, so I told them to put on Tanafax, the stuff we were supposed to put on burns. I'm told now it's one of the worst things you could put on a burn. I told Billy, 'Don't worry. You'll be all right,' got back in my aeroplane and taxied back to the squadron. Our adjutant went to see him in hospital at Chichester that night. Billy was sitting up in bed, perky as hell. The next thing we heard, he was dead. Died of shock.

From Readiness at Dawn, *a fictionalised account of the Battle of Britain, written in 1940 by 'Blake' (pseudonym of Squadron Leader Ronald Adam, Controller in the Operations Room at Hornchurch at the height of the battle).*

One of the new squadrons from the north was [codenamed] Amber. Its Squadron Leader was a neat figure with a quiet, diffident manner, shy eyes and a soft voice. Amber had been released from readiness to available and were at lunch. From over the entrance door to the dining room came the crackle of the loudspeaker as Operations Room switched on.

'Operations calling Amber. Operations calling Amber. Readiness. Readiness. Switching off.'

They dropped their knives and forks. They ran to the entrance where their cars were waiting for them. The last out of the mess galloped down between the cars, jumping on them as they gathered speed. As they reached their dispersal point, the loudspeaker was issuing its next message.

'Operations calling. Amber Squadron scramble. Amber Squadron scramble. Patrol base. Patrol base. 10,000 feet.'

They ran for their Mae Wests, their helmets and goggles and gloves and their parachute harness, and so to their aircraft.

'Amber Squadron taxiing into position,' lookout's voice said in the Operations Room. 'Amber Squadron A-flight taken off. Amber Squadron B-flight taken off.'

'Hallo, Tartan. Hallo, Tartan. Amber Leader calling. Are you receiving me? Amber Leader to Tartan. Over.'

'Hallo Amber Leader. Hallo Amber Leader. Tartan answering. Receiving you loud and clear. Are you receiving me? Tartan over to Amber Leader. Over.'

'Hallo, Tartan. Amber Leader answering. Receiving you loud and clear. Have you any instructions?'

'Hallo Amber Leader. Tartan answering. Patrol base 10,000 feet. Possible attack developing. Will keep you informed. Listening out.'

'Close up B-flight, ' Amber Leader could be heard saying to one of his flight commanders.

'OK, OK. Just behind you.'

[The Controller] watched the plots. It was the old business, or what in those full and hurried days now seemed old. From the south-east they marched, the steady long line of them as each observer centre gave its message. Fifty plotted, then a hundred, then another hundred just behind, with diversionary attacks north and south of the main road.

Cricket and the other new squadron, Falcon, had engaged the fighters far away, towards the coast. The bombers came on.

'Hallo, Amber Leader. Tartan calling. What is your height?'

'Amber Leader answering. 10,000. 10,000.'

'Hallo, Amber Leader. Many enemy bombers south of you now turning north. Height reported 13.'

'Hallo Tartan. Shall I turn away and gain height?'

[The Controller] paused for a moment. Height was everything. But the bombers had now left no doubt of their objective. It was to be the aerodrome.

'Hallo, Amber Leader. Base is likely to be attacked. Bombers very near. Leave it to your discretion.'

The quiet voice of the Squadron Leader answered. 'Hallo, Tartan. Will try and gain height here.' Another voice broke in.

'Hallo, Amber Leader. Ack ack fire due south of us. Ack ack fire. Twelve o'clock from you. Twelve o'clock.'

And then another voice. 'There they are – tally-ho! Twelve o'clock above us, coming towards us.'

Amber Leader's same quiet, unhurried voice spoke: 'Line astern. Amber Squadron, line astern. Going in. Head-on attack.'

From the rampart of the Operations Room the anti-aircraft puffs, woolly in the distance, crisp in the foreground, poised their snowballs in the sky. The crack of the guns and the woompf of the bursting shells were more and more audible. The group captain was at his vantage point, tin hat at the same angle, hands on hips, sturdy little figure, erect and gazing upwards. The anti-aircraft fire swelled to a roar. In that roar, the crackle of machine-gun and cannon fire was lost, and then suddenly the roar ceased and the crackle came through clear.

'They're turning away,' the group captain called back through the window. 'By Jove, they're turning away!' Amber Squadron had gone in. Climbing with every ounce of help their engines could give them, they had met the bombers as these had steadied their course for the aerodrome. There was no time for tactical manoeuvering. In a minute or two the bombs would be falling on their base. They went in, firing at the great obscene objects that were carrying destruction to their station. One voice after another spoke: 'Returning to base for more ammunition.' The anti-aircraft fire broke out again. But this time its noise was more distant and the puffs nearby became woolly while those far away were crisp. The enemy was retreating.

'Hallo, Amber Leader. Hallo, Amber Leader. Tartan calling. Are you receiving? Over.'

But Amber Leader had gone. No one found him or his machine ever again. He had led the squadron into the bombers as the anti-aircraft fire was at its densest. A shell had burst and a puff of billowing smoke marked where Amber Leader once had been.

Pilot Officer Roland Beamont

Pilots flying from Biggin Hill, Kenley and the other airfields in 11 Group were at the centre stations of the battle. They had to face the main onslaught each and every day. Further out in the battle area – in 10 Group to the west, where we were – the fighting was just as hard when it happened, but more spread out in time. For our squadron, number 87, battles occurred roughly every other day. We'd nearly always lose a pilot; often two. But there wasn't the pressure there was at Biggin Hill and those places. The thing that sticks out in my mind was the laughter. Some of the things we laughed at might be regarded as a bit macabre. 'Old so-and-so ended up on his back and they had to get a crane to lift his aircraft to get him out.' The fact that old so-and-so was in the hospital was neither here nor there. It was still a hell of a laugh.

We didn't take ourselves too seriously. If anybody was heard waxing a bit heavy, and asking if any of us would survive another week, he'd be laughed out of the room. It was taboo to admit that you were in any sort of personal difficulties. We were kids, but at the top of our profession. We were demonstrating that we were better than the enemy and were saving our country. We were climbing out of Exeter one sunny day with eight Hurricanes. None of the other planes in the squadron were serviceable. We were told on the radio that there were 100 plus Germans coming in over Cherbourg. Then the controller said it was 120 plus. Then we heard the enemy was 150 plus, plotted twenty miles south of Portland, heading north. We were ten miles north of Portland, heading south. All of a sudden, the sky was full of these black bees – a great mass of them. We were approaching them obliquely from the front. They were stepped up in formations from 1,500 feet below us and towering up above us in the distance, probably up to 18,000 feet. The front fifty or so were Stukas. [The Stuka was a particularly easy target for British fighters.] I just had time to think, 'This is going to be easy,' when behind we saw twin-engined planes that looked like Ju 88s. It was going to be a dive bombing attack on Portland naval base. While we were closing in, the first Stukas were peeling off and going into their dives, one after the other. I thought, 'What's the CO going to do? Is he going in behind this lot?' But I realized there was no going behind them. They were stretching out right across the Channel. He just eased off towards the second echelon of Stukas and said, 'Come on, chaps. Let's surround them.' And there were just eight of us! That was Lovell-Gregg. He didn't come back.

We shot down a lot that day. They produced tremendous boils of white water as they dropped like bombs into the bay. We just opened up, went into the lot, went through them firing, pulled up from underneath the formation, then came back and picked off individual ones.

Pilot Officer Desmond Hughes

Once, when we were down at Manston, one of our flight commanders wasn't able to start his engine when he was scrambled. His numbers two and three took off without him. In due course, he was able to get his engine going, took off and was tucking his wheels up when he looked into the circuit and saw two aircraft. He flew off towards them, got in front and waggled his wings to indicate, 'OK, I'll take over now.' He was very upset when they shot him down because they turned out to be 109s. To add insult to injury, the bullets from the German fighters, quite apart from forcing him to land, set off the Very cartridges in the turret. His poor gunner in the back of this Defiant was sitting there, as they went into a belly landing, with red, yellow and green signal lights whistling all around him inside his turret.

Pilot Officer Brian Considine

During time off, all we were interested in was booze and girls. There was a place we used to go to in Andover to booze up, and all the rest of it. There was a girl there we called the Gypsy. She was a black-haired, sultry type and used to go for the boys. She had quite a reputation. Our flight commander was Stuart Walch, an Australian, a marvellous fellow and an outstanding pilot. One night, he was out with the Gypsy, didn't come back until around five the next morning and then led B-flight up. I was about to go on leave, so I didn't go up that time which was fortunate for me because that was a disastrous day for us. We lost five out of the six in B-flight. The only one in the flight who came back was Jackie Urwin-Mann. He wasn't sure what had happened. I can't believe that Stuart Walch - he was too good - would ever have let them be caught napping up there the way they were if it hadn't been for his night out with the Gypsy.

Pilot Officer Christopher Currant

Our aircraft were parked just at the end of the gardens of the houses where we were billeted. There was a bell which they would ring when the squadron was to scramble. When it went, we would dash out, jump into our kit, jump into our aircraft and take off. This was happening a hell of a lot of times every day. Sometimes there'd be a false alarm. It got on our nerves. An order was issued that no one was to run down the garden or by the aircraft unless there was a real alarm because whenever we'd see somebody running, we'd think, 'This is us', and we'd all start to run. It was hypnotic.

Squadron Leader Sandy Johnstone

We relied at Westhampnett on telephone orders which came from the Operations Room at Tangmere. It was one of those cranking telephones. You'd turn a handle to make it ring. We were damn fools. Our system of signals was: one ring for A-flight to scramble, two rings for B-flight, three rings for the whole squadron, and four rings for a call through to the officers' mess. You used to get the chaps sitting there and on one ring, A-flight would jump up. Two rings, A-flight would sit down and B-flight would jump up. Three rings and we'd all get up. Four rings and it might turn out to be only someone in the Ops Room inquiring what there was for lunch. So we finally changed it all around and made it one ring for the mess.

Pilot Officer Bobby Oxspring

The idea of getting the Hurricanes in on the bombers while the Spitfires kept the German fighter cover busy often didn't work out. You couldn't get them all into action at the same moment. If you were only a minute apart, it was too late.

General Sir Hastings Ismay, Secretary to the War Cabinet

From the moment one set foot on the tarmac [of fighter stations in Kent and Sussex], one sensed the tension in the air – the pilots standing by 'in readiness' waiting to 'scramble' into their machines at a moment's notice. It was impossible to look at those young men, who might within a matter of minutes be fighting and dying to save us, without mingled emotions of wonder, gratitude and humility. The physical and mental strain of the long hours at dispersal, the constant flying at high altitudes – two or three sorties a day were normal, six or seven not uncommon – must have been prodigious. And yet they were always so cheerful, so confident and so obviously dedicated.

Pilot Officer Tim Elkington

I was given the usual training on biplanes before I was sent to join 1 Squadron in July. But I'd never flown a Hurricane before. They gave me forty minutes on a Miles Master trainer when I got to the squadron and then up in a Hurricane the next day. I did a lot of patrols, but I didn't see my first German aircraft close up until mid-August.

I was fairly frightened when it finally happened. I felt a nasty chill when I saw that black cross on the aircraft and thought, 'My God, it's going round the back of me.' I wasn't going to let it get on my tail. I worked very hard to make sure it didn't, doing a high speed stall getting around to follow it. Luckily I had a height and sun advantage. I chased it, fired at it and thought I got it. It was smoking, went on its back and went down through the cloud. But looking back, I'm sure that – as a nineteen-year-old newcomer – I was firing at it from far too far away to have finished it off.

I was shaking as I flew back to base. I kept seeing odd aircraft through light cloud cover and kept wondering, 'Is it a German or is it one of us?' I had shot my bolt, physically and mentally, and my main purpose was to get home as fast as I could. I wasn't looking to do any more fighting that day. When I landed, I didn't say very much. I didn't say much for a full half-hour. I was overawed by what had happened.

I was shot down the next day when the squadron went up to intercept a raid. I was top weaver. That was a very exposed position, going back and forth over the top of the squadron, looking everywhere for enemy aircraft. Suddenly I looked down and the squadron was gone! I was sitting up there all alone, wondering what the heck to do. Then I saw a 109 going out over Portsmouth, so I went after it.

Previously, I'd been jinking all over the place, waltzing all over the sky, making sure that nothing was sitting on my tail. But I straightened out to go after that 109 and that was a fatal mistake. Something hit my aircraft and it was suddenly on fire. I tried very quickly to get out, got half-way over the side and was thrown back in. I tried again and was again thrown back in. So I sat down in the cockpit and thought, and decided that if I really wanted to get out, I should undo the radio and oxygen connections that were attached to me. I undid them and looked at my watch. It was 1.40. I thought that was a good time to go and out I went.

My mother lived at the time at Hayling Island, which is right under where I was shot down. Against all the odds, she was on the balcony looking at what was going on above. She saw a Hurricane chased by two 109s. She saw it hit and she saw the pilot bale out. She didn't know it was me. I had an ambulance girl telephone her later to tell her I was all right.

11 Group Intelligence Bulletin

32 Squadron on patrol sighted several formations of Junkers 88s and Dornier 215s escorted by Messerschmitt 109s. The pilots report that the Messerschmitt 109s circled round on each other's tails and, when attacked from below, one would drop out from the most advantageous position for an attack, deliver a short attack and rejoin the circle, when another would take its place, and so on. It was found to be very difficult to combat these tactics.

Associated Press

Southern England, 13 August – Here in this part of England, against which the central fury of the Nazi attack has thus far fallen, life went on today at its accustomed strolling gait.

During one of today's raids in the Dover district, a correspondent found workmen continuing to repair the roof of a cottage damaged yesterday. A farmer went on feeding his pigs, and a small boy continued to pick green beans in his family's vegetable garden.

In a house that had not a window left, the family remained at the dinner table. A newspaper man pushing his head through a gaping window, apologising at the same time for the intrusion, was told by the father of the family, 'You aren't the first one. It's a bit public not having windows, but the fresh air is nice.'

Sussex Daily News, *17 August*

We have invested our money as a nation in the best material, the best machines and the best men, and the outcome is the Royal Air Force. The dividend on the investment is coming in. The loss of at least 169 enemy machines for a loss of 34 of ours is a return so impressive that some are sceptical ... Ours are better in quality against Nazi superiority in quantity. This is an almost elementary fact. Germany is outstandingly the nation of the cheap and nasty in the mechanical world. We must redress the balance but preserve the British quality. That is the way to victory.

Mrs Jean Cook
Letter to her nephew, Squadron Leader Sandy Johnstone

My dearest Sandy,
  You have no idea the excitement you have caused by having your photograph in the papers [when he received the Distinguished Flying Cross]. I am told the villagers feel a sort of reflected glory. The little boy next door is very disappointed that it is only your head and shoulders that is showing. I believe Jeannie had bought five *Bulletins* [a Glasgow newspaper which printed the photograph]. Mrs Patterson phoned from Greenock to say how pleased she was about your honour. We are all terribly proud of you. I hear your mother spent a whole day at the phone. I wish you would come north so that we can have a look at you. With all my love, dear,

Yours,
Jean

Notes on Conference of 11 Group Sector Commanders

The AOC illustrated (with graphs) the increase during the present phase of operations in the number of aircraft lost and, to a lesser extent, the number of casualties to pilots. It was generally agreed this was due to several causes: the employment of new squadrons with little experience of engagements with enemy fighters, an increasing proportion of new and inexperienced pilots on existing squadrons, and the better armour and armament of enemy bombers. There was also the fact that the enemy had practically ceased employing dive bombers, of which our squadrons had taken heavy toll in the past.

Flight Lieutenant Alan Deere

The radar was sometimes swamped by the incoming German raids. The filtering system on the radar wasn't entirely reliable in those days, nor was the ground reporting of the Observer Corps. I don't say that disparagingly, but that was the situation. We were under pressure. Raids did get in, not undetected but unplotted, and we were told to stand by in our cockpits and told to start up and told to switch off and eventually told to 'Scramble! Get off as quickly as you can!'

One time when that happened, there were about three new pilots in the squadron. I was leading the squadron then, the squadron commander having been shot down. The procedure for take-off was to go around the far side of the airfield and for the others to follow around on the other side of me. But one of the new chaps got lost and taxied across in front of me. So once I had swung around to take off, I couldn't move.

I shouted at him, 'Get out of the bloody way!' Eventually he did, by which time the rest of the squadron had gone off. Just as I was about to get airborne, with the other two in my section, the bombs started to come down from Heinkels above.

The first one landed to my right as I took off. Looking to my left on the far side of the airfield, I thought, 'He's missed us.' But the sticks of bombs were coming right across the field. The next bomb landed right in front of me. That's all I remember – the plane going up in the air and landing on its back, ploughing along the airfield, with me still strapped in the cockpit. My number two wasn't hurt, but he was blown clean into the air right off the airfield perimeter. He landed in a creek. My number three had his wing blown off. He skippered along on his side, but fortunately he was able to get out of his aircraft and get me out of my cockpit because I was trapped there upside down and there was petrol all over the bloody place. I was pretty badly concussed and he had dislocated his hip. We tried to help each other across the field. A 109 came down and strafed us, but missed.

Because an inexperienced man had cut across my path, we had lost three planes. The medical officer bandaged my head and told me to take the rest of the day off and to report to him the next day. But by the time the day had finished, we had lost a few more men and needed all the pilots we could find.

Squadron Leader Tom Gleave

When a sprogg came to your squadron from an Operational Training Unit, you had to nurse him; you had to bring him along. In the middle of the battle, you were always saddled with at least four of these sproggs, whom you had to look after while sending chaps off to intercept enemy aircraft. It was hard to put a lot of training in. You had a situation in which a couple of men might be on leave, two chaps were in the station hospital because they'd got shrapnel in their arms or some place. Group Ops would call and ask, 'What have you got?' They'd be told, 'We've got three aircraft and two pilots or four aircraft and three pilots.' You'd be told, 'Put a defensive flight around the aerodrome, just in case.' You'd take a couple of sproggs with you because they might be the only ones left on the ground. The flight commander would keep an eye on them, but when combat began, he couldn't keep an eye on anyone but the enemy.

Pilot Officer Peter Brown

When I was transferred south from 12 Group, the pace of events was a lot faster. The first mission I went on seemed uneventful. When we got back and had a debriefing, I learned that some of the pilots had seen 109s in the distance and some of the others had seen something else. I had seen absolutely nothing. The next time up, I happened to see a little bit of something. But it took me about four trips to get tuned in, to see what was going on. A lot of people were hit in their first flights and didn't know what hit them. If you look out the small window of a passenger aircraft today, you see there's a lot of space out there to look for an aeroplane. If you open up the whole area above and below you, there's an enormous amount of space for an aircraft to be in.

Operations Record Book, 141 Squadron

Sergeant Wickens ordered to carry out an operation patrol at 00.50 hours but in taxiing out he collided with a stationary aircraft, damaging both machines. Pilot Officer Smith was then sent up, carried out the patrol, but overshot in landing and damaged his aircraft by colliding with a gunpost at the edge of the aerodrome. Crews of aircraft (Defiants) are injured.

Pilot Officer Dave Glaser

I'd got two problems after I left training. One: I'd never fought in an aeroplane in my life. Two: the Spitfire was the fastest thing I'd ever been in. To me it was a bit of a handful. I'd got to try to steer this thing, shoot and do all the rest while this large number of enemy aeroplanes were coming in.

Jeffrey Quill was in the squadron when I joined it. He knew my father well. I was only nineteen. When I joined, he said, 'You fly as my number two.' He saw me through the early stages, when one learned fast and needed some sort of guidance. I was very lucky, though I think I gave him his first grey hairs. We were coming down through cloud one time, with Wigg on the left, Jeff in the centre, and me on the right. As we came down, we closed up and closed up and eventually you could just see the wing tip of the aeroplane you were formating on. But I lost sight of it in the cloud and thought the best thing I could do was break away. When I came out of the cloud, I finally spotted the other two up above, far to my right, looking around for me. I had cut under or over them in the cloud. Jeff told me later that all he could think of when he lost sight of me was, 'What the hell am I going to tell his old man?'

We'd do readiness for two days, and then we'd be down to thirty minutes, and then we'd be on release. Release would invariably be from midday one day to midday the next. Jeffrey, who'd been the chief test pilot at Vickers Supermarine, the people who built the Spitfire, used to get a Vickers car sent down to the base when we were due for release. He would take some of us up to London and then pick us up on the way back the next day. When we were released, everybody rushed right off, because if you didn't get away quickly, you might be caught for another do or something. We were waiting for this big Vickers limousine to arrive one day, but it was late. The phone went. Jeffrey answered it and was asked, 'Any of 65 Squadron there?' He said, 'There are five of us.' They said, 'Right. Get airborne immediately.' We rushed off and got airborne, with Jeff leading. We were vectored up. When we broke cloud, I couldn't believe it. All I could see was five of us and a damned huge formation of German aircraft. You looked at them and thought, 'Where the devil do we begin?' There was a cloud of bombers, with 109s wheeling above them. Jeff led us away to gain height to go into the attack. We picked up a German straggler and shot him down. Then we climbed up again, but the amazing thing was the sky could be absolutely full one

(RAF Museum)

Armourers reloading aircraft guns after a battle

(RAF Museum)

Pilots, back from a sortie, being debriefed by their squadron intelligence officer

Air Chief Marshal Sir Hugh Dowding

(RAF Museum)

Flight Lieutenant Alan Deere receives the Distinguished Flying Cross from King George VI. Air Chief Marshal Sir Hugh Dowding looks on.

(RAF Museum)

(RAF Museum)

Pilot Officer Roland Beamont

(RAF Museum)

Pilot Officer Dennis David

(RAF Museum)

Air Vice Marshal Trafford Leigh-Mallory

(RAF Museum)

Air Vice Marshal Keith Park

Defiants flying in line astern formation

(RAF Museum)

Hurricane being refuelled from a bowser

(RAF Museum)

(RAF Museum)

Squadron Leader John Dewar

(Wing Commander N.P.W. Hancock)

Pilot Officer Pat Hancock

(Squadron Leader M.P. Brown)

Pilot Officer Peter Brown

(F.S. Perkin)

Sergeant Jack Perkin a few months after the battle

minute and the next minute there was not a thing in sight, and that was the situation then. We were vectored around, looking, but didn't see another thing and eventually returned to base. When we landed, the Vickers limo was waiting and we went off to London like a shot!

Flying Officer John Bisdee

We had three Americans in our squadron – Red Tobin, Andy Mamedoff and Shorty Keogh. Shorty Keogh was an ex-professional parachute jumper and barnstormer. These three had volunteered for the Finnish air force when Finland was fighting the Russians in 1939, but Finland packed in. They had then volunteered for the French air force, but the French packed in. They had got to Bordeaux, I think, where they were taken pity on by the skipper of an English freighter and brought back to England.

At this stage, America was neutral and England wasn't awfully keen on taking Americans into our armed forces. There was an enormous number of Germanophiles in America at the time. They would have made hay with the idea that the American boys were being subordinated to the dreaded British.

But these three were really down and out in England. They went to drown their sorrows in a pub in London, where they met an air commodore one night. They explained their sad predicament to him and he said, 'Get in touch with me tomorrow.' They got in touch with him the following morning. By noon, they had been commissioned in the Royal Air Force and sent off with some money to buy uniforms and that kind of thing. I don't know whether they did any training before they came to our squadron. They must have had some. They were a grand lot, very picturesque characters. Red Tobin, a long, gangly chap, used to dash out to his aircraft with his long legs, shouting, 'Saddle her up boys. I'm riding!'

Shorty Keogh was four feet ten inches. He was so short, we had to give him two lots of cushions on his seat, so he could see out of the cockpit. But they all did very well in the squadron. They were fine pilots. Towards the end of the battle, they all went off to Eagle Squadron – the American squadron that was formed here in England at that time. All three of them were later killed.

Pilot Officer David Crook

Shorty was last seen spinning into the sea near Flamborough Head during a chase after a Heinkel. Red crashed behind Boulogne, fighting like hell against a crowd of Messerschmitt 109s, while Andy hit a hill in bad weather and was killed. As Red once remarked with the usual grin, pointing to the wings on his tunic, 'I reckon these are a one-way ticket, pal.'

Flying Officer Jeffrey Quill

I didn't want to stay at being a Spitfire test pilot when the war began hotting up. I went to see Air Vice Marshal Keith Park and persuaded him to post me to 65 Squadron. The squadron commander was killed the day I arrived. We were based at Rochford, but went every day to Manston, right down on the southeastern tip of England, so close to the Germans across the Channel that we never spent the night at Manston. It would have been easy for them to pull a surprise raid on us. We'd fly to Rochford. But we operated out of Manston and sometimes got beaten up there, often on take-off.

When the bloody great bombing raids started forming up over northern France, with their fighter escorts taking off from different fields to join them, our Controllers would know what was happening. The radar would pick them up. We'd sit at dispersal at Manston and the telephone would ring. The Controller – they were usually very chatty – would say, 'There's something big brewing up over Abbeville, so be ready.' Sometimes they'd tell us to get into our cockpits. We'd get all strapped in and be ready to take off. Taking off from Manston, we were too close to the incoming raids to go climbing out to sea for a direct interception. We'd never have been able to get enough height. So we'd take off and climb inland before we could get into position to turn back and attack from above. We got fed up with this. We used to ask, 'Why the bloody hell do we have to start from here?' They'd say, 'You've got to be at Manston because if we start pulling the fighters out of southeast England, local people might think we're evacuating the area.' Public morale was a big factor in keeping us there. In fact, when we went in to land at Manston around 5.30 in the morning, we were instructed to fly low over the nearby towns and give them a jolly good buzz. I don't know what people thought about being awakened by the noise at that time of day, but at least they knew we were there. If it had suddenly ceased, with all the invasion scare going on, it would have been bad.

There was another reason why we stayed at Manston. The air force said, 'This is our airfield. We're bloody well not going to be moved from it by the ruddy Germans.' People weren't going to be pushed around. But for us, tactically, it would have been better to be based further back. This was especially true when it came to the squadron forming up after take-off, which was quite a business. It involved a lot of chatter on the R/T. Somebody might get left behind. And the squadron leader got a bit tetchy because people weren't forming up more quickly, so we thought it was much better to form up in squadron formation on the ground. When the squadron commander said go, we all went. We took off in formation and got back into combat position once we were in the air. It was quicker and neater – when we had the time – but it was more unwieldy, particularly when you were on the ground.

That's how we got comprehensively dive bombed while we were still stationary one day. We were waiting there, all engines running, everybody watching the squadron commander, waiting for the whole thing to start rolling. The next thing we knew we were being bombed by 110s. We all, of course, opened up and took off and to hell with the formation! We were very lucky to survive. Everybody got up except one. He was a New Zealander called Wigg. He was a bit slow getting started. Perhaps his engine was slightly on the choke situation. A bomb dropped right behind him and the blast from the bomb, coming from behind, blew his propeller around backwards and stopped his engine. He nipped out of the cockpit and had to run like hell to get clear. Bloody bombs were dropping all over. It was funny because he was usually a deliberate, slow-moving sort of chap who'd never hurry for anything.

Pilot Officer Dave Glaser

Wigg would never run. When we'd all rush out for the scramble, Wigg would come strolling out eating an apple. On the ground, his main interest was digging his ditch. He was always digging that ditch. Every time we landed, he'd be back digging a few more spadefuls of earth. In the end, that thing was so deep that when he was in it, still digging, you couldn't see him. All you'd see was the shovel suddenly appearing and earth flying in all directions. He wanted that ditch to be ready for him to get into if he was on the ground when the Germans strafed the airfield.

One day, a Dornier, shot up and looking for a field on which to crash land, headed for our base at Rochford. We were coming back from an interception when Nicky Nicholas saw it, tucked in behind it and fired away. All that chap apparently wanted to do was get the damned thing on the ground before he lost control of it and he finally managed a belly landing on the field. When he got down, all defensive guns – machine-guns and things – on the base opened up at him. One of the Germans had started to get out of the plane, but he shot back in again. The stuff was flying in all directions. Wigg had landed by then and was getting out of his plane. When the shooting started, he jumped into his ditch. It was so deep by then that he sprained an ankle.

Eventually, the shooting subsided and the chaps came out of the Dornier just as a local copper arrived on his bicycle, wanting to know what was going on, because when Nicholas had been trying to shoot down that Dornier, a bullet had gone through the billiard table at the village police station and they weren't very pleased about that.

Sergeant Dick Kilner

We'd been told at Manston that a raid was on the way and to get ready to scramble to meet it. We were in our cockpits. I found that my oxygen bottle hadn't been replaced. It was empty, so I told someone to get a fresh one for me. If you were going to 30,000 feet, you needed oxygen. Just then, one of the groundcrewmen standing on my wing looked up and saw the enemy aircraft already coming right for us out of the sun. All the groundcrew disappeared down a dug-out. I thought the best thing was for me to do the same. I hopped out of my aircraft and ran like bloody hell. I'm sure my athletic club would have been very proud of me for the speed I got to that dug-out.

It was a frightening quarter of an hour there. Some of our planes were destroyed on the ground. We could hear the bombs coming down, louder and louder. We just waited for one to land on us. When the raid was over and we came out, we could see a line of bombs had dropped and one had dropped on either side of our dug-out.

Pilot Officer Richard Jones

One day when we were at Hawkinge near Dover and were scrambled, I raced for my aircraft, hopped in, but it just wouldn't start. I was left behind as the others took off. No sooner were they gone than German bombers swept in and the aerodrome was bombed. There was only one very small shelter in the area where I was. And there were four or five times more people around than could fit into it. Everybody rushed for the entrance. When I got in, I was quickly pushed to the back. We all were being pushed to the back and out the rear by people pushing in from the front. We came out the back and tore around to the front and pushed our way in again. I think we all went around about four times while the aerodrome was being bombed. It's funny now. It wasn't at the time.

Squadron Leader Sandy Johnstone

Westhampnett, the satellite field where we landed when we came south from Scotland in mid-August, was just three large fields knocked into one. There were no airfield buildings at all on it. The place still looked like three fields. You could see the marks where they'd taken the hedges down. A windsock flew at one corner and there were a few Nissen huts. That's all there was, aside from a burning Messerschmitt as we flew in and, in the middle of the airfield, a Hurricane lying on its back.

We'd been told we were coming south for only a short period, so we hadn't brought much stores with us. It was a blow when the station commander at Tangmere, who was in charge of Westhampnett too, came across to see me and said, 'By the way, I hope you brought plenty of stores with you. We've got nothing but Hurricane squadrons, so we don't carry any Spitfire spares.' Middle Wallop was the nearest airfield that had Spitfires operating from it. I rang the Sector commander, a chap named Roberts, and told him our predicament. I asked him if he could let us have a few spares to keep us going. He said, 'Certainly. Send over a lorry and we'll see what we can do for you.' We were jolly busy and I couldn't spare an officer, so I picked a young corporal, Murphy by name, a tough little Glasgow Keelie, and three other chaps, and sent them over, with Murphy in charge. It was the first time he'd been in charge of anything. He was cock-a-hoop.

I gave them strict instructions. They were not to dally. They were to get there, make themselves known, get as much spares as they could and come straight back. They were two miles short of the airfield at Middle Wallop when it came under attack. They suddenly saw the German aircraft diving on the field. Murphy stopped the lorry and got all his chaps out and into a ditch. A Messerschmitt 110 flashed over their heads, on fire, and disappeared over a hill and crashed. Suddenly they saw a parachute coming down close to them. They rushed over, collared the German, tied him up and put him in the back of the lorry.

By this time, the raid was over, but Middle Wallop was in an awful mess. Hangars were on fire. People were running about. They drove to the guardroom. All they found was one young and very frightened airman who'd been left in charge when everyone else had gone off to help with the fires and the damage. This young airman wasn't very keen to take charge of the German, who was getting angry about being tied up. But a sergeant appeared, took charge of the prisoner, locked him up in the cells and told our fellows how to get to the equipment station.

They drove off with fires going on all around them, backed up to the stores section and, just as at the guardroom, found that all the senior people had gone off to help. They had left the place in charge of a couple of inexperienced airmen who didn't know our fellows weren't from their station. When they heard they'd come for Spitfires spares, they began bundling the stuff out. We got enough stuff almost to build two new Spitfires, including wings and everything. We were delighted. When I rang up Roberts to thank him, he said, 'What for?' I said, 'All the stuff you gave us.' He was amazed. Nobody in charge had even known Murphy had been there. Roberts said, 'That's all right. We'll write it off against the bombing raid.'

We needed those spares. Things got busy for us very quickly and stayed busy. We were off at lunch one day when the phone went and we were told, 'Get airborne!' It wasn't, 'Come to readiness,' or anything nice and calm like that. We just rushed out, ran across to our aircraft willy-nilly. Spitfires were taking off from all corners of the airfield. Why there were no collisions, I'll never know. But we all got airborne while Stukas began diving down on the base. Some of them were pulling out of their dives right in front of us. One of my chaps – Finlay Boyd – he'd just taken off. He hadn't even started to pull his wheels up when a Stuka dived right in front of him. He just turned his firing button and blew this aircraft into the ground. It just exploded in front of him. That was his first big action. He was so shaken, he just continued to circuit and landed back at Westhampnett. He hadn't even pulled his wheels up. The rest of us had meantime got together as best we could. We were in a tremendous mêlée of aircraft. We just fired blindly at everything that was nearby. We got a fair bag that day and, amazingly, no casualties ourselves.

Sylvia Yeatman

My husband, who was engineer officer at the Bomber Command base at Detling, was due for leave. He kept saying he couldn't possibly take it, in view of what was happening. I said, 'You must. It's probably the last chance you'll get for a long time.' So I bought tickets for sleepers on the night train to Scotland and we set off to Argyllshire to stay with my cousin, taking along bikes and dog and all. Just as we arrived, a message came through. My husband was recalled. No reason given. We went right back to London by train from Glasgow. I went to stay with my sister-in-law while he went on to Detling to see why he was recalled. He told me he'd send a coded message to tell me what it was about. He said if he'd made a mess of things, he'd say in the message, 'I lost my uniform.' If it was the aerodrome, he'd say, 'I've lost my vest.' If it was a general recall, he'd say something else – I can't remember what that was.

I went out to dinner. When I came back, my sister-in-law said, 'I've had the most extraordinary message from Harry. He said he's lost his vest but he's really left his string jersey on the train.'

When I got to Detling, I realized he wouldn't have been there at all if I hadn't taken him off to Scotland. The Germans had bombed it. The CO had been killed. The Ops Room was gone. His office, his bedroom, everything had gone.

Detling was a silly place to have an airfield. We were up on a hill. When the Germans started bombing it, they had things all their own way. We used to call the German attacks our medicine – they came at eleven in the morning, three in the afternoon and seven in the evening. Of course, they didn't always come as regularly as that, but they did raid us often. My husband had a lot of fights with the Air Ministry, which he finally won, to take his men down and get them workshops in Maidstone, so they could get on with the job of repairing damaged bombers. They couldn't get much done at Detling. They were always going in the bunkers during the raids.

Flight Lieutenant Tony Miller

While we were working at Tangmere Aerodrome on developing airborne radar that would be effective, we had a system in case there was an enemy raid. If the tannoy announced a raid was imminent, we would rush to the hangar and allocate crews for the Blenheims we used for experimenting. The idea was to get them off the ground and out of the way as soon as possible, so they wouldn't be damaged. One day, I went to the mess at lunchtime and there was Bing Cross, a pilot who'd been in the Norwegian campaign. He'd been on the aircraft carrier *Victorious* when it was sunk and he'd been in hospital. I bought us drinks and just then the tannoy sounded off. I said, 'Hang on to my beer. I'll be right back.'

I got down to the crew room and was saying to the others, 'You fly with so-and-so. And you fly with so-and-so,' when somebody shouted, 'Good God, they're here!' There was an awful explosion and all hell broke loose. It was Junkers 87s. Down they came, one after the other, loosing off thousand pound bombs. Several landed near us. There was so much bloody noise. Debris was flying in the air, coming down through our tin roof. I nipped out of the crew room and pressed up against the earthen revetment outside. But I was showered with debris anyway.

The raid didn't last very long. When I looked around, I saw our CO, Willy 'The Wasp' Chamberlain, had leapt into one of our experimental Blenheims and was trying to start the thing, to take off and get it out of the way in case the Germans came back. I jumped up on the wing beside him and pointed to the tail of the aircraft, half of which was now missing.

So much of our experimenting depended on using electrical apparatus so we were more or less limited on the ground to the length of a long trailing cable you could feed out from the hangar where the electrical supply was. So all our aircraft were unhappily closely clustered together, which meant we copped it fairly well that day.

I spotted an airman on top of a flat roof of one of the nearby hangars. He didn't look well. I nipped up a ladder and saw he was shell-shocked. He had apparently kept on firing his gun at the raiders right through the raid, though thousand-pound bombs had been landing close to him. I said, 'Let's go down.' He took no notice. I swore some good round oaths at him which finally penetrated and he came to and I got him to sick bay.

Aside from our planes, damage wasn't too bad on the aerodrome that day. But there were casualties. Some airmen had dived down a trench carrying electrical cables round the station. A bomb landed nearby and the blast travelled down the trench and killed them. Three or four civilian workmen who'd made a run for it to get out of danger were also killed by a bomb. Bing Cross, whom I'd left with our drinks, was gone when I got back to the mess. It was four years before I saw him again.

Squadron Leader Peter Devitt

As squadron leader, it was my job to write letters of bereavement to the parents of the pilots in my squadron who were killed. And you got parents coming down to see you when you'd been fighting all day and were dead tired. The officer of the watch would ring through and say, 'We've got Mr so-and-so here and he'd like to see you.' You had to go down and go through the whole thing with them, and tell them how it had happened. That was the worst part, though on the whole the parents took it well.

One of my flight commanders got shot down fairly early on and his wife was down there. She was about to have a baby. I had to go and explain to her what had happened.

Everybody was expecting it anyway. I expected it too. I refused to have my wife there. If she had been there, she would have known when I was taking off, flying up, this that and the other. She might panic and ring up and bother people when they were busy. Anyway, I had a small son and she had to look after him. She had a sister whose husband was away in the navy, so they found a place to live together.

Flight Lieutenant Frederick Rosier

The really good fighter pilot had a gift. He could scan the skies, take it all in, know how long he had to do something, and then do it. Very few people had that gift. I think I was an exceptional pilot in peacetime, but I didn't have that gift. Eyesight was terribly important. You could pick things out long before anyone else. But when you were in the middle of combat, it was the facility to look around and instantly put it all into your mental computer to produce the right answers. Most people who looked around could take in only a certain amount.

Pilot Officer Dave Glaser

There was one chap – McPherson – who, in a scrap, sometimes even when he was right in the middle of it, would shout suddenly to one of us, 'Look out, there's one on your tail!' He was incredible. He was an old regular flight sergeant. He seemed to know what was going on up there all the time.

Pilot Officer Bob Kings

There were a combination of factors which made a successful fighter pilot – the ability to fly skilfully, the ability to shoot accurately, and luck. The best pilot in the world with the first two qualifications only had to be unlucky for two or three seconds and somebody behind him would blow him out of the sky. It happened to many aces.

Pilot Officer Bobby Oxspring

Nearly every time you were jumped and had to break sharply to get away, you blacked out. You didn't lose consciousness, but you lost vision. When you had about three or four 'G' on you, your heart couldn't pump blood to the brain and it affected your eyesight. First there was a grey mist over your vision and, as you increased the 'Gs', as you reefed sharply to get away from someone on your tail, you blacked out. It was like being with your eyes open in a dark cellar with no lights on. As soon as you eased off, you could see again, but while it was happening you felt tremendous pressure on your body.

Squadron Leader James Leathart

There was nothing abnormal about being exhausted. It happened to all of us. We were under such pressure. One morning, after a sortie, Johnny Allen fell asleep while eating his breakfast and fell face down into his bacon and eggs. Once, I counted the operational sorties I did in a four-week period during the battle and it came out to eighty-four. Almost all of those involved combat. And I didn't go up as often as some of my men.

Michael C. Tagg, Department of Printed Books, Royal Air Force Museum
Letter to a German woman who, after the war, requested details of how her husband, a Luftwaffe pilot, had been shot down during the Battle of Britain by, she had been led to believe, Flying Officer Ben Bowring

I have been able to locate Squadron Leader [as he was by then] Bowring, but he tells me he cannot remember details of individual combats, which is not surprising as he had flown approximately 156 hours in twenty-seven days before being shot down.

Flight Lieutenant Eustace Holden

At dawn one day, the squadron went to 30,000 feet and, on landing, I started to walk to the mess for some breakfast when I was recalled for standby. Relieved ten minutes later, I again made for the mess but just as I got to the door, I was called back and had to go to 30,000 feet again. Back at the aerodrome in due course, I tried again to get a meal. I was half-way through it when I was wanted for another standby. When that came to nothing, I made for my quarters to have a shave. I'd just lathered myself when the loudspeaker called, '501 Squadron – readiness.' So up to 30,000 feet again. Later, I finished shaving and actually had lunch before being called for another standby. Then, about five o'clock, at 30,000 feet again for the fourth time that day.

Pilot Officer Dennis David

The days were long, starting at 3.30 in the morning. At Tangmere, sometimes we'd go into town, to Chichester, after dark. We went to a pub, 'The Dolphin', to have a few drinks. Legal closing time was 10.30, but the police would look the other way and let the boys down a few beers after hours, and then they would drive them back to dispersal. You had the feeling the whole country was behind you. There was tremendous kindness. It was a lovely feeling. I've never felt that Britain was like that again.

You didn't get much sleep after dawn, even if you weren't on readiness. You'd be sleeping in the dispersal hut, but the bloody engines were warming up and the ground crew was all around getting things ready. If the weather was bad when we awoke in the morning, we thought it was marvellous. The big raids wouldn't be coming through.

Pilot Officer Birdie Bird-Wilson

We'd be awakened before dawn by the noise of the ground crew starting up the engines of the aircraft. We went back to sleep again.

Some lazy buggers would carry on sleeping until we were actually scrambled. Then they'd scramble straight out of their beds, into their boots and Mae West and maybe their trousers and off they'd go.

Winston Churchill
War Cabinet Memorandum, 26 August

The air battle now proceeding over Great Britain may be a decisive event in the war and must dominate all other considerations . . . We cannot tell what new form the enemy's attack may take; nor what our losses will be; nor what damage will be done to our factories both of output and repair. We do not know with any certainty the size of the air force which the enemy may bring against us. It is certainly very much larger than our own.

*   *   *

The men who went into combat in the air lived with death and it frightened them. But what frightened them most was something else. They were petrified by the prospect of being trapped in an aircraft that was ablaze and being roasted alive before they could bale out. There were many third-degree-burns victims among the pilots. But to the good fortune of many of them, there was a remarkable doctor on hand who, during the summer of 1940, pioneered major improvements in the treatment of serious burns and in plastic surgery for burns victims. Archibald McIndoe, later to be knighted by King George for his services to Britain, was a New Zealander who set up the trailblazing burns unit at Queen Victoria Hospital at East Grinstead an hour south of London.

Leading Aircraftsman Cyril Jones

I was an operating room assistant at the hospital. We were a specialized unit for treatment of burns and reconstructive surgery. We received pilots and groundcrew who were burnt as a result of German bombings and accidents on the airfields. The pilots came mostly because of flash burns caused by high octane spirits from their fuel tanks. The burns were up to sixty to seventy percent of their bodies. The difference between being burnt to a cinder and coming to us might have been just three seconds of exposure to the flames in a burning plane.

On Monday mornings, McIndoe would fly around to all the main hospitals to decide which cases would be brought back to us for treatment. After Dunkirk, we started treating burn victims with saline baths. We found that people with burns who had been immersed in saltwater at Dunkirk did very well. Before that, there were some terrible things done. They had been using tannic acid and tannic jelly, which solidified over the burns. It was thought that if you could cover a burn by excluding the air, it wouldn't hurt as much. The tannic acid formed a film. But in addition to sealing out the pain, it sealed in the bacteria. All the germs and pus were locked inside and we had a terrific infection rate.

Another treatment was with gentian violet, a violet dye that looked fluorescent when it was painted on. What it did was to make everything go rigid. We had one Canadian boy in the RAF whose leg we had to take off above the knee because of the infection caused by the gentian. McIndoe stopped all that sort of treatment when we went over to saline baths treatments, though there was still the danger that the burn victims might die of toxaemia or shock during the first ten days.

Most of our patients were young men, in the prime of their lives. Most had been good-looking. The pilots who came to us were also well educated. To suddenly look the way they looked after being badly burnt was very shaking. It hit them hard. The advantage of our unit was there was always someone worse off. You may have lost a leg, but right next to you might be a chap who'd lost his hands. A man might have no ears but there was another chap who was blind.

McIndoe insisted on putting these men together. He'd never allow rank to get special privilege. He was always asked by other services to take special cases. We once had a captain in the Royal Navy who needed treatment. The navy in those days was all posh. There was a lot of tradition and this, that and the other and, of course, the under ranks weren't even spoken of. This captain came to us one day. He'd lost an eye and McIndoe was asked to rebuild his eye socket. McIndoe admitted him into a ward with ordinary airmen who had suffered bad burns. This captain, who expected VIP treatment, was put into a ward with forty men. On one side was a leading aircraftsman. On the other side was a sergeant. Well, this navy captain was in high dudgeon about it. He went straight to McIndoe and said, 'It is ridiculous for me to be nursed in a ward where I've got ordinary ranks around me. I must have a private room of my own.' McIndoe told him, 'You asked to be treated by me. If you wish to be treated by me, you will take the treatment I am offering. If you don't like the ward, then go and find someone else to treat you.'

There was terrific camaraderie among the patients. You'd often see fifteen wheelchairs being pushed to town, all going to the pub. McIndoe wanted the men to be accepted by the general public as normal human beings. He wanted to give them back their normal functions and their dignity. In the early days, we had to go through the stage of men not wanting to live. They were terrible to look at. But to see them now, after so many years – they are accepted and have been for years, though some had to go through as many as sixty operations. Some decided, 'Right – my wife accepts me and that's good enough.' This is where many of the women played an important role. Some of our nurses – good-looking young girls – married those men when they were at their worst.

In his treatment, McIndoe paid most attention to eyelids and hands. He would take a single layer of epidermis from the arm of the man to replace his eyelids. He wasn't looking to give a man back his looks. It couldn't be done. He was aiming at restoring their normal functions – opening and closing of the eyes, opening and closing of their mouths, restoring their noses, and restoring the use of their hands. They went through phases. From healing the burns to starting reconstructive surgery could be anything from three days to three years.

Dan Attwater, currently Director of Nursing Services, Queen Victoria Hospital

Some of the men became our customers for life. Scar tissue contracts so people feel a tightening of eyelids and puckering of the mouth. So they had to keep having corrective operations.

Nurse Ann Standen, Queen Victoria Hospital, East Grinstead

It would be wrong of me to say we weren't horrified. Inwardly, you'd say, 'Oh my God, what will they do with them?' You didn't recoil in horror but you wondered what could be done. Faces were just horrible – even the man I would later marry. He was injured when his bomber was in a collision. The injuries were horrific. By the time he called a halt to the treatment and said enough was enough, he had new eyelids, a new nose, new lips. They couldn't do much for his hands because they were too badly burned. It was amazing what they did do. He had sixty operations.

Relatives of the patients would come to the hospital to see the men. Some took it well. Some didn't. It was a shock. They'd seen a perfectly normal being one day. The next time they saw them, they were a mess. They could recognize them, but it was a shock.

Some of the men showed a tinge of bitterness, 'Why did it happen?' they asked. 'I'm finished now,' they'd say. That sort of thing. But they were soon made to realize they were not the only ones.

Squadron Leader Tom Gleave

There were long lines of Ju 88s, Dorniers, possibly Heinkels as well – huge grills of them stretching out in the sky. We had come too late to get above them, but we wanted to get them before they unloaded their bombs. We were climbing higher and higher. I could see everything on the aircraft above me, even their rivets. I broke my chaps away for the attack. I got on to number five bomber on the outside line and fired, just underneath the nose. I couldn't get number four, but I gave number three a burst. As I went over the top of him, I saw glycol pouring out of his engine. But as I went down to do number one bomber in the line, I got a clink in my starboard tank – an incendiary, and it burst into flames.

It burnt so quickly, it was unbelievable. I tried to get the cockpit hood open. Though I'd always been a stickler for drill, I forgot that all I had to do was pull the toggle. I finally managed to get the hood open. By then, I'd undone my belt. As the hood came back, there was a God Almighty explosion. I went straight up in a huge sheet of flame. The aircraft just disappeared. I came down head over heels, pulled my ripcord and my parachute opened. My hands were swelled up, and my face and legs. Most of my clothes had gone. I was pretty badly burnt – about thirty percent burns. I lost all the skin off my right foot. I still get holes occasionally, things sometimes come out, bits of bone. I lost all the skin off my hand and most of my face. My eyelids and nose went. We carried loaded guns. We could have shot ourselves and I would have had I got to the state where I hadn't a hope in hell. No doubt some pilots did.

Pilot Officer John Fleming

We'd had three or four false alarms in the morning. We were in our cockpits and then stood down. And, about five to one, the whistle went. I was tail-end Charlie, zig-zagging, sweeping the back of the formation. I saw in my mirror that we were being jumped. I could see the German fighters coming down. I just had time to call out to everybody, 'We're being jumped from behind! I'll go and look at them!' I turned around, flew towards the Germans and made them split up. We had a private party there, with me in the middle. I reckon I got a couple of them – the way things were happening there was no evidence – and then they got me. They knocked off my wing tips. My radiator was under my feet. That got shot up and I was more or less on a red-hot footplate. A string of bullets ripped through my instrument panel. There was a reserve tank of forty-five gallons of petrol behind that. The petrol poured onto this red-hot plate and onto me. So me and my forty-five gallons went up in one big whoomph, which was quite interesting. I found I couldn't open my hood. I turned the plane upside down, twice, but still couldn't move it. I was still being shot at. I could hear the bullets. The third time upside down I pushed off from the floor. I was thirteen stone ten and very fit so the hood came off its runners and out I went. I was above the rest of the squadron by then. I was seen by some of them coming down, smoke pouring from me, with my cockpit hood round my neck. I knew the cloud base was 2,000 feet that day and the Germans had been reported to have shot people parachuting down, so I didn't pull the rip cord till I could see the ground and steered myself towards a field.

The next thing I knew there were bullets whistling all around me – farm labourers on the ground, thinking I was a German, were shooting at me till they heard me cursing down at them in English. Being a New Zealander, they heard some curse words they had never heard before. Everything was burnt off me. I had no clothing on me. My fur-lined flying boots were burnt down to slippers. I had no skin left to be transferred to burnt parts. I've been wearing a harness around my middle ever since I came out of hospital, more than forty years ago. My legs are tied on to me. The surgeons wanted to take my legs off at the hips, and give me a pair of roller skates to get around on, I suppose. But I was fortunate. I had no relatives in Britain. So they couldn't get authorization from my next of kin. I wasn't going to sign. I wanted six-foot-two of ground when I was buried. I'd fought for it. I wasn't going to be short-changed on the coffin. Sir Archie McIndoe saw that I wouldn't be.

Flying Officer Peter Davies

My hands were badly burnt and very painful when my aircraft was shot up. I had to bale out. They sprayed them with tannic acid. It formed a dark brown hard casing over my hands. The skin began to grow back over some of the fingers together. They had to be separated. One or two things went septic, but I recovered pretty quickly and was fortunate compared to some of the men. There was another pilot officer named Davies who was brought in. His mother was upset seeing him – he was so badly burnt, his eyes were just slits. They brought her in to see me to show how burn cases could recover.

Squadron Leader Tom Gleave

Sister came in [at the hospital] and said my wife had arrived. I was well enough to worry about her seeing me as I was: my hands, forearms and legs were encased in dried tannic acid. My face, which felt the size of the proverbial melon, was treated in the same way, and I peered through slits in the mask. I heard footsteps approaching the bed and then saw my wife standing gazing at me. She flushed a little and said, 'What on earth have you been doing with yourself, darling?'

I found it hard to answer. 'Had a row with a German,' I replied.

Sergeant Jack Perkin

The extraordinary thing was that for the only time in my life did anybody have to say to me – as my fitter did the morning I was shot down – 'Don't forget your leg straps, Sarge.' I looked down and to my surprise, I'd forgotten to put the parachute leg straps through the loops and into the central buckle. If I hadn't, I'd have slipped right through the parachute when I had to bale out.

When we took off, I took my position in the leading section on the right of Flying Officer Smith, who was leading the squadron. We climbed to 20,000 feet over the Chelmsford area. We were told over the radio that twenty escorted bandits were approaching the east coast at 20,000. So we patrolled over there, but didn't see anything. Five minutes later, we were told to descend to 5,000 feet, where fifty escorted Jerries were said to be approaching the coast. We dived down and almost immediately were ordered back to 20,000 feet, where masses of enemy fighters were said to be. I could almost hear Smithy swearing at our having lost height for no reason. But we started up again and climbed towards London. We'd almost reached 20,000 feet. The sky was perfectly clear and the sun was shining brightly. I was flying very near to Smith, about five feet away, concentrating on keeping station with him. I hadn't seen any enemy aircraft at all, but suddenly there was an explosion and my whole cockpit was enveloped in flames. A petrol flame is more intense, hotter and fiercer than almost any other fire I know of. In the Hurricane, you had the reserve tank of petrol right in front of you, in between the engine and the cockpit. You had that straight in your face. You can only think, 'I must get out of this.' People who stayed in a burning cockpit for ten seconds were overcome by the flames and the heat. Nine seconds and you ended up in Queen Victoria Hospital in East Grinstead in Dr Archie McIndoe's burns surgery for the rest of the war. If you got out in eight seconds, you never flew again, but you went back about twelve times for plastic surgery.

I reckon that, undoing my straps, I got out of that burning plane in four to five seconds. I thought that, in my hurry, I had kicked off my parachute at the same time. With the flames all around me, I didn't care. I got out of the plane, but found myself held in place by my oxygen lead and my radio lead, both of which were still attached to my flight helmet and to the inside of the cockpit. I actually was going down with the plane, outside it. It was spiralling down in flames and I was outside, at the side of the cockpit, my legs towards the tail, being held there by the two leads which were still firmly attached inside the cockpit. But as we gathered speed spiralling down, my helmet was wrenched off. As I fell free, I had this lovely feeling of cool air. I was away from the burning plane. I thought, 'This must be heaven.' I just let myself fall. There was nothing else to do. There was nothing else I wanted to do. I thought I was falling to my death, with my parachute kicked off, but I didn't mind. I was glad to be away from the flames and I was also dazed by the shock of one instant being in close formation with my leader and the next instant being in a fiercely burning cockpit. The lovely cool air was marvellous. I just fell. Then I began to feel sick. I later turned out not to be badly burnt, but at the time there was a nasty smell of burning flesh and burning hair. And I was somersaulting. I saw the ground and then the sky and then the ground and then the sky. I thought, 'I can't stand this any longer.'

And I thought, 'I wish I still had my parachute.' I reached for the ring and it was there! I felt for the pack and it was there also, behind me. I hadn't kicked it off! I pulled the ring and there was an enormous jerk on my crotch as the main chute opened and I was pulled up. The feeling was not relief or exultation – it was surprise.

Aircraftswoman Second Class Edith Heap

I know people who still have nightmares about being shot up and baling out. That was a time that taught me a lot about people. It taught me not to take people at face value. You found that some people you thought were going to be pretty terrific in a crisis were useless and some people who didn't seem to have much to offer turned up trumps in emergencies.

CRISIS

As August drew to a close, the Germans, led by faulty intelligence into believing Fighter Command was on the verge of collapse, moved in for the kill. Ranging far and wide over southern England, the Luftwaffe sharply stepped up its attack, particularly on RAF airfields. The raids came over in such numbers that Operations Room Controllers had trouble determining which deserved priority attention from the limited defence resources at their disposal. It had by now become routine for sections of three aircraft or flights of six to be sent up against thirty, fifty, a hundred or more attacking aircraft. Such odds inevitably meant mounting casualties. Before long, only the very lucky squadron in the south still had enough men to put twelve planes aloft.

This third phase of the Battle of Britain lasted fourteen days, from 24 August to 6 September. During that brief episode, British defences came close to collapse. The stress of combat encounters several times a day every day from first light to last exhausted Fighter Command pilots. There were mistakes and accidents. Morale began to slip among the veterans, who saw friends with whom they had flown since the outbreak of hostilities fall one by one to enemy action. During this two-week period, Fighter Command lost one quarter of its pilots – killed or seriously wounded.

Air Chief Marshal Sir Hugh Dowding

A fresh squadron coming into an active Sector would generally bring with them sixteen aircraft and about twenty trained pilots. They would normally fight until they were no longer capable of putting more than nine aircraft into the air, and then they had to be relieved. This process occupied different periods according to the luck and skill of the unit. The normal period was a month to six weeks, but some units had to be replaced after a week or ten days ... By the beginning of September, the incidence of casualties became so serious that a fresh squadron would become depleted and exhausted before any of the resting and reforming squadrons was ready to take its place. Fighter pilots still could not be turned out by the training units in numbers sufficient to fill the widening gaps in the fighting ranks. Transfers were made from the Fleet Air Arm and from the Bomber and Coastal Commands, but these pilots naturally required a short flying course on Hurricanes and Spitfires and some instruction in formation flying, fighter tactics and interception procedure.

Flight Lieutenant Alan Deere

Our morale was getting a bit low because there were only three of us – George Gribble, Colin Gray and me – left in the squadron who had any combat experience. We had been there the whole time and were pretty tired. Each time we went up, there seemed to be more and more Germans up there. We'd gone through two squadron commanders. The new pilots who came in – they just went up and came down! You'd say to them, 'Now, look, don't get yourself lost. Stick with us. Don't bother about shooting to start with.' But, of course, they couldn't resist peeling off and some of them didn't come back and some had to crash land.

One day, the adjutant rang me up and said, 'There are two new pilots reporting for 54 Squadron.' I said, 'Thank God. Send them over.' They turned out to be two New Zealanders, like me, who'd been three months at sea coming over. They'd only flown Wildebeests, a very old-fashioned aircraft, in training. They'd been sent to an operation conversion unit and given five or six hours on Spitfires. And that was it! They hadn't even seen a reflector sight. They both got shot down the second day, were fished out of the Channel and ended up in the hospital together.

Flying Officer John Dundas
Letter to his brother, Flying Officer Hugh Dundas
Royal Air Force Station, Middle Wallop, 25 August

Very sorry to hear that a 109 – or rather twelve of them – inflicted grievous bodily harm on you over Dover two days ago. Mummy sent me a wire yesterday, and you were mentioned as wounded in an 11 Group Intelligence Summary this morning. I haven't heard any details, but I do hope the damage isn't too bad. Write and tell me about it as soon as you're well enough to do so. Anyhow, you'll now get a nice spell of sick leave which I rather envy you.

The 109s nearly made hay with us over the Isle of Wight yesterday. They sent us off too late to do anything about the bombing of Portsmouth and too low to do anything about the myriads of 109s who were hovering around the scene and who, when they saw poor old 609 [Squadron] painfully clambering into the sun, came down on us. The result was that one of our machines was shot to hell, two more damaged and not one of us succeeded in firing a round. I was reduced to the last resort of a harassed pilot – spinning. It was humiliating. But fortunately we didn't lose any pilots.

John Dundas was killed in action one month after the Battle of Britain. Middle Wallop Sector Commander, Wing Commander David Roberts, recalls: 'He was one of my best chaps. I was controlling at the time. He called up and said, "Whoopee! I've just shot down a 109!" That was the last we heard from him. He'd shot down one of the German fighter aces and the chap's number two got him.'

Flying Officer Christopher Deanesly

I was shot down at the end of July, spent some time in hospital, had some leave and returned to the squadron at the end of August. The squadron had changed a lot in my absence. It had been engaged in almost daily combat. Men were tired. Morale was drooping. We'd lost our best flight commander, Carr Withall, an Australian. We had all greatly admired him. We'd lost a lot of people, some of whom had been with the squadron from the beginning.

Flight Lieutenant Tony Miller

Experimenting with new airborne radar equipment made me feel sometimes that I was out of the war. So I asked for a posting to a fighter squadron. Willie the Wasp said, 'I can't recommend you for posting unless you "put up a black"', which meant doing something terrible. I don't know what happened then. Perhaps backdoor channels worked. But suddenly a signal arrived posting me to 17 Squadron, which was relieving a squadron which was going up north to recover, and, to my horror, to command the squadron! They had lost their CO – Taffy Williams – who had been killed in combat a few days earlier.

My new squadron had gone through about five squadron leaders in the past three months. Then I appeared, quite green. I met the senior flight commander and he took me around and introduced me to the men and then a klaxon went. I said, 'What's that?' He said, 'That's take-off. There's your plane. Off you go.' This was my first ten minutes as commander of the squadron.

Pilot Officer Dennis David

In those desperate days, if you were twenty-one, you were an old man. It was horrifying to see the youngsters coming along. Some were only eighteen years old, but it wasn't their age which scared you. They were so inexperienced. They'd had only eight or nine hours on a Hurricane. We needed chaps with thirty or forty hours of operational training. We needed chaps who could match the German pilots, who were jolly good.

Pilot Officer Jas Storrar

I was nineteen and I felt that chaps of twenty-two and twenty-three were much more experienced and worldly wise. Not that we youngsters lacked any normal, healthy pursuits like drinking and that sort of thing. As fighter pilots, the senior men who had got where they were by promotion before the war were either no bloody use at all or very good indeed. The ones who were no use at all were lucky if they survived. They didn't remain fighter pilots. They went off to staff jobs. Twenty to twenty-one was the age to be. Some of the older pilots didn't have the daring and irresponsibility that was needed for the kind for combat we were in.

Pilot Officer Richard Jones

We aged faster than the average person. Towards the end, I was becoming more careful and that, in a fighter pilot, is a dangerous thing. I started to consider my neck, which I hadn't considered before. I had thought nothing could happen to me. But I began to realize that things *could* happen to me. I became more cautious. Later on, just after the battle, when I learned I was going to be posted away for a rest the following week, those were the worst days I had. The week was absolute hell. Whenever we were scrambled, I'd think it would be just my bloody luck not to make it. I got very careful and where earlier I'd always made perfect landings, I began making a cock of landing. I'd overshoot and have to go around again.

Elizabeth Cook

Richard [Pilot Officer Richard Jones] and I were engaged during the battle. I was away at Reading, working at a hairdresser's. When I had a long weekend off, I'd go down and find digs or a hotel room near where he was stationed. I was very much aware of the situation he was in. I knew of the day-to-day danger he faced. There was always the possibility that he'd not come back, that he'd be killed. Men were being killed every day. The husband of one of my best friends, also a pilot, was killed. It could have been Richard. We just lived for the day. I lived for the time we could be together.

Squadron Leader Sandy Johnstone

The veterans, if you could call them that – I was only twenty-three – could concentrate on fighting. The younger chaps had two battles to fight. They were fighting the Germans and they had to battle to concentrate on simply handling their aircraft. It made them much more vulnerable to the enemy. We did our best for them. You tried to pair off an experienced chap with a newcomer. But one by one the experienced chaps were promoted to other squadrons or got shot out of the skies themselves. Newcomers sometimes were only there a couple of days. There was a young sergeant named Sprague, a very serious lad. He was good. I knew he was good. I always took the new ones up before they went into battle to make sure they could at least fly the aeroplane. Sprague went missing within a week – shot down and killed, we later learned. He'd only got married the week before. His wife came down and waited on the road running on the side of the airfield. Day after day, she just waited there, hoping her husband would come back. She just wouldn't go away.

Flight Lieutenant Bob Stanford-Tuck

You told the new man all you could. If you had time, you'd take them up and show them what you meant. You'd show them how to turn correctly, and evasive manoeuvres. Then you'd let them fly alone for a bit and you'd get up sun and make a dummy run at them. If they just floated along, wondering, 'Where is he?' and you knew they hadn't seen you, at the last instant, when in combat you'd open fire, you'd say over the radio, 'OK. You've had it.' They learnt very quickly from that not to fly down sun if possible. If they got through the first two or three combats, I thought they'd be all right. But it was always the new boys who copped it first. Suddenly something would come up their backside and wham!

I used to watch the newcomers in the van taking us down to dispersal from the mess. They would fiddle with their scarves. They were so obviously nervous.

Air Vice Marshal Keith Park

My first aim was not to have my squadrons caught on the ground and destroyed, as happened in Poland, Holland and France in 1940. At the same time, I had to conserve my fighter strength by not being drawn into the air by false alarms or feint attacks by German fighters.

I was worried daily from July to September by a chronic shortage of trained fighter pilots and it was not until the battle was nearly lost that Air Staff at the Air Ministry assisted by borrowing pilots from Bomber Command and the Royal Navy. Incidentally, [after the Battle of Britain] when I was posted to Flying Training Command, I found that the flying schools were working at only two-thirds capacity and were following peacetime routines, being quite unaware of the grave shortage of pilots in Fighter Command.

Pilot Officer Roger Hall

I'd been a regular officer in the Royal Tank Regiment, but I'd always wanted to fly, so I was willing to drop a rank when the chance came to join the RAF. After preliminary training, I was sent to an Operation Training Unit near Liverpool to be taught to handle a Spitfire. We were supposed to have twenty-five hours on the plane. A lot of the men completed the course in just two days and were sent right off to squadrons. They were needed so urgently. It took me four days. It was very sketchy training. Target practice was firing our guns into a sandbank in the Mersey Estuary. The first time I was in combat, we got to a German bomber formation as it was coming in. I fired at a Dornier with which I then nearly collided. I didn't wait to see what happened to it. I broke away to follow my section leader, Ferdie Holmes. We were attacked by some German fighters. Trying to get away, I began turning madly. I called on the radio to ask Holmes where he was. He said, 'I'm on your tail. Just keep turning.' He was killed later in the war.

The odd thing was you didn't really learn to fly until you were in combat. You jolly well had to then. I never had a very high opinion of my talents either as a pilot or a fighter pilot. But you did all sorts of things with the aeroplane you'd never dreamt of doing – flick rolls, looping-a-loop, all sorts of tricks to outmanoeuvre the enemy. The others in the squadron tried to teach me. I never felt nearly as good as they were. I was usually more concerned with keeping my aircraft in the air than in keeping the enemy out of it. I developed some confidence later on. After a bit, it came naturally. You learned what you had to learn to survive.

I had a smart little sports car. One of the fellows in the squadron said, 'If you're killed before I am, can I have it?' I told him I didn't care what happened to it if I was killed. I thought my chances were fifty-fifty.

Pilot Officer Desmond Hughes

When our squadron was posted down from Lincolnshire to Horn-church towards the end of August, we faced the tragedy almost immediately of losing our CO, Philip Hunter. He was last seen going out over the Channel in pursuit of planes that had bombed the town of Ramsgate. We never found out what happened to him. It did our morale not much good. There'd been a certain amount of hero worship about him. He was so good. He was a brilliant pilot. Everybody thought the sun shone on him. He seemed to be invulnerable. It was a hell of a shock when he went.

The leading of the squadron had to come down to people who weren't experienced. We had an inexperienced replacement as CO and two inexperienced flight commanders. They felt they had to lead though, under the circumstances, they weren't the very best people for that task. The fact was our Defiants were out-turned, outclimbed and outgunned by the Messerschmitt 109s. In the last week in August, we lost nine gunners and five pilots. We'd lost a CO dead, the acting CO shot down injured, both flight commanders shot down injured.

When we were scrambled one day, there were only two of us with serviceable aircraft. The others had been lost or so shot up they had to be grounded for repairs. We just managed to find our way through the craters on the airfield, which had just been bombed. As we climbed up, it was interesting to be told that the two of us were being vectored against thirty plus. We climbed on. When we got to about 12,000 feet, the Controller came through terribly apologetic. 'Terribly sorry, old boy, but they've turned away.' I can't say that Richard Stokes or I or our gunners wept when we heard that. When we went back up to Kirton-in-Lindsey in Lincolnshire, we were led by our most experienced surviving pilot, Samuel Richard Thomas, only a pilot officer and not yet twenty-one years old.

Sergeant John Burgess

We hadn't seen much action when we were at Coltishall in 12 Group. There were two squadrons there – 264 Squadron, who reckoned they were the cat's whiskers, having done very well at Dunkirk, and 222 Squadron, of which I was a member. Late in August, 264 Squadron – they flew Defiants – was sent down to Hornchurch to relieve one of the frontline squadrons there. In one week, they suffered fantastic casualties. The squadron was virtually decimated. We had waved them off as heroes going to add new laurels to their victories over Dunkirk. A week later, they were finished and we were sent down to replace them.

Funnily enough, we weren't worried. We hadn't had much combat experience ourselves. We thought we'd just go down to Hornchurch, do a few circles around the sky, a few Germans would conveniently fall to the ground and that would be it. At the age of twenty, you don't think too deeply. I had the feeling that I was sort of going to be part of a live newsreel. You'd go up and everything would be lovely. You'd see aircraft shooting at each other and you'd shoot at one or two, and perhaps one or two of the Germans would shoot at you, but the bullets would miss you and that would be it.

But the first week at Hornchurch was hell. Just after we got there, in the early afternoon, we were ordered to the satellite aerodrome at Rochford, about fifteen minutes away, to stay there for twenty-four hours. We took all our operational aircraft along – fourteen Spitfires in all. On the way, we were told to start climbing. A heavy German raid was building up. We got up to 22,000 – 23,000 feet and were told to patrol Maidstone–Ashford, one of the major RAF patrol lines on the approach to London. German bombers were said to be coming in with their fighter escorts. When the CO spotted the enemy formation, we went into line astern, getting reading to attack. I couldn't see the enemy, but the CO said, 'Going down! Going down! Going down!' and down he went, turning on his back. The others followed after him, on the attack, one by one. I was last in line – number fourteen, and I still couldn't even see the Germans we were attacking. Eventually, the chappy ahead of me – number thirteen – rolled on his back and went screaming towards where the enemy was supposed to be. I went after him. As I rolled over on my back and straightened out, I looked down and there they finally were – massed patterns of greeny-brown aircraft with little white crosses on their wings. It was a very large formation of Messerschmitt 110s – maybe thirty or forty of them. I dived down. I had no fear. They wouldn't hit me, just like Errol Flynn never got hit in his films. As I dived down, one group of the 110s formed a big defensive circle, going round and round. I straightened up and went for that circle. The 110s were passing in front of me, one by one. I kept firing. I kept my finger on the button. Finally, I had to pull away. I don't know if I hit anybody. But there was a bullet hole in my wing tip. I thought, 'Jolly good. I've got a souvenir.' That was my first taste of combat.

That evening, we were sent up again, to patrol Dover. We were over Dover when suddenly there was a bang and a bullet whistled between my legs. I looked out over the nose of my aircraft and saw little white dots appearing there. Bullets were puncturing the skin of my aircraft. I looked up and not more than twenty or thirty feet above me was a duck-egg blue wing with an Iron Cross on it, a Messerschmitt 109. We were being bounced by 109s. The man I was formating on was in flames. I pulled sharply away and found my engine overheating badly. I went down and just managed to get back to base when my engine seized.

It was then that I realized finally that the Germans were intent on killing me and that it wasn't a great big game or a newsreel and that if I didn't keep my wits about me, I was going to die pretty quickly.

During that first week in the front line, our squadron suffered maybe twelve losses. On 31 August, I was the most junior pilot in the squadron. Within two weeks, I was one of the most experienced. I got a book recently listing the names of all who had been in our squadron during the Battle of Britain. Some I couldn't remember. They passed through and had been shot down before I could get to know them.

CRISIS

Sergeant Iain Hutchinson

I know it sounds crazy, but I believed I'd be warned in time by something hitting my aircraft and be able to take evasive action to save myself up there. I'd developed a tactic which I thought was perfect for making the attacking aircraft lose sight of me. It was an awkward manoeuvre, the first bit of a bunt, an outside loop, when an enemy got on your tail. You just pushed the stick forward hard. The chap behind you would then have trouble following you. In order to make a deflection shot at you, he had to point his nose lower than you. But he couldn't do that if you were bunting hard. Then, if you did a series of downward spirals, it would be very hard for him to follow you. You'd then climb up and resume combat. I was convinced that device would always save me.

But when we were moved south, we had a lot to learn. On our first sortie as a squadron in the south, we lost half the squadron – not all killed – but half the squadron shot down. I myself was shot down the next day when I got split off from the squadron. I saw three 109s coming out from underneath me and opened fire at them. But I didn't look back and somebody came up behind and shot me up.

I was going to bale out, but realized that my parachute harness was slack and that my aircraft was still capable of flying so it would be safer to put it down in the field, and it would cause less damage. As I came down, I saw a man ploughing the field with two horses. I had a momentary vision of him looking extremely surprised as I flew past him, hit the ground and came to a halt.

I was flying again the next day, but I was shot down five times during the next month, though I didn't end up in hospital until the last time. Until then, I felt I couldn't miss a sortie. It's hard to explain, but the feeling was that as long as I kept going up, it was going to be OK, but the moment I broke the sequence, something might happen. The first time I broke the sequence and missed a sortie, a friend of mine, Ramshaw, took my place in the squadron and was killed.

People were quick on the trigger. You daren't wait for the other guy to shoot. One time, I saw another aircraft in the sky and went straight towards it because it could have been a German. When I got near enough, I could see it was a Spitfire so I turned away. As I turned, a shower of tracer went right past my nose. As the plane went past me shortly afterwards, I saw not only that it really was a Spitfire, but that it was someone from my own squadron taking a shot at him.

He'd recognized me, but his impulse to fire had been quicker than his recognition.

The last time I was shot down, I'm quite sure it was by a Spitfire. That was a traumatic moment. I tried to get out of the plane as it went down, but my parachute was stuck against part of the cockpit just behind me, I was stuck with the bottom part of my body inside the aircraft and the top part of me flattened against the outside of the aircraft by the airflow, with the plane going down at about 400 miles an hour. I remember wondering which part of me – the part inside the plane or the part outside – would be more intact after I hit the ground.

Flames were coming out of the plane and I was being frizzled. The next thing I knew, I was floating free in the air. I couldn't see very well because my face had been burned. I pulled my ripcord – my parachute was there – but it was rather late and I hit the ground with a thud.

My recollections of what happened next are hazy. Some ladies came along to help me. They brought some tea but they wouldn't let me drink it. They brought some brandy but wouldn't let me drink that either. I remember trying to make some funny cracks, but nobody seemed to appreciate my sense of humour. I must have looked a horrid sight. My uniform was all burned. My face was burned. My eyes were bloodshot because I'd bounced my skull off the tail of the plane when I was thrown out.

Flying Officer Ben Bowring

By mistake, our squadron was sent the first Hurricane 2s. These had the twin superchargers. They were really meant to go to a maintenance unit to be modified so that as soon as they got to 9,000 feet, the second supercharger would come in and give it extra boost, so we could have more power at height and go much higher. Though these aircraft came to us by mistake, we used them and the first time you took off in one of them, you were getting something like sixteen pounds boost for take off, so you went off like a shot.

We got used to it. When you got to 9,000 feet, you pulled a plug out and that gave you the new boost. We had these for four or five days before they found out we had them by mistake, but the battle was so fast and furious at the time that by then we had only one left. The others had been shot down or damaged. We reported that we'd finished them all, but decided that we'd all fly the Hurricane 1s.

We'd been posted a new squadron leader. He'd been in France and he wasn't very keen to fly any more. But we didn't have many pilots left and I said to him he just bloody well had to fly. He said he would, but insisted on flying the Hurricane 2 we still had left. I was to fly as his number two. Of course, when he got to 9,000 feet, he opened his tap. He got extra boost, went soaring off and we couldn't catch him. We kept shouting at him, asking him to slow down and then we saw the Germans coming. By then, we were up in Spitfire country, where Hurricanes really shouldn't have been, and got mixed up with 109s. He got back all right. I didn't.

Pilot Officer David Looker

Me 109s came at us just as we came out of the clouds. My plane was hit by cannon shells and I went into a spin. I managed to straighten out and finally came safely through a balloon barrage, pulled up and found myself at about 600 feet with a big hole in my right wing and the right side of my cockpit shot away. I was about the bale out when I saw Croydon airfield below. So I decided to try to crash land, but as I came over the road to the airfield, our anti-aircraft guns opened fire at me. They thought I was a German plane and blew my tail off. Instead of crash landing, I went in head first and ended up in hospital.

Two years later, I was out in Canada and met a squadron leader who'd been commandant at Croydon at the time and remembered the incident. He told me, 'It got me posted to Iceland because I'd complained so much about the army being unable to tell the difference between a Hurricane and a German aircraft.'

Corporal Claire Legge

Behind the Controller's dais in the Ops Room there were four cabins which were monitoring the four radio channels we had. For reasons I've never understood, these were jobs they gave to girls. They monitored these channels and recorded what was said by the pilots in the air. The doors of these cabins were open most of the time. That's how the Controller sitting in front of them found out how the battle was going. Once he'd got the men onto the enemy with his directions, it was up to them. What they heard often distressed the girls very badly. They knew the pilots and they heard them screaming and going down. It was horrid.

SCRAMBLE

Elaine Leathart (wife of Squadron Leader James Leathart)

I had got to know the men of 54 Squadron very well. I felt deeply when people like Johnny Allen were killed. I remember saying to James's father, 'I don't think there will be any of them left.' It was sad for the wives. The men were right in it, doing something. But we were just sitting there waiting.

There were always cars in our family. They were of prime importance. During the battle, James said, 'I'm going to get killed. You'd better have a car.' So he bought Johnny Allen's car when Johnny was killed and had an airman drive it up to me in the north.

Pilot Officer Peter Hairs

You'd be drinking in the mess one night. And you'd be drinking in the mess the next night. You'd look around and see that two or three who'd been there the first night weren't there anymore. You tried to accept it as normal. It *was* normal! I remember seeing my own flight commander – Flight Lieutenant Stoney – crash. We'd been up on some action. When you met the enemy, you'd pick an aircraft, go after it and fire at it. He'd fire at you and you'd have a bit of a dogfight. In the process, we'd all be separated. Afterwards, each section commander would wiggle his wings so we could pick him out and formate on him again. I saw him on this occasion and started flying towards him. He was flying quite normally, but suddenly he did a half roll, his nose dropped and he went straight down and crashed into the ground. Whether he'd been shot in action, I don't know. These things did happen. Sometimes they were seen to happen, sometimes not.

Pilot Officer Robert Doe

Every time I was in action, I managed to get hit. Everytime I'd land, there'd be bullet holes in the plane. Half the time I didn't know about them till I was on the ground. To my knowledge, I should have been shot down on two separate occasions, when another pilot shot a German off my tail whom I hadn't seen and who was about to shoot me down. You almost always got shot down by the ones you didn't see.

I never gave much thought to the enemy pilot. I just saw an enemy plane and attacked it. Once I saw a 109 going out low over South-ampton. I set out after him. It took me a long time to catch him up because he was going flat out. Eventually I was close enough to shoot at him, which I did. Parts of his plane fell off and his engine stopped as I flew up alongside him. He was a tall, blond man in sky blue sort of overalls. Nothing I could do. I waved at him and watched him go down and crash into the sea.

We had a bunch of new pilots sent in, but not many had a chance to fly with us because we were losing too many aircraft as well as pilots. We just couldn't spare anything to let them fly in. A couple of them did fly with us and just disappeared, virtually on their first trips.

Flying Officer Christopher Foxley-Norris

The fact that you had not been killed or wounded did not mean that you were combat-ready. You could be exhausted. Some people, like Al Deere, appeared to be inexhaustible, but others weren't. It wasn't lack of moral fibre or cracking up. You just got so tired that you were useless.

I still don't like the telephone because you'd be sitting there in the dispersal hut, playing cards or reading a book or something like that and the telephone would ring. Everyone froze. An orderly answered. It might be 'Squadron scramble', or something quite unimportant – so-and-so to see the equipment officer or something like that. But the tension which built up between the ringing of the phone and learning what it was is my hangover from the Battle of Britain. I still don't like telephones.

Flight Lieutenant Alan Deere

You never could tell. Some of the least likely chaps turned out to be best and sometimes you got things wrong in sizing men up. I had a pilot who came to me one day and said, 'I can't fly today. I'm not feeling well.' I said, 'You've got to fly. We're short of men.'

He said, 'I just can't.'

I called the doctor and told him, 'Take a look at this chap. I think he's lost his nerve.'

It turned out he had malaria. I was unable to judge because I was so tired myself.

Sergeant David Cox

There was one sergeant, Jack Roden, who should never have been a fighter pilot. He was one of the bravest men I ever knew. He was dead scared from the beginning, but he kept on flying. I used to say to him, 'Go to the CO or to your flight commander and get taken off.' He wouldn't.

He used to crash Spitfires in all sorts of silly ways – three or four of them. He was frightened of the plane. He never shot anything down. One day, he got shot up and badly hurt trying to land his damaged Spitfire in a field. If he had crash landed with his wheels up, he'd have been all right. He'd have come to a grinding halt quickly. But he landed with his wheels down. The field was too small and he ran into a tree and was badly injured. He was conscious enough at first to be asked why the heck he had put his wheels down when he should have crash landed. He said it was because he didn't want to damage another Spitfire. He died three days later. It was unnecessary. He should never have been a fighter pilot.

There were others who were also ill-placed. It was inevitable. We were so short of pilots. And there were a few who didn't really want to be there. The one who was easiest to spot was the one who always came right back with something wrong with his aircraft – the radio had gone or the revs were dropping or it wasn't flying right or it was overheating. If it happened often, the flight commander or CO would say, 'The next time it happens, have it tested on the ground or have someone else take it right up again.' If the plane was found to be all right, the pilot would be quietly posted away.

Squadron Leader Ted Donaldson

If I thought it was a rest a man needed, I'd give him a fortnight's holiday. If I felt the war had really got to him, I'd get rid of him. There weren't many of them. There was one chap who said one day, 'I think I'd better stay down today because I've got double vision.' He was obviously fatigued; we all were, though we didn't use that word for it then. I looked at him and his eyes really were pointing in different directions. I said, 'Look, the Germans don't know you've got double vision so you'd better come with us. The Germans will see twelve Hurricanes, not eleven with one extra chap who can't see straight.' Someone said, 'You're a shit, sir.' But he survived. I saw him not long ago.

Pilot Officer Roland Beamont

A chap was occasionally removed from the squadron and posted to a non-operational job if he didn't appear to be worth his place. It wasn't any good having a formation of eight Hurricanes going up to face a hundred Germans if on the way up one of them veered away from the formation without saying anything. When you got back you'd find he'd landed. He'd say his engine was U/S [unserviceable], but the engine fitter couldn't find anything wrong with it. If that happened once, OK. If it happened twice, you had to do something about it. Without any vindictiveness at all, that chap had to go, because his presence was going to lower the morale of the entire squadron.

Pilot Officer Peter Brown

I went up with the squadron one day and my undercarriage would not retract. So I reported on radio to my squadron leader that I was returning to base, I landed and taxied straight to the maintenance hangar to have it serviced. They put the plane on the jacks, jacked it off the ground, operated the undercarriage and it retracted without any trouble at all – it slammed straight up. They tried it eight or nine times and said there was nothing wrong with it. Of course, retracting in the air was different. There were different pressures. I taxied back to dispersal to await the squadron's return.

Later, we went off again and again I couldn't get the undercarriage up. So I called up the CO again and said, 'Red two returning to base. Undercarriage won't retract.' By this time I was desperately worried. It was getting to look as though I really didn't want to stay with the squadron. I taxied to the maintenance hangar again and they jacked it up again and tested and found it absolutely perfect.

I started getting some strange looks and I taxied over to flight dispersal again and again waited for the squadron to come back. When we went off on the third trip of the day, I prayed to God harder than I had ever prayed in my life that the undercarriage would come up so that I could prove that I wasn't trying to stay out of action. To my intense relief, the undercarriage finally came up.

I was desperately frightened of being thought a coward. Every mission during the Battle of Britain was potentially a life or death situation, but I was much more concerned about that than about risking my life fighting the Germans.

Flight Lieutenant Peter Brothers

There was one pilot who, when we were sitting on the ground waiting to be scrambled, had beads of sweat on his forehead. He said he wasn't feeling too good. I rang up the station doctor and took this chap to sick quarters. Then he rang me up in the dispersal tent and said he wasn't even to fly his aeroplane back to Biggin Hill from the forward base at Manston where we were at the time. We never saw him again. He'd cracked up.

But you couldn't call that chap a coward. He later got a job testing rebuilt aircraft. He had the most ghastly crash in a Hurricane, but went on testing. He had a different sort of courage. He couldn't face up to the Germans, but he could face death in the job he had moved on to.

Squadron Leader Jack Satchell

I interrogated personnel of an army detachment stationed near where Pilot Officer Carter crashed. They saw his plane come out of the clouds. An object left the cockpit and then became two objects, one of which was Carter. The other object was his parachute. We found it thirty yards from his body. Why his parachute was not strapped to him was a mystery. I assumed that, in his haste to get out of the plane, he did what he was accustomed to do when he landed after a sortie: he undid both his fighting harness *and* his parachute straps. He probably baled out before he realized what he had done. Poor devil – his agony of mind during those few seconds must have been frightful. His brain must have been working pretty fast on his way down.

Pilot Officer Mike Heron

We were on readiness one day – Flight Commander Ken Gillies, myself and Pilot Officer Watkinson. A call came through that there was a German bomber stooging around; would we try to intercept it. We took off into very low cloud – I suppose 600–700 feet cloud base. We climbed up through cloud which was more or less continuous and were vectored while climbing up. Ken Gillies was leading. I was flying on his right hand, starboard side – number two. Watkinson was number three on the port side.

When we came up on top of the cloud, we were again given a course to fly and spotted a Heinkel 111 maybe two or three miles away and went towards it. When we were within a mile of it, it must have spotted us. It changed course and started jinking in and out of the cloud. Had the chap the sense to remain in cloud, we wouldn't have been able to locate him and we did lose him for a minute or two. But then, because of his stupidity in coming out, we altered course and, though we lost him again once or twice, we got nearer and were able to attack him – first Gillies, then myself, then Watkinson.

Then Gillies suddenly said over the radio, 'I am obliged to break off combat.' That was all. I don't know what happened to him, whether he was wounded or there was some damage done to his plane. People's voices in combat situation were usually excited or strained. I couldn't tell whether he was in pain from the way he sounded. I never saw him again. His body was washed up on the coast several weeks later.

Flying Officer Ben Bowring

Some pilots got so tired they probably went straight into the German bombers they were attacking. The pace was exhausting. If you weren't already in the air, you'd sit down to breakfast to eggs and bacon, the horn would blow and you were off and it wouldn't let up. There was a squadron commander at Manston who was so battle fatigued that it's practically certain he knew what he was doing when he crashed into a German aircraft. There were masses of them coming over. He told us, 'If I have to, I'm going in.' I think he was so tired he just couldn't cope. It was like swimming against a strong tide. You could go on for so long, but eventually some of us had to go with it.

Investigation of Psychological Disorder in Flying Personnel of Fighter Command by Air Vice Marshal Sir Charles P. Symonds and Wing Commander Denis J. Williams, 1942

Lagging or breaking away from formation may be noticed. Deterioration in flying, bad landings and general carelessness were commented upon – 'His flying isn't as good as it was ...' 'He begins to lose his appreciation of danger and thus either gets killed or else merely piles up.' Common to all these stories was an account of the development of fear to a degree which called for an increasing effort of will to control it. Some degree of fear was admitted as natural and stimulating, increasing alertness and sharpening judgment. Any effect fear might have had in claiming attention and impairing efficiency was in the earlier stages of the operational career offset by the interest of the job, the desire to do well at it and perhaps win a decoration, and the offensive spirit. The experience of a few successes added to the weight of these balancing factors, and the balance was such that once airborne the pilot was relatively fearless. The cumulative stress, both mental and physical, weakened the inhibitory effect of the balancing factors, so that fearlessness was gradually lost. An effort now had to be made to control fear. One officer ... described himself as getting into a state in which you don't care whether you are shot down or not ... He thought that a number of pilots were lost in the Battle of Britain from getting into this state. Another noticed that he was becoming jumpy and irritable, and that he had a sudden craving for leave, though previously he had not wanted it or taken it. Another found himself waking tired in the mornings, and feeling jumpy when a show was on ... Discipline was held to be of great value for 'discipline on the ground reflects itself in the air; if you can't keep together on the ground, you can't keep together in the air.' 'Individualism is frowned upon and the pilot is only an individual while he is pressing his button. The individualists are soon missing.'

Pilot Officer Richard Jones

I later had a lot to do with a Bomber Command crew. It was important for bomber people to be part of an operational unit. But I was a bit of a loner. A lot of the Fighter Command pilots were. When we were in the air, we operated individually. If we were in trouble, it was up to us alone to get out of it. I remember one of our men – a very likeable person – who, at readiness in the crew room, would sit and read and when you spoke to him, he wouldn't answer, wouldn't hear you. He was very much alone. When we were under stress, we tended not to speak much. I was like that. I still am.

Pilot Officer Birdie Bird-Wilson

Yes, I was afraid. It came out at night mostly, when I was asleep. I had terrible nightmares. It seemed as though I was flying half the night although I was still in my bed. I think anybody who says he wasn't afraid is a bloody liar – unless he was a chap like Sailor Malan, a superb pilot, an excellent leader and a man of great mental stature. But people had to put a shield around themselves. Externally, some were hale, hearty, debonaire. They showed a couldn't-care-less attitude. But I'm convinced they got down on their prayer mats many, many times. When they were by themselves or before they went to sleep, I believe they had a quick conversation with God Almighty.

Pilot Officer John Ellacombe

There were fourteen, fifteen hours of daylight each day. You were on duty right through. Chaps were being lost all the time. We had seventeen out of twenty-three killed or wounded in my squadron in less than three weeks. We had another eight aircraft shot down with the chaps unhurt, including myself, twice. It was a fight for survival. There was tremendous 'twitch'. If somebody slammed a door, half the chaps would jump out of their chairs. There were times when you were so tired, you'd pick up your pint of beer with two hands. But no one was cowering terrified in a corner. My greatest fear was that I'd reach the stage where I'd show fear. But it took me years after the war to get rid of my twitch.

Sergeant Mike Croskell

At Exeter, there was no mess on the base. The officers went to live at the Rougemont Hotel. The rest of us stayed with local people. The days were very long. We'd go to work at the crack of dawn and stay on duty till last light. I was billeted with very pleasant people in the town of Honiton. I got very tired. I'm not normally bad tempered, but I got very irritable and the people I stayed with said something about it, it was so obvious. Those were rough days.

Sergeant Dick Kilner

There was always the fear that there might be a Jerry behind you. Generally if you could see the bombers and their fighter escort, you knew what you were up against. If you didn't see the fighter escort, that was when you had to look around because they'd be there somewhere and it was time to worry. Half your mind would be on attacking the bombers; the other half would be on looking around for the fighters you couldn't see.

Pilot Officer Peter Parrott

Once you were in action, you were too busy trying to shoot something down or trying not to be shot down yourself to be frightened. But there was tenseness, fear, apprehension right through, from the first time I was jumped by a 109 – that was over France at the very beginning – and realized what was happening was real. Some of the worst of it was sitting on the ground waiting for the telephone to ring and for someone to shout 'Scramble.' You came to accept it as normal.

There was a lot of laughter. It was an escape mechanism. If you got back from a trip and had had a bit of a hairy time in action, you didn't tell it as the hairy time it was; you'd tell it as a joke.

You had to put up a front, particularly if you were in a position of command and the way things were happening, it wasn't long before I was a deputy flight commander, leading the flight when my flight commander was away. You had to hide your own feelings so as not to upset the others. You'd resort to humour and bravado. You'd laugh things off.

We did some very strange things on the ground. My flight commander, Adrian Boyd, was a man of ideas. We were very conscious of the fact that England might be invaded and we would not necessarily have an aeroplane to fly with when it happened. We might have to get involved in guerilla warfare. That was very much in the air at the time. Adrian was all for improvising weapons we might use. He reckoned you could kill somebody with a Very flare pistol, which you could, though a Very cartridge wasn't the best missile for the job. So he got a cartridge, took out most of the gunpowder, but left the detonator and projection powder in. He then filled it up with rusty nails, tin tacks, small bits of old metal he could find. He was going to make some sort of blunderbuss, something like a shotgun. He tied it to the back of a Nissen hut and aimed the thing at the remains of an old windmill not far away.

There was a chap named Guy Branch lying in a deckchair nearby, waiting for the telephone to ring and to be scrambled. That blunderbuss went off with an enormous bang and Guy, who hadn't been in on this, literally went six inches out of his chair. It made quite a noise, but we weren't convinced it had done much to advance the war effort.

Pilot Officer Jas Storrar

Coming back from an interception, Guy Branch was shot down and landed in the sea off Poole Harbour. He was about a mile from the coast. The rescue people had seen him coming down and a lifeboat was on its way out to him. I saw him in the water. He waved to me. I circled over him, and stayed as long as I could. The lifeboat couldn't have been more than fifty to a hundred yards from him so when I got back, I reported that he had been picked up. I telephoned his wife and told her he was all right.

Being a bit of an offshore sailor in the years since the war, I can see now how, with a bit of rolling sea, they were able to miss him. But at the time I simply couldn't understand how somebody in the water, wearing a green Mae West, couldn't be spotted. But he wasn't. For a long time, his wife lived in hope that he'd been picked up by the other side. But he hadn't been. He died that day. He shouldn't have gone then. His number wasn't really up yet.

Pilot Officer Christopher Currant
From Memories of a Fighter Pilot

Once again he took the air and Croydon was the base
To fight it out in fear and sweat so many times each day
To smell the burn of cordite flash, to see the flames of war
High up above the fields of Kent, the dive, the zoom, the soar.
Returning from a clash of foes one day he came across
A sight which burnt deep in his soul and never can be lost
A pilot dangling from his chute towards the earth did drift.
He circled round this friend or foe, so hopelessly alone
To keep away who ever dared to fire on such a gift.
It was a useless gesture though, as round and round he flew
He saw as in an awful dream first smoke and then flames spew
Curl up his back as arms he waved and burn the cords of life
Snapping his body from the chute, snatching him from war's strife.
With sickened horror in his heart he landed back at base.
He cried himself to sleep that night and thanks to God's good grace
That he was spared yet once again to live and fight this fight
Against the things he saw as black for things he believed were right.

Winston Churchill

This ... period 24 August–6 September ... seriously drained the strength of Fighter Command as a whole. The Command lost in this fortnight 103 pilots killed and 128 seriously wounded, while 466 Spitfires and Hurricanes had been destroyed or seriously damaged. Out of a total pilot strength of about a thousand nearly a quarter had been lost. Their places could only be filled by 260 new, ardent but inexperienced pilots drawn from training units, in many cases before their full courses were complete.

* * *

British ground defences were strengthened during the course of the summer. The troops ferried home from Dunkirk were rested and regrouped. Additional forces had been recruited and were being trained. Armament factories were churning out equipment to replace what had been abandoned on the beaches of France. Preparing to repel the enemy became the watchword as reconnaissance planes brought back word that the Germans seemed about ready to launch their cross-Channel attack.

Vessels of all sorts had been requisitioned by them throughout Germany and occupied Europe and brought to dozens of ports along the Channel coast facing England to take part in or support the planned landings. RAF bombers had attacked them, as had the Royal Navy. But intelligence reports made it clear that the German threat remained undiminished.

The enemy had gathered thirty-one divisions of infantry and armoured troops for the first three waves of their landings on English beaches. They were engaged in rigorous landing training. Their paratroops were primed to be the vanguard of the assault.

In their public pronouncements, British officials taunted Hitler for failing to make good his threat to invade. In private, they knew too well that the invasion remained a very real danger, and possibly was imminent.

GHQ Intelligence Summary
5 August

German light tanks up to six tons may be carried in land planes and up to nine tons in flying boats. It appears that the German Ju 90 land plane (of which some fifteen exist – 6 July 1940) could carry one or more tanks up to a total weight of something between nine and ten and a half tons ... It has now been reported that Ju 52 aircraft usually used for troop transportation, of which a large number are available, will be used to transport 'tankettes', and that special 'tankettes' are being constructed.

New York Times

Berlin, 14 August – Foreign correspondents were informed this afternoon that dancing would be forbidden again throughout the Reich, beginning at once. A dancing prohibition was effective during the entire Western campaign, but it was modified after the French capitulation to permit dancing two evenings a week. The reason for the modification, it is believed, was to enable victorious Reich soldiers home on vacation to enjoy and rest themselves. Reimposition of the ban appears to indicate that this period of relaxation and vacation is ended and that serious warring is imminent.

W. F. Leysmith, New York Times

London, 15 August – Fifty German parachutes without owners were found yesterday spread over a wide area in Scotland and the English Midlands, and today one of the biggest manhunts in British history was under way. As yet, no parachutists have been run to earth, and a Midland farmer who picked up several parachutes on his land said there were no marks to indicate any Germans had descended there.

Unofficial sources in Berlin were quoted by the United Press as saying 'suicide squads' of German parachutists had been landed in the Midlands to sabotage British industry. An Associated Press dispatch from Berlin, however, said Germans called British reports of finding Nazi parachutes 'a midsummer night's dream' and added that, 'the English mind is full of fantasy'. The parachute 'attack' is believed by many to have been a German ruse, the purpose of which is not yet clear, except that it was possibly meant to create panic.

Alfred Duff Cooper, Minister of Information
Radio Broadcast to the Nation, 17 August

We should not have liked him [Hitler] to come before we were ready to receive him, but we are quite ready to receive him now and we shall really be very disappointed if he does not turn up. We can assure him that he will meet with that welcome on our shores which no invader has ever missed. This was to have been a week of German victory; it has been a week of British victory instead.

War Cabinet
Chiefs of Staff Committee, 26 August

An analysis of recent German air reconnaissances had shown that a great interest was being taken in aerodromes in the extreme south-west of England, and that certain aerodromes had sometimes been visited two and three times daily.

It was suggested that the Germans might be contemplating a diversion in this area in order to draw our forces away from southeast England, which was at present the focus of our attention.

A report ... has been received through the military attaché, Washington, of a German plan to land a force of rubber motor boats in southwest England, with the object of cutting off Devon and Cornwall and then advancing up the Severn Basin and down the Thames Basin, thus cutting off the south of England. The Commander-in-Chief, Home Forces, has regarded this report as unreliable.

Commander-in-Chief of the German Army
30 August

INSTRUCTIONS FOR THE PREPARATION OF OPERATION SEA LION
Task: The Supreme Commander has ordered the services to make preparations for a landing in force in England. The aim of this attack is to eliminate the Mother Country as a base for continuing the war against Germany, and, if it should be necessary, to carry out a complete occupation ...

PROPOSED METHOD OF EXECUTION:
  a) The Luftwaffe will destroy the British Air Force and the armament production which supports it and it will achieve air superiority. The navy will provide mine-free corridors and, supported by the Luftwaffe, will bar the flanks of the crossing-sector.

b) The army's landing forces will first win local bridgeheads with the specially equipped forward echelons of the first wave divisions. Immediately afterwards, they will widen these bridgeheads into a connected landing-zone, the possession of which will cover the disembarkation of the following troops and ensure early uniform control on the English shore. As soon as sufficient forces are available, an offensive will be launched towards the first operational objective, i.e. Thames Estuary – heights south of London – Portsmouth.

From Cabinet War Room Summary
7 September

A German soldier parachutist, dressed in civilian clothes, was captured by a farmer at 17.20 on September 6. He was in possession of a receiving and transmitting wireless set, automatic pistol, £200 in notes, a Swedish passport and British identity card dated 6-11-1939. The man's name is Gosta Caroli and he lived formerly in this country and went to Birmingham in October 1939, and left England in December when he volunteered for the German army. His mission was to report on damage to aerodromes.

War Cabinet Memorandum
Home Secretary, 7 September

DUTIES OF THE POLICE IN CASE OF INVASION
1. The general principles governing the position of the police in the case of invasion are:
   a) that the police are not part of the armed forces of the Crown and that therefore, in the event of a landing and effective occupation of an area by the enemy in force, the police should not use arms, nor carry arms, in the occupied area; but
   b) that in the event of a landing by isolated parties who do not form part of an occupying force and whose object is, or must be assumed to be, to attack civilians, destroy property and cause confusion and devastation, neither the police nor civilians are debarred, either by international law or domestic law, from resisting and, if possible, destroying the enemy in order to prevent him carrying out these objects.

Gunner Philip Coad

Other people may have felt differently, but I was immensely happy. I was being trained to be in a field artillery regiment. I was doing what I wanted to do. I was contributing to the war effort. If the invasion took place, I thought I might be given a rifle and shoot somebody or be shot myself. It didn't worry me. I knew it was desperately important that we win the battle, but I never thought we'd lose it. I may have been foolish not worrying, but I wasn't alone in that.

Pilot Officer Robert Doe

It never entered our heads that we might lose. When people said we might be invaded, we talked about what a wonderful time we'd have shooting up the German landing barges.

Pilot Officer Peter Parrott

We were in the Caledonian Hotel in Aberdeen one Sunday night when we were stationed at Dyce Aerodrome. Not a lot was happening up there. In those days in Scotland, to buy a drink on a Sunday, you had to be a bona fide traveller and to have travelled at least three miles. That was the law. We were in uniform and they knew our aerodrome was just three miles away, so that was all right. A police constable suddenly appeared and went around whispering something to various people there, including some army officers. He came up to us and all we heard was, 'Sunrise tomorrow morning.' It didn't mean a thing to us, but we assumed it meant there was a risk the Germans would invade the following day. It didn't happen, of course, and I still don't know what that constable was talking about. But there was very much a sense of expectancy about the invasion those days.

Gunner Robert Angell

We were twenty-four hours on, twenty-four hours off at our anti-aircraft unit at Dover. When we were off duty, we slept in caves under the cliffs of Dover that had been converted into air-raid shelters. One night, we were called out and told the German invasion had started. There was nothing we could do. There were about sixty of us and about twenty rifles and the rifles were antiques, earlier than First World War vintage. We were just standing there, feeling totally exposed, nineteen miles from the French coast and wondering what the hell was going to happen and what the hell we would do when it did. That was the only time in the whole of the war that I was really frightened. We stood there for an hour, peering into the darkness. Nothing materialized. We were stood down and that was that.

Afterwards, rumours began to fly around that there had either been a major German exercise on the French coast, preparing for the invasion, or there had been an attempted invasion. There were stories of Churchill's secret weapon of pouring oil on the sea and setting light to it. There were rumours that charred bodies had been washed up along the coast.

Fighter Command Headquarters

The fighter pilot in dealing with enemy aircraft during an attempted invasion should, subject to any special task allotted to him at the time, observe the following priority whenever he has the choice of target:
  a) Dive bombers operating against naval forces
  b) Tank-carrying aircraft
  c) Troop-carrying aircraft
  d) Bombers
  e) Fighters

* * *

During this period, many British civilians were bombed for the first time. It was for them the initial experience of death and destruction raining down from the skies. In some places, concern was expressed about the failure of the RAF to stop the German raiders from reaching them. Of far greater significance for Britain, however, were the raids which had increasingly been concentrated on the airfields. Biggin Hill, Debden, Hornchurch, Hawkinge, Manston were hit again and again. The damage done was sometimes so crippling that the consequences were deemed to be potentially catastrophic.

Air Vice Marshal Keith Park

The enemy's bombing attacks by day did extensive damage to five of our forward aerodromes and also six of our seven Sector Stations ...

There was a critical period between 28 August and 5 September when the damage to Sector Stations and our ground organization was having a serious effect on the fighting efficiency of the fighter squadrons, who could not be given the same good technical and administrative services as previously ... The absence of many essential telephone lines, the use of scratch equipment in emergency Operations Rooms, and the general dislocation of ground organization, was seriously felt for about a week in the handling of squadrons by day to meet the enemy's massed attacks, which continued without the former occasional break for a day. Biggin Hill was so severely damaged that only one squadron could operate from there, and the remaining two squadrons had to be placed under the control of adjacent Sectors for over a week. Had the enemy intensified his heavy attacks against the adjacent Sectors and knocked out their Operations Rooms or telephone communications, the fighter defences of London would have been in a parlous state during the last critical phase when heavy attacks were directed against the capital.

Pilot Officer Peter Hairs

We'd taken off from Gravesend. My CO was leading. I was his number two. Our squadron codename was Mandrill. Just after we took off, I heard the Biggin Hill Controller, whose codename was Sapper, calling. 'This is Sapper calling Mandrill leader.' He didn't get a reply so he came on again. 'Mandrill leader. This is Sapper calling,' and he told us to fly vector so-and-so and angels such-and-such. 'Mandrill leader, are you receiving?' No reply. We found out later the CO's radio wasn't working properly. I didn't want to butt in and say I was receiving, because I might have upset things. After a while, I heard the Controller again. 'Bandits approaching Sapper! They're approaching Biggin Hill! They're bombing Biggin Hill! They're bombing me!'

We eventually arrived at Biggin Hill, but were too late to intercept. The Germans had come in low, dropped their bombs and made off again.

Pilot Officer Wally Wallens

Where it was possible, a section of three aircraft was kept on the ground till the very last moment when our airfield was attacked.

Those planes were the last defensive reserves for the airfield, the rest of the squadron having already been scrambled to intercept a raid downriver or somewhere. There you'd be, on the field, with the trolley-accumulator to start your engine attached to your plane, the groundcrewmen under the wings and you sitting in the cockpit feeling like a sitting duck. Sometimes, the bombs would begin coming down on the airfield before you were sent up. The airman would press the button on the trolley-ac, you'd press your button and your engine would start. The airman would then pull the trolley-ac away and race for shelter while the bombs came slamming down. You'd start taxiing across the field and hope there wasn't a bomb crater in your path. It was bloody unpleasant.

Assistant Section Officer Felicity Hanbury

As the battle grew more intense, we knew we were going to be bombed at Biggin Hill. We were preparing for it all the time. We had drills on what to do when it happened. There were two air-raid warnings. We heard the civilian warnings from Westerham and Bromley, the two towns on either side of Biggin Hill. We didn't take any notice of them. Civilians there needed more time to get to their shelters than we did. But when the station warning went, we did what we had to, often simply taking cover in preparation for what we might have to do afterwards. When the bombing began and the Germans came down and machine-gunned the station, I think the girls were most frightened of showing they were frightened. They were determined not to let anyone down, however terrified they were.

It was a hot summer. The ground was very hard so that when bombs fell, it was very difficult to get people out who had been sheltering in a trench that had been hit, after they had been hurt or killed. Once, they bombed a trench in which some WAAFs had taken cover and which I'd nearly gone into myself. I was on my way to my office. When I was half-way between two trenches, the station warning went and I went into the other trench. As soon as the aircraft noises quietened down, one didn't wait for the all clear. One wanted to see what had happened. My first move was to see how the airwomen were getting on in their trench. Half-way there, I discovered it had been hit. Somebody shouted that it had been bombed. There was a frightful smell of escaping gas; they'd hit a gas main. When I got to the trench, I saw it was sort of half bombed. The

WAAFs had all been blown to one end of it. Luckily, only one was killed, but there were a lot of serious casualties, some of whom have had a fairly miserable time since, I'm afraid.

They'd destroyed most of the airwomen's quarters and we had to find some place for them to live. We went around knocking on people's doors round the station and asked if they could take in one, two, three or whatever of the airwomen. They were tremendously co-operative.

I was posted to London soon after the bombing of Biggin Hill was over. It was heaven being bombed in London after that. You were part of such a vast target in the big city. You could lie in your flat and hear bombs going off not far away, but feel safe. I suppose the difference was that you knew they were after you on a little target and, my goodness, you could *see* them coming at you, diving right down, and the wretched machine-gunning. I never went to an air-raid shelter in London.

Pilot Officer Dennis David

The groundcrew – the fitters, the riggers, the others – kept working on aircraft while the Germans were attacking the airfields. Naturally, they broke off when things got too hot. But they made planes serviceable when it looked like it couldn't be done. They kept us flying.

The bowser drivers were amazing. What could be more dangerous than driving a 900 gallon petrol tanker when bombs were falling, and they did it, refuelling us under fire so that we could take off again to go for the bombers. The armourers who reloaded our guns and the radio men who saw to our radios – they all kept us going when things were darkest.

Aircraftsman Second Class Albert Hargraves, Bowser driver

It was my birthday, 25 August, when the big raids on Biggin Hill began. The Germans came in with the sun at the back of them. They came over bombing and strafing. Four of my pals in the M/T section were going to go out with me for a drink at night to celebrate my birthday. I never saw them again. They were killed. The celebration was cancelled.

The biggest raid was a few days later. It was a Sunday, around teatime. We'd just come out of the canteen. The station commander announced over the tannoy that everybody who wasn't essential should go to the shelters. But so many dashed for the shelter than not everybody could get in. I dashed back to my bowser to drive down to flight where there were some trees. I'd just got clear of the main camp part to get onto the perimeter to go around when the Dorniers came down the middle of the aerodrome. They looked like they were only fifty feet off the ground, though they must have been higher than that.

The cab doors of the bowsers had been taken off to let us get in and out in a hurry. I pulled up sharp, jumped out and ran like bloody hell to a hedge and lay down. The bombs were exploding and you could hear the machine-guns and cannon fire from the Dorniers and Messerschmitts. Then it went quiet. The main shelter, the one where not everybody could get in, had been hit. There was a hell of a crater there.

We rushed over and tried to get people out. There were a lot of casualties. There were heads lying around and arms sticking up out of the crater. We were digging away there until three in the morning. We got about fifty bodies out and there were still some left. The next day, they got a load of miners in to help dig the shelter out. They found some more bodies. After they thought they'd got out as many as they could, they just bulldozed the area over.

Headquarters were demolished with all the service records. They didn't know who was on the base. If anyone had absconded then, they would have got away with it.

Assistant Section Officer Felicity Hanbury

Joan Mortimer was a sergeant in charge of the armoury. As soon as the bombing stopped, she wouldn't wait for the all clear. She'd rush out on to the aerodrome to mark all the unexploded bombs and the bomb craters so that when our aircraft came back, they could see where not to land. Goodness knows how many lives she saved by doing that.

Aircraftsman Second Class Albert Hargraves

There were so many little flags marking off the unexploded bombs, they looked like flowers in a field. We were all commandeered to work at bomb disposal. We got threepence a day extra for it.

Flight Lieutenant Peter Brothers

We'd see the damaged buildings and craters when we got back to the aerodrome after it had been bombed while we were elsewhere, intercepting other raids. And we'd see the little flags stuck in the ground to mark off unexploded bombs. We'd either land on the perimeter path or make a path of our own through them all.

Operations Record Book
Biggin Hill, 30 August

A low level bombing attack was carried out by the enemy on the station and very serious damage was done to buildings and equipment. The raiders dropped sixteen big HE [high explosive] bombs, estimated 1,000 lbs weight each, of which six fell among the buildings rendering completely useless and unsafe workshops, transport yard, stores, barrack stores, armoury, guardroom, meteorological office and the station institute and shattering by blast part of the airmen's married quarters, which were being used as accommodation for WAAF personnel. 'F' type hangar in north camp was also badly hit. One shelter trench received a direct hit and two other near hits. The total casualties were thirty-nine killed and twenty-five wounded and shocked. All power, gas and water mains were severed and all telephone lines running north of the camp were severed in three places.

Aircraftsman Second Class Albert Hargraves

The station commander at Biggin Hill, Group Captain Grice, wanted to get the aerodrome operational again as soon as possible. He went up and had a fly-around to see what it looked like from above. It looked terrible, but he saw that one of the hangars, which was just a shell after the bombing, still looked undamaged from up there. When he came down, he had it blown up so the Germans wouldn't want to have another go at us.

Right through the worst of it at Biggin Hill, the Salvation Army was there. You'd be at dispersal at eleven at night, just in case. There'd be at least two pilots on standby in their cockpits and the Salvation Army would be there with their van and their tea and wads. Wads were buns, a little on the sweet side. You were lucky if you found a currant in one of them. A penny for a cup of tea. A halfpenny for a wad. It was fantastic.

Squadron Leader Harry Hogan

When we were operating out of Gravesend, we were controlled from Biggin Hill. When Biggin Hill was bombed, and the Ops Room there was knocked out, we had to set up an emergency system for getting our flight instructions. The trolley-accumulator, which was used to start the aeroplanes, was plugged into planes on the ground and I assigned pilots so that there would always be one of them in his cockpit with his radio on, with the trolley-accumulator providing the necessary power so that he could pick up messages from the Ops Room at Hornchurch. The Controller there relayed messages to us from Group. 'Scramble' and the rest of it. That kept us operational for at least two days until Biggin Hill was able to set up an emergency Ops Room.

Wing Commander David Roberts, Sector Commander, Middle Wallop

There was a fair bit of damage when Middle Wallop was hit. A stick of bombs came right across the hangar area. Two chaps were killed while shutting the doors of one of the hangars. One bomb hit an air-raid shelter and killed a workman there. Two or three aircraft were damaged on the ground and lost. Thank God, the Ops Room wasn't hit. It was only a wooden hut. I stayed there. I was controlling at the time and I had everything in the air. More raids were coming in and they had to be met. When the bombs came down near us, we all went flat on the floor. The WAAFs were under the table. My flight sergeant, the senior NCO in charge of the Ops Room said, 'This is where we're all on the same level, sir.'

Pilot Officer John Ellacombe

When I went to bury Jim Johnston who'd been shot down, I took along Johnnie Comar, a Canadian who had trained with me. We flew to Hawkinge Aerodrome, where the local people had laid on a padre and a firing squad of six RAF airmen. While the good padre was saying the final bit of his service, we could hear a scream above and looked up and saw these Junker 87s heading down our way, shedding their bombs as they dived. The airmen disappeared in a flash. I told the padre to run like hell and Johnnie Comar and I jumped into the grave on top of Jim's coffin, which still gave us four or five feet of slit trench. The whole place thumped and banged for about a minute. When it was quiet, we climbed out. We couldn't see the padre. We couldn't see the airmen. Even the gravediggers had disappeared. It was horrifying, that raid being mixed up with saying farewell to a friend.

Aircraftswoman Second Class Edith Heap

The Germans made quite a mess of Debden before they were finished bombing it. There was one Scottish girl who was in the bath when a raid came in one time. She wasn't sure what to do. So she let the water out of the bath, put on her tin hat and just sat there in the tub till the raid was over.

When it was busy, it was chaotic in the Ops Room. On one particular day, when Winifred Butler and I were just coming on duty, the sirens went when we were on the other side of the parade ground. We ran like hares and shot into the Ops Room. I said to the girl I was going to relieve, 'Right, give it to me.' Winifred did the same. And the girls we were relieving stayed on to help.

We didn't worry about the bombing. We didn't have time. We were too busy. All you'd think about was getting the aircraft up in the air to do something. But we knew the Ops Room at Detling airfield had received a direct hit.

When you didn't have your earphones on, you could hear what was happening in the air. That's where I learned all my bad language. You could actually hear the battle taking place. It was awe-inspiring hearing the pilots call out to each other over the radio. 'Look out! There's someone behind you!' 'Break off!' That sort of thing. It got fast and furious. We could hear it while we were plotting.

There was an Irish girl – a plotter like me – who had hysterics when we were being bombed. We thought that was frightful that she wasn't able to control herself. Poor girl. It showed a lack of understanding on our part. I understand now, but at the time we thought, 'English people don't behave like that.'

We stayed on at Debden until they decided it was too dangerous because of the bombing. After Detling had been hit, they decided it was too much of a risk. So they moved the Ops Room off the station. They put it first in a wooden hut in a chalk pit not far away. We felt terribly brave at one point, because there was an unexploded German bomb on the road. The road was closed, but we had to go along it in a bus to get to our new Ops Room. We were soon moved again, to a school in Saffron Walden. The night after we moved, when it would have been my watch on duty, there was a direct hit on the chalk pit Ops Room.

Corporal Claire Legge

We used to sleep with trousers and things beside the bed, absolutely ready. Normally, the air-raid warning went up in stages – 'Prepare to take cover', that sort of thing. On the morning we were bombed at Tangmere, the advance warning did come – 'Prepare to take cover.' That meant get up and put your clothes on. I was only half-way through when the call came, 'Take cover! Take cover!' There was absolute panic. We had one girl, a plotter, Hyacinth, who was tall and elegant. She used to walk around willowy, like a model on show. She decided, when 'take cover' was sounded, that she would take a bath. She *always* had a half water, half oil bath. Well, she was in her bath and wouldn't get out. So another corporal, Frances Turner, and I had to physically take this blasted woman out of the bath and get her dressed. As a result, the first bomb had in actual fact fallen by the time we got into the shelter. Poor old Frances, she came in after me. I got in first and all the time she was pushing this woman down the stairs.

We were in the shelter a long time. I was right by the entrance. One of the male sergeants from the plotting table came tumbling down the steps into the shelter in a most terrible state. 'Oh my God,' he said. 'It's awful up there.' I gave him a swig of brandy from the flask my father had given me and which I always carried in my gas mask.

I don't think any of us felt frightened until suddenly a rumour went round that the trench had collapsed and somebody's head had been severed by some wood or something right at the end of the shelter, which we couldn't see from where we were because it went round a corner. In fact, it hadn't really happened, but it made one feel a bit sick.

Anyway, when it was all over, out we came and you never saw such a mess in your life. The Germans had seemed to be going for Portsmouth and Southampton. We had got all our fighters up, ready and waiting over there, but instead of going there, the Germans did a turn and came straight for Tangmere. We had 1 hangar, 2 hangar, 3 hangar, 4 hangar and the Ops Room. They went *bop, bop, bop, bop,* and missed the Ops Room. How? God only knows. The hangars were flattened. There were mattresses all over the road – one of the hangars must have been a storeroom. There was a monumental mess.

Flight Lieutenant Bob Stanford-Tuck

The single-storied mess at Martlesham was very old-fashioned, rather like a bloody great bungalow. My bathroom was on the outside wall. I'd been flying a bit the night before and I'd done one patrol early in the morning, got back and was in the bath when the sirens went.

The German bombers came in and plastered our aerodrome. The stuff was really coming down. I jumped out of the bath and ran out through a side door to the nearest slit trench with just a towel round me. As I dived in, my towel came off and I was starkers, absolutely starkers, taking a header into that slit trench. There must have been about fifteen WAAFs in there. I landed on top of them without a stitch of clothing on. Most of these young WAAFs were our waitresses in the mess. In the days afterwards, everytime I walked into the dining room, you could see them all giggling away. I got used to it after a bit.

Assistant Section Officer Molly Wilkinson

We were ordered to evacuate our station at dawn and dusk every day because the German raids were so bad. They'd sound a hooter and all personnel who were not involved in flying left the base for about an hour at those two times. That was when the Germans chose to come in because it was difficult to see them then, with dawn breaking or dusk falling. I used to go with Basil Embry, the station commander. He had what is now called an estate car. He would have a machine-gun. As we got off the base, outside the gates, he'd say, 'Right, we'll stop here. You get down in the ditch.' And he'd set up his machine-gun on top of his car and wait for the Germans to fly over. He'd shoot at them. I don't think he had any success. But he was a real fighting man.

Gunner Robert Angell

To try to bring down the attacking German bombers, we had three-inch anti-aircraft guns down at Dover, within sight of France. Those guns were of First World War vintage. They were so old it was said they had to be drawn from the Imperial War Museum in London. Along came August and the first waves of German bombers came over. At that time, nobody in the country had seen aircraft in such numbers. It was phenomenal to us and, at Dover, we were the first to see them. You'd hear their distant drone and then there they were, all in perfect formation. It was an amazing sight and even more amazing when the formations grew bigger and bigger.

The joke was they were flying at – I can't remember exactly – maybe 23,000 feet. The range of our guns was 16,000 feet! It was hopeless. We could do nothing but watch them going over. To where? We knew not. It all seemed terribly remote. Heinkel 111s. Dornier 17s. The fighters which escorted them gradually came out of range and peeled off to come back. Sometimes they'd have a little sport around Dover. There were about sixteen barrage balloons on wires protecting the harbour, to prevent low level bombing attacks. The German fighters would swoop down on them on their way back to their bases, fire bursts of machine-gun fire and down the lot. It was like a game – could they down all sixteen barrage balloons with three aircraft? When they did, they came within range of our guns; for about two or three minutes all hell was let loose around Dover. These characters roared in and shot down the barrage balloons, which produced the most marvellous fireworks display, while all the guns in the harbour let fly, including our First World War Lewis machine-guns. It really was pandemonium.

Occasionally, one of those German fighters would give off smoke and go off in the distance and we'd claim a victory. It seemed like a game – nothing like war. It wasn't until we read it in the papers the next day that we learned that the bombers had been heading for the airfields.

Prime Minister to Secretary of State for Air, Chief of the Air Staff and Secretary to the War Cabinet
29 August 1940

I was much concerned on visiting Manston Aerodrome yesterday to find that although more than four clear days have passed since it was last raided the greater part of the craters on the landing ground remained unfilled and the aerodrome was barely serviceable. When you remember what the Germans did at the Stavanger aerodrome and the enormous rapidity with which craters were filled I must protest emphatically against this feeble method of repairing damage. Altogether there were one hundred and fifty people available to work, including those that could be provided from the Air Force personnel. These were doing their best. No effective appliances were available, and the whole process appeared disproportionate to the value of maintaining this fighting vantage ground.

All craters should be filled within twenty-four hours at most, and every case where a crater is unfilled for a longer period should be reported to higher authorities ... After the craters had been refilled camouflage effort might be made to pretend they had not been, but this is a refinement.

Air Commodore Gerald Gibbs, Senior Staff Officer, 11 Group

We had trouble with the civilian labour employed to repair runways and so keep our vital airfields in action at this critical time. Every time there was an 'alert' at some of these airfields, the labour would go into the shelter and refuse to carry on. Victor Beamish, that fine character, killed a little later ... tried everything with them – blandishments, exhortation, rewards, insults, all to no avail. They said this was a free country and they weren't going to work. Victor pointed out that it wouldn't be a free country much longer if we didn't get the airfield going, but no good. We put parties of our airmen on the job.

Air Vice Marshal Keith Park

When the German air force had concentrated on bombing my fighter aerodromes, I got such little help from the Air Ministry to repair the bomb damage that I had to borrow some thousands of troops from the British army to fill bomb craters and keep the aerodromes serviceable. For doing so, I was severely criticized by the Air Ministry at the time for accepting army assistance. Had my fighter aerodromes been put out of action, the German air force would have won the battle by 15 September.

E. B. Sharpley, Town Clerk, Stoke-on-Trent
To Major General Sir Robert Gordon-Finlayson, Officer
Commanding Western Command

As you may possibly be aware, for some days past now we have, in this area, been having air raids. Enemy planes have commenced their raids at 10.00 p.m. and have stayed in the area in some cases for several hours. On no occasion has there been, so far as we are aware, the slightest attempt to interfere with their presence or operations, and it is difficult to come to any other conclusion than that the enemy must know that there are, in this area, no defences, and is taking advantage of it. Cannot some steps be taken to afford to the area some degree of protection, even though that degree is a small one?

Sir Charles McGrath, Clerk of the Peace, West Riding of Yorkshire To Air Chief Marshal Dowding, 2 September

You will have received a report of the enemy air attack on Bradford and the extensive damage done to industrial, shop and house property in the centre of the city. I spent some hours there yesterday and was informed that the Fire Brigade, Rescue and Repair Parties and other Civil Defence services and Home Guard behaved splendidly. But there was grave concern about the complete absence of any air defence. There are no anti-aircraft guns guarding the city and during the protracted time that the enemy took to deliver his attack – roughly from 10.30 on the Saturday night to 4.00 on the Sunday morning – there was no interference whatever by our air force and the enemy was left to have it all his own way. That this is a 'people's war' has become commonplace, and the people are told that we cannot lose the war unless the civilian population lose their nerve. The morale of the people of Yorkshire is very high, but the absence of protection from air attacks puts an added strain on them, and they would be considerably heartened and enabled to view a continuance of the nightly air attacks with more composure if they could be assured that measures will be taken to defend them from the enemy by adequate ground and air defences.

Letter marked by Dowding's office, 'Routine reply despatched.'

Fighter Command Headquarters

Air Chief Marshal Sir Hugh Dowding wishes to state that he is in receipt of numerous communications from public bodies, industrial firms and private individuals, containing criticisms of the defence, particularly at night, and suggestions for improvement.

While such communications are carefully perused and receive

detailed consideration, Sir Hugh regrets that the very great pressure on his duties precludes his entering into correspondence with individuals. He would, however, offer the following general comments:

i) The limited defence resources of the country must be concentrated on decisive points.

ii) Not every aeroplane heard at night is necessarily hostile. Successful night interceptions are not infrequent, and efforts to effect night interceptions are never relaxed.

iii) Neither side is at present capable of putting a stop to night raiding on the part of the other.

iv) Scientific advances give promise of a greatly increased percentage of successful night interceptions before very long.

Mrs H. E. Miles
War Journal, 4 September

There was an air raid today just as we were sitting at lunch. The charwoman and I went down to the cellar and invited the postwoman (who was calling at that moment for ten shillings due on a big parcel from America of Guava jelly, tins of soup and ten pounds of sugar) to come down also. R. stood by the open front door and was amazed at the speed of the dogfight. One plane came down on Netley Heath. We saw the smoke coming out over the hill. Later, R. went up there and a Canadian soldier told him how they went to secure the airmen, as it was quite near their camp. Apparently some of the crew were blown to smithereens and a hand of one of the Hun fliers was proudly carried round the tents by a French Canadian soldier, on show. How terribly sad – how often had that boy's mother held his hand tenderly!

War Cabinet Minutes
4 September

The importance of adequate sleep should be emphasized. The people should be told that it was up to them to see that the enemy did not succeed, by sending over a few planes each night, both in directly holding up production and in affecting it indirectly by depriving workers of their sleep ... The 'red' warning should be given sparingly at night, the 'purple' warning being used to ensure the adoption of essential safety measures.

Ruth Roberts

My daughter Susan, who was about five at the time, was playing with her little friend, Katie, outside our house in Nether Wallop when Southampton, which was about twenty miles away, was attacked by German bombers. I remember Katie stopping playing and asking in awe when she heard the explosions, 'Was that thunder?' Susan said, 'Don't be silly. That's only bombs.'

Our black spaniel, Donald, gave us early warning. He could hear the planes coming towards us before we could and would run upstairs to hide under the bed.

Frank Banham, Air Raid Precautions Officer, Gillingham, Kent
7 September

Following any enemy raid, there is a definite probability of unexploded bombs being present. It has to be assumed, for the purposes of public safety, that they are all of the delayed action type.

For this reason, it is necessary that the area around any unexploded bomb should be kept clear for at least eighty hours, preferably longer. On open ground, the position of an unexploded bomb is quite often marked by a clean round hole a foot or more across, depending on the size of the bomb, with no sign of any crater or discoloration due to smoke and fumes, but identification is far less simple if the unexploded bomb falls on buildings, pavement and so on.

Mrs Gwladys Cox
War Diary, 6 September, 10.00 a.m.

During this morning's raid at 9.00 a.m., we watched an air battle in the sky to the northeast, over Hampstead and Camden Town. Not a plane was to be seen, but remarkable tracings, straight lines, curves, spirals, all twisting and turning in the sky, marking the swift passage of aircraft in battle. The heating and cooling of the air caused by the progress of fast planes is said to produce these vapour trails – a really beautiful and symmetrical pattern was made on this occasion.

9.45 p.m. A raid is on, the alert having sounded during the nine o'clock news. We feel it risky to retire, if you can call it that, so sit in the drawing room reading and writing, listening for guns and crashes. This is the fourth alert since breakfast. It has been a marvellously fine day, very hot, but not oppressive. Jane rang up to inquire, 'How are we enjoying life?' She said a bomb had fallen in the Harrow Road, at the end of her road, last night. She heard the plomp!

Housewife Magazine

Have you packed a kitbag or basket ready to take into the shelter with you, along with your gas mask, when the sirens sound? It is a good plan to have ready: 1) some cotton wool for swabbing cuts; 2) absorbent gauze for dressing a cut; 3) a kitbag to hold all these oddments; 4) a triangular bandage in case of fractures; 5) safety pins; 6) sal volatile; 7) tannic acid jelly for treating burns; 8) sticking plaster; 9) bleach ointment for blister gas casualties; 10) small bandages; 11) boric lint for application to wounds; 12) scissors; 13) elastoplast dressings; 14) ear plugs to deaden noise (cotton wool does just as well); 15) iodine; 16) a metal mirror and comb; 17) a bottle of antiseptic; 18) a pencil for use in making a tourniquet; 19) a jemmy (a useful tool in case of the door jamming, or if there is some debris to clear); 20) toys for the children; 21) a reliable torch (include a spare battery as well); 22) chocolate; 23) chewing gum to soothe the nerves of smokers who must not smoke in the refuge room. Some cold food and something to drink might also be added to this list.

New York Herald Tribune

London, 31 August – In twelve months of war, the face of London has changed ... In their homes and at work, in shops, restaurants and theatres, by radio and by newspaper and by the sound of pulsing engines overhead, the men and women of London are continually reminded that Europe is at war, that the empire is in danger and that their country requires of them hard work and sacrifice until the Battle of Britain and the war of which it is part are brought to a successful end.

Looking at the sky during the day, the Londoner sees countless silver-grey balloons tugging at the cables which hold them at sentry duty over the city. At night, he gropes his way along darkened streets, in danger of stumbling over sandbags piled in front of every second house, or of running head-on into a camouflaged pillbox at some strategic corner.

* * *

During this moment of crisis for Britain, a simmering clash of views and personalities within the upper echelons of Fighter Command came to the boil, and though it had no bearing on the outcome of the battle, it generated bitterness still felt by men who experienced the sometimes dramatic consequences.

11 Group Commander Keith Park, whose squadrons were most heavily engaged in the defence of Britain at the time, was in full accord with Fighter Command Commander-in-Chief Sir Hugh Dowding on strategy and tactics. Dowding and Park were given access to reports from ULTRA, the very hush-hush operation in which a special, top secret British intelligence unit monitored and decoded streams of German secret military communications. They, therefore, had some prior knowledge of Luftwaffe plans and operations. This knowledge reinforced Dowding's determination to disrupt and repel the German onslaught by intercepting raiders whenever and wherever they appeared over Britain. With British forces outnumbered and the raids growing in frequency and coming in at short notice, that meant regularly sending up small numbers of defenders to clash with and try to disperse large enemy formations.

10 Group Commander Quintin Brand agreed there was no acceptable alternative to this approach. But 12 Group Commander Trafford Leigh-Mallory, who, like Brand, knew nothing of the ULTRA secrets, thought Dowding's tactics were fundamentally mistaken. Leigh-Mallory was convinced the German assault could be more quickly and more decisively thrown back if the attackers were challenged by big wings of British fighters, consisting of several squadrons fighting as a unit. He also bridled at the relative inactivity imposed on the squadrons under his command by Dowding's insistence on keeping his reserves intact in case the Germans, with their vastly superior numbers, suddenly exerted even greater pressure than they had already.

One of Leigh-Mallory's squadron leaders was the remarkable, thirty-year-old Douglas Bader. Bader had lost both his legs in a flying display accident nine years earlier but, with the aid of artificial legs and an indomitable will, he had returned to active flying duty with the RAF when the war began. A forceful personality and, like Leigh-Mallory, frustrated at having to perform only a secondary role in the battle, Bader insisted 'Big Wing' tactics, which would finally bring him into the centre of the battle, were right and energetically promoted them. He was able to persuade Leigh-Mallory to authorize the formation and dispatch of the 12 Group 'Duxford Wing', which

Bader led, though it was contrary to Dowding's ideas and orders and infuriated many people in 11 Group, where the battle was being fought. Park later charged that the 12 Group Big Wing 'on several occasions allowed my fighting aerodromes to be heavily bombed' because, in effect, forming it up delayed the dispatch of requested back-up.

Flight Lieutenant Sir Archibald Hope

The theory of the Big Wing was: if you had a raid of say fifty 109s coming in with a lot of bombers below it, one of our squadrons of twelve aircraft couldn't do very much against them. You might shoot down four or five 109s. You might shoot down a couple of the bombers. But you couldn't really stop the raid. However – so the theory went – if you had twenty-four or more aircraft up there, you'd stand a better chance of stopping it. But Leigh-Mallory and Douglas Bader were absolutely wrong about the Big Wing. Keith Park had no option. The way the Germans were coming in, he hadn't got time to form up Big Wings. He hadn't got enough squadrons. He had to get his aircraft airborne as quickly as he damn well could, in such numbers as he could.

Aside from that, Leigh-Mallory and Keith Park hated each other's guts. They couldn't stand each other. If one said it was the right way to do something, the other would be quite certain to say it was the wrong way.

Squadron Leader George Darley

The Big Wing was a damned silly idea. It was an offensive rather than a defensive formation – and we were on the defensive. It was far too unwieldy. Everybody would be in the air at the same time and then everybody would be landing at the same time. We'd all be down re-arming and refuelling when the next wave of Germans came in and we'd be caught on the ground.

The success of the Big Wing came later, when we went on the offensive over France. Then we held all the cards in our hands, and not only in greater numbers of fighters. We had all the tactical advantages then, as well. We were able to select our own weather, time, routes, targets, concentration of forces and, above all, surprise. We had none of those during the Battle of Britain and, therefore, the Big Wing was a mistake at that time.

Not only that. We in 10 Group were often called on to help 11 Group, guarding their airfields when most of their squadrons were away or re-arming and refuelling on the ground. Keith Park would call our AOC, Quintin Brand, and say, 'Please can I have a couple of your squadrons.' Of course, Brand sent them along. Park also called Leigh-Mallory for help, but Leigh-Mallory wanted to have his aircraft in the air at the same time as the 11 Group squadrons. He didn't like being out of the limelight. It would have meant all 11 and 12 Group aircraft re-arming and refuelling on the ground at the same time, an easy target for the German bombers. Dowding should have told Leigh-Mallory to pipe down. Unfortunately, instead he told Park and Leigh-Mallory to sort it out among themselves. Dowding was a tough nut, but wasn't up to dealing with Leigh-Mallory.

Air Vice Marshal Keith Park

On a few dozen occasions when I had sent every available squadron of 11 Group to engage the main enemy attack as far forward as possible, I called on 12 Group to send a couple of squadrons to defend a fighter airfield or other vital targets which were threatened by outflanking and smaller bomber raids. Instead of sending two squadrons quickly to protect the vital target, 12 Group delayed while they dispatched a large wing of four or five squadrons, which wasted valuable time ... Consequently, they invariably arrived too late to prevent the enemy bombing the target. On scores of days I called on 10 Group on my right for a few squadrons to protect some vital target. Never on any occasion can I remember this Group failing to send its squadrons promptly to the place requested, thus saving thousands of civilian lives and also the naval dockyards of Portsmouth, the port of Southampton and aircraft factories.

Flight Lieutenant Brian Kingcome

In those days, you didn't want one vast flying circus to meet the Germans. You wanted to cover as much of the big sky as possible. You didn't need thirty-six or forty-eight aircraft to break up a bomber formation. You needed six or eight or twelve aircraft flying straight through the middle of it.

219

Squadron Leader Tom Gleave

Apart from the fact that we didn't have enough aircraft to keep putting a Big Wing aloft, there was a question of the time it took. If you wanted to send one squadron, it took fourteen minutes for it to get to 20,000 feet. Two squadrons took eighteen minutes. Three squadrons – about twenty-six minutes. Four squadrons – thirty-four to thirty-six minutes. And five squadrons, which is what Leigh-Mallory was aiming at, took forty-five to forty-eight minutes to form up and get to 20,000 feet. By then, the raid it would have been sent to meet would have been over and by using so many squadrons, subsequent raids coming in would arrive unchallenged. The result would have been catastrophe.

12 Group was supposed to cover Biggin Hill, Kenley, Northolt and the other 11 Group airfields while 11 Group squadrons were off the ground meeting the Hun coming in. It failed to do this. I know of at least one occasion when Keith Park rang up 12 Group and said, 'You're supposed to look after my airfields.' He got no change out of that. Of thirty-two Big Wings sent off by 12 Group, only seven met the enemy and only once did the Big Wing get there first, before the bombs were dropped.

Pilot Officer Wally Wallens

The Wing always arrived too late. Had those planes in the Wing come to our help in sections or flights or even squadrons, they would have got where they should have been much more quickly and we would have got the support we should have got.

Pilot Officer John Ellacombe

We knew the 12 Group Big Wing got airborne on a few occasions. But it never got down to where we were in time. On a day that the North Weald aerodrome was bombed – and I, incidentally, lost all my kit in the raid – we were off over the Thames Estuary, trying to fight off a German raid. The rear of our sector, including North Weald, should have been guarded by the Duxford Wing but it was still forming up at the time and missed the bombers.

Marshal of the RAF Sir John Slessor, Chief of the Air Staff, 1950–1952

One cannot help admiring old Stuffy. He had his faults and was never an easy man to deal with. My only criticism of his handling of Fighter Command in the Battle is that the first essential of a C-in-C is to see that his subordinate commanders (a) understand and (b) fall in completely with his strategic instructions – and sack them if they do not ... L-M was an old friend of mine ... and I liked him. But he never should have been allowed to take the line he did ... I like to think that if I'd have been in Stuffy's place I would ... much earlier have told L-M to shut up and get on with commanding his group in accordance with what he knew quite well was my policy.

Flying Officer Hugh Dundas

I don't think either the critics or the proponents of the Big Wing had it quite right. The Wing was too big and was probably operated from the wrong place and by the wrong headquarters. It should have been operated by 11 Group, not 12 Group. Some sort of wing tactics could have been made to work and to work effectively.

Flight Lieutenant Gordon Sinclair

We felt the Big Wing was the correct way of operating because you were able to give yourself cover; for example, up sun. If you were flying blind as a single squadron or flight or section and had no cover up sun, you were terribly vulnerable. Flying as a wing, you could move people out to protect your tail, which is what we did.

We were generally late when called into 11 Group, but we were operating from eighty miles north of London while the bombs were being dropped mostly around the Thames Estuary and on the airfields. There was no hope of our getting there if we were alerted late, had delays on the airfield and then had to get to 20,000 feet, which took a very long time. Even if the squadrons had gone off in flights, there still would have been those ridiculous delays when we were waiting for clearance to get off the ground. We'd be all ready to take off, pointing into the wind, ready for the word to go. But we had to wait. Our engines would get overheated and our tempers would get frayed. I think it was because of hesitation between the two Group headquarters, saying do we want them off or don't we want them off. There were terrible differences of opinion about who should be called in and when.

And when we did get off and got down to North Weald, we'd circle there for ages, knowing there was a bloody great battle going on further south. We certainly had the impression that, for reasons we couldn't understand, we weren't called in quickly enough.

But I was only a pilot, commanding a flight. I wasn't particularly involved in major thought about it all. One didn't feel called upon to think ahead. One of the few people who did think ahead was Douglas Bader, who looked at things totally differently. He wanted to get mixed into the battle and realized that unless he fought like hell to get mixed in, he'd be left out.

F. W. Winterbotham, Chief of the Air Department of the British Secret Intelligence Service during the Second World War

If, as Göring and Leigh-Mallory had wanted, Dowding had sent up mass formations of our own fighters, not only would they have been far less manoeuverable in attack on the German formations, but the balance of losses, which was in our favour when small formations of RAF fighters got in amongst the massed German aircraft, would have been lost.

From where I sat, there was no adverse doubt at all about the way in which Dowding was fighting the battle, and his understanding and interpreting of ULTRA was obviously an important contribution to our success in this part of the war. Security dictated that only a very few people should get Göring's signals (which ULTRA intercepted), and no doubt some of the young pilots in the Midlands felt the other fellows in the south were getting the glory. I watched Dowding and Park handle the ULTRA with supreme care, never hinting that the top secret alerts, which were given to the key sector aerodrome commanders, had come from intercepted signals.

Dowding's strategy of always having some fighters available to go up and meet every raid not only foxed the Germans as to our actual fighter strength, but also gradually wore down the morale of the Luftwaffe.

Sergeant David Cox

There was a feeling among us in 12 Group that 11 Group was trying to keep the battle to itself. We wanted to see more of the action. It was ridiculous if you knew the enemy was a few miles south and you weren't supposed to intercept or pursue them. We often didn't take any notice. We went south of the Thames anyway and it caused a row.

As for talk that 12 Group didn't provide cover for 11 Group when it was asked to, it wasn't as simple as that. Sometimes there was faulty information. Sometimes, when we were asked to cover an airfield and we spotted the enemy not far away, we went after them. It may have been a diversion to get us away. There were mistakes.

Once Debden airfield was bombed from 1,000 feet, below cloud, while we were sitting up at 15,000 feet. That was a mistake, but not ours. The Observer Corps reported the Germans were coming at 1,000 feet. But the 11 Group Controllers just didn't believe it because it had never happened before and they thought a nought had accidentally been left off the report coming in. So the report they passed to us was German bombers at 10,000 feet instead of 1,000. We were waiting up there, above the cloud. The Germans came in below and we didn't see them. We got the blame. That was unfair.

You had to admire Douglas Bader. You couldn't like him – there was this element of snobbishness about him. I don't think he thought much of sergeant pilots. But he was an inspiration. His voice over the radio, when we were outnumbered in the air, gave us all confidence. He knew how to say the right thing at the right time up there.

Squadron Leader Jack Satchell

Douglas Bader was a great man. I knew him before he lost his legs. He was an impossibly cocky young man because everything he tried to do, he did brilliantly. There were five squadrons at Duxford. Woody Woodhall, the station commander, said each of the squadron commanders would lead the Big Wing in turn when it was operational. But the four others of us agreed that Douglas was such a damned good leader that he should be regular wing leader.

When we arrived at Northolt towards the end of the Battle of Britain, Keith Park came to welcome us to 11 Group, which was a very good show. But he spoilt it on learning that we had been operating in the Duxford Big Wing, of which he most strongly disapproved. He treated me to a long dissertation on the uselessness of the Duxford Wing and how any little success it had was due entirely to the kindness of heart of 11 Group in inviting us to come and join in after most of the job had already been done by 11 Group squadrons. He said every time the Big Wing had seen any action, the 11 Group squadrons had already broken up the Hun formations and we had merely been cleaning up Hun stragglers.

That was different to my view on the subject. I remember those huge formations of Germans we ran into. Maybe they were stragglers, but I doubt it. There was a shocking amount of petty jealousy going on between 11 and 12 Group. I think it was chiefly due to Park, which was a great pity because he was a very fine AOC and the man who really saved Britain. Leigh-Mallory was almost as fine an AOC, but he had little opportunity to do much except push out those balbos.

'Balbos' were named after Italo Balbo, the Italian aviator and military tactician who pioneered the deployment of large formations of attack aircraft.

Pilot Officer Dennis David

Pilots were killed in 11 Group who would not have been killed had 12 Group taken a greater part in the battle. We were screaming for them. But they weren't there. They had a lot of good chaps in 12 Group. Many of them wanted badly to be down with us.

Pilot Officer Peter Brown

We were doing patrols at the end of August, but we weren't getting much action up in 12 Group. We wanted to get into the battle. We knew what was happening in 11 Group. There was a sense of frustration. I went to the CO and asked, 'Why can't we get transferred down?' He said, 'We'd all like to go.'

Pilot Officer Bobby Oxspring

Our squadron commander was a great personal friend of Douglas Bader. Sometimes, after an action, Bader would land at our airfield and come to have a cup of coffee and chat about tactics. He was a bit frustrated because Keith Park never seemed to ask for help from 12 Group. He certainly didn't ask for help as much as he might have. Bader said that many a time, when he was in a nice position and could hear on the radio what was going on, he'd want to sally forth and help out, but was told not to go.

Squadron Leader Tom Gleave

Douglas Bader was completely wrong on tactics at the time. He was very brave. But he'd been out of the air force for ten years. He lagged completely behind in modern concepts. All he could think of, as far as I could see, was the old First World War flying circuses, which had nothing to do with what we were up against in the Battle of Britain.

Pilot Officer Denis Crowley-Milling

For my part, there has never been a leader to match Douglas Bader. As young, relatively inexperienced pilots we were completely captivated by him and his indomitable fighting spirit. He never ceased to encourage us and, most of all, he helped us to conquer our fears. In the air over the radio, he kept up a constant flow of talk, cracked jokes and made us all feel twice the men we were. I have always thought how lucky I was to have been under his guidance throughout the Battle of Britain.

Flying Officer Barrie Heath

People in 11 Group told us, 'We don't know what you buggers are doing in those great big balbos. You'd do a damn sight better if you did some real fighting instead of going around in a huge formation, being nothing but a bloody nuisance.' Normally, my response was, 'Balls!' or words to that effect.

Take-offs of the Wing were always fairly fraught because Douglas Bader was short-tempered. He was always in a hurry. He always had a good aircraft. He'd whiz off and expect everybody to stick with him and be able to climb as fast as he could. When you were manoeuvering three or four squadrons, it wasn't easy keeping in the same piece of air at the same time. You'd be going flat out one minute, throttling back the next, trying to stay in some sort of formation. There wasn't a lot of radio help in those days. VHF radio was just about coming in.

I'd known Bader before the battle started. He was a bombastic, aggressive CO. We had eyed him with great suspicion. I don't think our feelings towards him turned to admiration until the time he was leading the Duxford Wing. We all came together under his leadership. We suddenly realized he was a bloody good leader and not a bad chap. But he was a very hard taskmaster.

* * *

Differences over the Big Wing remained pronounced and bitter and relations between the 11 and 12 Group commanders continued to be strained. But circumstances did not permit the luxury of indulging in intra-mural squabbles. With Fighter Command wondering, as each gruelling day came to a close, whether it would have the men and the planes to turn back the Germans when the next dawn broke, Britain's situation was extremely precarious.

Kept for the most part in the dark, the British public remained almost casually confident of ultimate victory. But awareness of how desperate things really had become was not confined to the upper echelons of the government and the military services in London. In Washington, United States Secretary of the Interior Harold Ickes noted in his diary that there were reports that Britain might be forced by the German onslaught to sue for peace. However, no one knew more than the men of Fighter Command exactly how close to the brink of disaster their country had been brought.

Air Chief Marshal Sir Hugh Dowding

When the Germans found that our fighters could deliver a well-timed attack on the bombers before their fighters could intervene, or when our fighters attacked from ahead or below, each move was met by a counter-move on the part of the Germans so that, in September, fighter escorts were flying inside the bomber formations, others were below, and a series of fighters stretched upward to 30,000 feet or more. One squadron leader described his impression of the appearance of one of these raids. He said it was like looking up the escalator at Piccadilly Circus.

Flight Lieutenant Alan Deere

I thought towards the end of August that we were on a bit of a loser. Each time we went up, there seemed to be more and more Germans up there.

Squadron Leader Sandy Johnstone

If the airfields had got another heavy thumping, I'm not sure we could have stood it.

CRISIS

Pilot Officer Pat Hancock

Had they gone on bombing the airfields, I might have been speaking German instead of English today, except I wouldn't still be here.

LONDON'S BURNING

German bomber pilots were instructed to steer clear of London unless specifically ordered to attack the British capital. Their primary target was Fighter Command, its bases and its supply installations. Destroying those would give the Luftwaffe mastery of the skies over England and pave the way for the conquest of Britain. Bombing London would be a pointless diversion which might create problems.

But on the night of 24 August, German bombers, seeking designated targets near London, lost their way in the dark and, without knowing exactly where they were, jettisoned their bomb loads over the centre of the city. The British did not intend to let such an incident, and the impact it might have on public morale, pass without a suitable rejoinder. RAF Bomber Command was instructed to retaliate against Berlin. It was one of the most important decisions of the Second World War.

For several nights, British bombers struck at the German capital, which Göring had solemnly promised would never be a target of enemy aircraft. Damage done to Berlin was not extensive, but damage done to the pride of the Nazi leaders was enormous. They were furious and vowed that the British would pay for their effrontery with the destruction of their cities.

On 7 September, the Luftwaffe launched its first mass raid on London. It marked the beginning of the fourth phase of the Battle of Britain. Commercial and residential areas of the densely inhabited metropolis were blasted that day and in the days and weeks that followed. London's docks were turned into roaring infernos. There were many casualties and widespread devastation. Bombs fell on Westminster Abbey, the Houses of Parliament and Buckingham Palace. The people of the British capital were beginning to experience what the people of Warsaw, Rotterdam and other cities had earlier suffered. But coming at a time when the Luftwaffe had finally brought Fighter Command to the verge of collapse, the bombing of London had a far different significance – for Britain, for Germany, and for the direction the war would take.

Flight Lieutenant A. D. Murray

11 Group commander Keith Park summoned his station commanders, senior squadron commanders and Controllers to a conference.
He said, 'Gentlemen, I don't know how much longer we can keep this
up. But somebody has dropped a bomb on Berlin.'

It didn't mean much to me at the time. 'Bombed Berlin. Good.'
But he obviously meant the higher command believed that as soon as
Berlin was bombed, the Luftwaffe's target would shift from our
fighter airfields to London, which would give us a breather.

Reichsmarshal Hermann Göring

AN IMMEDIATE REPORT IS REQUIRED IDENTIFYING THOSE CREWS
WHO DROPPED BOMBS WITHIN THE PERIMETER OF LONDON. LUFT-
WAFFE HIGH COMMAND WILL ITSELF UNDERTAKE THE PUNISHMENT
OF EACH AIRCRAFT CAPTAIN INVOLVED. THEY WILL BE POSTED TO
INFANTRY REGIMENTS.

Adolf Hitler

Mr Churchill is demonstrating his new brainchild, the night air raid
[on German cities]. Mr Churchill is carrying out these raids not
because they promise to be highly effective, but because his air force
cannot fly over German soil in daylight. For three months I did not
answer because I believed that this madness [the war] would be
stopped. Mr Churchill took this as a sign of weakness. We are now
answering night for night. When the British air force drops three or
four thousand kilograms of bombs, we will in one night drop two
hundred, three hundred or four hundred thousand kilograms. When
they declare they will increase their attacks on our cities, then we will
raze their cities to the ground. We will stop the handiwork of these
night pirates, so help us God ... The hour will come when one of us
will break, and it will not be National Socialist Germany!

Pilot Officer Steve Stephen

One German bomber formation stretched from over London right
out towards Southend, twenty miles long or more and, I suppose,
about a quarter of a mile wide. And with an escort of fighters above.

It was a breathtaking sight. You couldn't help feeling you'd never again ever see anything as remarkable as that.

Squadron Leader Sandy Johnstone

I'd never seen so many aircraft. It was a hazy sort of day right up to about 16,000 feet. As we broke through the haze, you could hardly believe it. As far as you could see, there was nothing but German aircraft coming in, wave after wave. We lost Harry Moody and Roger Coverly that day. We never discovered what happened to Harry. They found Roger's aircraft the day after, I think, but it was two weeks before they found his body. He'd come down by parachute. He was very much dead, caught up in a tree about ten miles from where his aircraft had come down.

Pilot Officer Jan Zumbach

We were climbing at full speed when I saw a burst of ack-ack fire over London harbour and then, a little to the right, below us, a formation of German bombers escorted by a surprisingly large number of Me 109s. Coming from the south, the bombers approached the Thames to drop their bombs and then turn north. I thought we were going to rush at the enemy, but this was not so. It seemed that the squadron leader, a British officer, did not realize exactly which direction the bombers were taking. Then I heard someone shout in Polish, 'Attack! Follow me!' It was Lieutenant Paskiewicz, a very experienced pilot, who shook his wings to show the others he was leaving the formation. He started to attack and was immediately followed by the other sections, and also by the leader, who now understood the manoeuvre.

In front of me, two Dorniers were already on fire and parachutes were opening in the sky. The German bombers were approaching at tremendous speed. My leader was already firing. It was my turn. I pressed the button. Nothing happened. I swore violently. Already I had to move out. Tracer bullets were whizzing by on all sides and then I realized I had forgotten to release the safety switch.

Turning violently, crushed down by centrifugal force, bent in two, I found myself on the tail of a stream of bombers, with a Dornier 215 in front of me growing bigger and bigger in my sights, until it blotted out everything else. I saw the rear gunner aiming at me. I pressed the button and the rattle of my eight machine-guns shook my plane. A long cloud of smoke came out of the Dornier's left engine. Another burst and it was ablaze. Over the radio, everyone was shouting, in English, in Polish.

I saw a Hurricane having trouble with a bandit. I was about to rush to his help when the Hurricane burst into flames. A parachute opened up almost immediately. It was Flying Officer Daszewski who had been able to bale out after losing half of his left buttock to a burst of Messerschmitt gunfire. Flying Officer Pisarek also had to jump, leaving one of his boots stuck in his burning plane. He landed in a suburban garden full of roses. A man came over to him and said, 'Sir, I would like you to know this is private property,' and then invited him to tea. Pisarek was terribly embarrassed because he was without that missing boot and he had a hole in his sock.

Cabinet War Room Summary
Enemy Aircraft Activity, 7 September

At 11.30 about seventy aircraft crossed our coast near Folkestone, thirty turning west towards Hastings, the rest spreading out over east Kent ... Enemy formations totalling some ninety aircraft commenced an attack on London and Thames Estuary areas at about 16.30. These were followed half an hour later by a second wave involving 250 aircraft and by 18.00 a heavy attack had been made on industrial and dock property on both sides of the Thames ... At dusk, enemy activity recommenced and from 20.10 until 04.30, a stream of single aircraft crossed the coast between Beachy Head and Dungeness, their main objectives being docks, railway and power stations in the Greater London area ... A few aircraft also reached Liverpool, Birmingham and South Wales ...

Preliminary reports do not permit an accurate review of the damage caused in the London area, but a great number of key points were hit and probably damaged, affecting chiefly food storage, flour mills, granaries and oil installations. In dockland, severe damage was caused to the Royal Victoria and Albert Docks, the East and West India Docks, Millwall and London Docks and serious fires necessitated the complete evacuation of Silvertown. In the case of railways, many lines in east and south London have been blocked and approximately nineteen stations hit and damaged. The southern entrance to the Rotherhithe Tunnel has been blocked.

Associated Press

Berlin, 8 September – An unending German offensive by all types of planes hurled 'several million pounds' of bombs on London yesterday and last night in an onslaught so gigantic that the Nazis said it put everything previous 'in the shade'. German sources emphasized the strength of British defences, but said the British were unable to stem the continuous waves of attacking planes.

Chicago Sunday Tribune

London, 8 September – The mightiest aerial assault ever made upon this capital raged on early today amid fire-reddened skies and exploding bombs in the heart of the city. Flames touched off by Nazi incendiary bombs set the sky aglow ... The Germans struck the most savage blow yet to fall in the battle for Britain at 8.32 p.m. last night, after a heavy daylight raid of hundreds of planes, which itself broke through the city's inner defences.

Anthony Weymouth
Personal Journal, 8 September

We are alive, but we have passed a night such as I never wish to spend again. We have been lying in the dark on our mattresses for eight hours listening to the characteristic drone of the German aircraft. They seemed to be flying round and round our flat. How close are they? Have they passed? Yes. No – for the exhaust, which was becoming less loud, is now increasing again. And then – the first bomb fell. I could hear the swish and then the explosion, which shook even this apparently sturdy building. I switched on a torch and I heard Audrey say, 'Steady, peoples.' It seemed a matter of seconds only before a new sound reached us. The clanging of bells, as one after another, the fire-engines raced along the Marylebone Road. The sounds grew in intensity, then became less and less ... I switched out the torch and lay down. I could hear Hod [his son] turning over on his mattress. Quite suddenly, I heard the drone of an aeroplane, and almost immediately, the shattering noise of a bomb exploding. How near was it? We had no experience by which to judge. All I knew was that the building shook, and my heart raced. Subconsciously, I was waiting to hear the crash of falling masonry. But silence followed the shattering crash. Once more, I lay down, my heart thumping against my ribs. Would this nightmare never end? It was only just after two o'clock. The Huns could – and doubtless would – keep it up till daylight.

And they did. A constant drone and bomb after bomb. We heard the 'All clear' about 4.30 and promptly went to sleep on our mattresses.

Pilot Officer Denis Wissler
Diary, 8 September

What complete swines these Jerries are.

Mrs Gwladys Cox
War Diary, 9 September, 7.45 a.m.

What an awful night! Last evening, after a fairly quiet day, we settled down at 8.00 p.m. to listen to the National Prayer Day Wireless Service, when the sirens wailed. Almost immediately, we heard the nearest and most intense gunfire yet. From the windows, we saw ... large fires and as we gazed, holding our breath, swift stabs of flame shot down from the sky in quick succession. Every stab sent up a vivid flash of flame while, already, a high wall of pure lightning-coloured fire glowed for miles along the eastern horizon. The rest of London was aflame with searchlights, bursting shells, floating flares and the quaking radiance of Molotov bread baskets – and *the noise*! Booms, bangs, pops, crashes, screams, warden's whistles – while below, in the inky street, the traffic crawled, dim-lit, ghostlike. I gasped, shut the window and suddenly felt we should no longer remain in the flat.

Hurriedly packing Bob into his basket and collecting rugs and pillows, we made for our basement shelter. Here we remained till 5.30 a.m. The place, though dusty and gloomy, is dry, and being below ground and surrounded by walls, comparatively protected. We were soon joined by Mr and Mrs Veasey, she lying on a mattress on the floor, he sitting bolt upright in a chair. We used our deck chairs, covered with rugs and eiderdowns, while a boxstand did for a table to hold our only light, a candle. Before we settled down, Mrs Samuels, warden of the shelter next door, looked in and seemed rather disgusted with conditions, declaring the place altogether 'too stuffy'.

SCRAMBLE

Helen Kirkpatrick, Chicago Daily News

London, 9 September – It is pretty incredible to find people relatively unshaken after the terrific experience. There is some terror, but nothing on the scale that the Germans may have hoped for and certainly not on the scale to make Britons contemplate for a moment anything but fighting on. Fright becomes so mingled with a deep almost uncontrollable anger that it is hard to know when one stops and the other begins.

Squadron Leader Sandy Johnstone

It's a terrible thing to say, but it was an immense relief when we realized they weren't coming for the airfields again. They were going for London. I thought, 'Sorry about this, London,' but it was the thing that saved us. By taking it, the Londoners gave the fighter chaps a chance to recover.

Winston Churchill

We never thought of the struggle in terms of the defence of London or any other place, but only who won in the air ... If the enemy had persisted in heavy attacks against the [airfields] and damaged their Operations Rooms or telephone communications, the whole intricate organization of Fighter Command might have broken down.

Joyce Atwood

When the docks were bombed, they were devastated. Whole areas north and south of the Thames – Millwall, East India Docks, Silvertown – were so badly damaged that many of the people living there had to be moved. In our own area, South Woodford, we had people brought to us who were cared for in our church hall. They were fed and found places to sleep until they could be rehoused in more suitable accommodations.

Daily Mail, *9 September*

It would be foolish to underestimate the severity of the ordeal. It would be unfair and foolish for the British public to be allowed only to read frank accounts of the damage after they have appeared in United States newspapers. The *Daily Mail* urges the Ministry of Information to tell the daily story with the utmost candour consistent with national safety. For one thing, the whole truth is never so alarming as fiction, passing from mouth to mouth, bred on half-truths or a suppression of the truth. For another, the full story of the fortitude of the people who have suffered and may suffer is to our race a noble inspiration, to the world an example, and to the Nazis a bitter and ominous report.

Lord Mayor of London
Broadcast to America

The city of London has never in her long annals been called upon to face an ordeal so cruel and so searching as that through which she has in these days been passing. Her long established traditions of safe and settled ways have been assaulted as never before, and her peaceful citizens have been subjected to the ruthless cruelty of an embittered foe bent upon her destruction. Today London stands as the very bulwark of civilization and freedom as we know it. It is the greatest responsibility that the world has ever known. It is the endurance of Londoners – that courage which they are showing – which will save the civilized people of the world.

Edward R. Murrow, CBS Radio News

London, 10 September – We are told today that the Germans believe Londoners, after a while, will rise up and demand a new government, one that will make peace with Germany. It's more probable that they'll rise up and murder a few German pilots who come down by parachute. The life of a parachutist would not be worth much in the East End of London tonight.

The politicians who called this a 'people's war' were right, probably more right than they knew at the time. I've seen some horrible sights in this city during these days and nights, but not once have I heard man, woman or child suggest that Britain should throw in her hand. These people are angry. How much they can stand, I don't know. The strain is very great.

Sergeant Tom Naylor

When London was being bombed, a pilot from one of the squadrons at our airfield had to bale out over east London. He came to earth in a little front garden of a house in Goresbrook Road. The first thing he saw when he disentangled himself was the door of the house opening and a large woman coming out holding a brass fireplace fender. She thought he was a Hun. There he was, in a dogfight a few minutes before, and now running down Goresbrook Road with a woman chasing him with a brass fender till he found a policeman to straighten things out.

Flight Lieutenant Gordon Sinclair

We were in a very tight formation. Johnnie Boulton was in the section behind me. We suddenly saw all these bombers and started to break up to go after them. I was getting ready to attack a Dornier. I don't really know what happened next. I don't know whether I pulled the throttle back too quickly, whether I hit Johnnie or he hit me. But our wings hit. I lost a wing. Johnnie went down and was killed and I think I collided with the Dornier. I was in too much of a panic about getting out to realize exactly what was happening.

I got out and parachuted down, landing on Coulsdon High Street near Croydon, spraining my ankle landing on the edge of the pavement. I lay there rather surprised to find myself still alive. Then a toe sort of turned me over in the gutter and a chap said, 'Good God, Gordon, what are you doing lying there?' It was a chap I'd been at school with. He was in the Irish Guards at Caterham Barracks not far away. He'd seen a parachute coming down and was rather hoping for a German prisoner.

War Cabinet Memorandum
Chief of the Air Staff, 12 September

Prime Minister

As you are aware, there has been a considerable amount of enemy bombing of railways and termini in the London area ... The following points are apparent:

 i) congestion of rolling stock now building up in marshalling yards; and

ii) most of the trouble is caused by delayed action or unexploded bombs which paralyse movement until they are blown up or removed ...

The sooner the bombs are exploded, the sooner the lines will be reopened to traffic. I have mentioned this matter to the Minister of Transport, and apparently there is a serious shortage of skilled gangs capable of dealing with these bombs.

Daily Mail, *13 September*

The lesson of the raids is this: there is no such thing as 100 percent safety. But if you are in a shelter or a protected lower room of your house, it needs a direct hit – the 'million-to-one-shot' – to cause death or severe injury. If even a high explosive bomb falls a foot or two from your house or your shelter, it will probably cause spectacular damage and perhaps a fire – but you will be there the next day to tell the tale.

Harold Nicholson, Parliamentary Secretary to the Minister of Information
Diary, 13 September

There is a great concentration of shipping and barges in France, and it is evident that the Cabinet expect invasion at any moment. A raid starts at about 11.00 a.m. I go upstairs and go on with my work. At about 12.15 I meet Walter Monckton in the passage. He whispers, 'They have just dive-bombed Buckingham Palace, and hit it three times. The King's safe.' The raid continues till about 2.30. There are delayed action bombs in St James's Park and the whole park-side of the Foreign Office has been evacuated. I cannot find any trains at all running to Kent and I have to give up going home. Another raid begins about 3.45. Bombs are dropping close to us in Howland Street and without warning. We go down to the dug-out. I then go up to the sixth floor and look over London. There is a triumphant double-rainbow circling the city and basing itself upon St Paul's which shines in the evening sun. At 9.15 the sirens start to yell again. It is a wonderful night with a full moon. When I get back to the M of I, I start typing this and as I do so, the guns boom.

Squadron Leader Sandy Johnstone

We feared they were going to use gas. They never did, but it seemed a thing they might do – wait until there was a good, strong wind, let off a gas attack and then follow it up with an invasion. We carried our gas masks and had them on quite often, and we had these little anti-gas panels. They were yellow and if any chlorine gas came over, their colour was supposed to change, to red I think. They were on buildings, poles, everywhere. We used to look at them all the time. I even had one on the bonnet of my car, where I could see it through the windscreen.

War Cabinet
Chiefs of Staff Committee, 14 September

The Committee had before them a memorandum by the Joint Intelligence Sub-Committee on the possibility of the isolation of London and the paralysing of the central machinery of government by enemy airborne troops. General Sergison Brooks said that in addition to his central reserve of regular battalions, he had a number of mobile detachments of approximately 250 men round London. Their primary task was to deal with airborne landings. Of the Home Guard in London, approximately 80,000 were available and not required for guarding vulnerable points ... He mentioned that he had only twelve guns of various types.

General Paget said that Home Force would endeavour to allocate more artillery to the London area.

War Cabinet Memorandum
Lord President of the Council, 14 September

Serious damage has been done to particular installations, including four electricity supply stations and the Beckton plant of the Gas, Light and Coke Company. As regards both water and gas, the damage to the mains has been more serious than the damage to central installations, water mains in particular having proved more vulnerable than was expected ... Up to the present, while serious damage has been sustained by individual installations or services, nothing has happened which points to a continued impairment of essential services. But everything turns on whether we get a breathing space to repair the damage already done, or whether the rate of damage is intensified.

Mollie Panter-Downes
London War Notes, 14 September

For Londoners, there are no longer such things as good nights; there are only bad nights, worse nights, and better nights. Hardly anyone has slept at all in the past week. The sirens go off at approximately the same time every evening, and in the poorer districts, queues of people carrying blankets, thermos flasks, and babies begin to form quite early outside air-raid shelters. The Blitzkrieg continues to be directed against such military objectives as the tired shopgirl, the red-eyed clerk, and the thousands of dazed and weary families patiently trundling their few belongings in perambulators away from the wreckage of their homes. After a few of these nights, sleep of a kind comes from complete exhaustion. The amazing part of it is the cheerfulness and fortitude with which ordinary individuals are doing their jobs under nerve-racking conditions. Girls who have taken twice the usual time to get to work look worn when they arrive, but their faces are nicely made up and they bring you a cup of tea or sell you a hat as chirpily as ever. Little shopkeepers whose windows have been blown out paste up 'Business as Usual' stickers and exchange cracks with their customers.

Ralph Ingersoll

One is not in London forty-eight hours before being extremely conscious of the fact that one is living with a people who are fighting for their lives – whether they fight by sleeping uncomfortably in a shelter so that they may work again tomorrow, or fight by putting out fires or by sucking oxygen out of a mask so that they do not lose their depth perception when aiming machine-guns at high altitudes. And one feels there is a quality of indecency in the eagerness of one's curiosity, an intrusion on something extremely personal and intimate of which one is not really a part.

War Cabinet Minutes

ESTIMATE OF CASUALTIES IN RAIDS ON LONDON
Period from 0600 Hours 7 September to 0600 Hours 14 September

September		Killed	Injured
7–8	Saturday–Sunday	306	1337
8–9	Sunday–Monday	286	1400
9–10	Monday–Tuesday	370	1400
10–11	Tuesday–Wednesday	18	280
11–12	Wednesday–Thursday	235	1000
12–13	Thursday–Friday	40	58
13–14	Friday–Saturday	31	224
Total		1286	5699

These figures must be regarded as approximate.

Winston Churchill

We cannot tell when they will try to come. We cannot be sure that in fact they will try at all. But no one should blind himself to the fact that a heavy full-scale invasion of this island is being prepared with all the usual German thoroughness and method, and that it may be launched at any time now – upon England, upon Scotland, or upon Ireland, or upon all three.

If this invasion is going to be tried at all, it does not seem that it can be long delayed. The weather may break at any time. Besides this, it is difficult for the enemy to keep these gatherings of ships waiting about indefinitely, while they are bombed every night by our bombers, and very often shelled by our warships which are waiting for them outside.

Therefore, we must regard the next week or so as a very important week for us in our history. It ranks with the days when the Spanish Armada was approaching the Channel, and Drake was finishing his game of bowls; or when Nelson stood between us and Napoleon's Grand Army at Boulogne. We have read all about this in the history books; but what is happening now is on a far greater scale and of far more consequence to the life and future of the world and its civilization than these brave old days of the past. Every man and woman will, therefore, prepare himself to do his duty, whatever it may be, with special pride and care.

These cruel, wanton, indiscriminate bombings of London are, of course, a part of Hitler's invasion plans. He hopes, by killing large numbers of civilians, and women and children, that he will terrorize and cow the people of this mighty imperial city, and make them a burden and an anxiety to the Government and thus distract our attention unduly from the ferocious onslaught he is preparing. Little does he know the spirit of the British nation, or the tough moral fibre of the Londoners, whose forebears played a leading part in the establishment of Parliamentary institutions and who have been bred to value freedom far above their lives.

This wicked man, the repository and embodiment of many forms of soul-destroying hatred, this monstrous product of former wrongs and shame, has now resolved to try to break our famous island race by a process of indiscriminate slaughter and destruction. What he has done is kindle a fire in British hearts, here and all over the world, which will glow long after all traces of the conflagration he has caused in London have been removed. He has lighted a fire which will burn with a steady and consuming flame until the last vestiges of Nazi tyranny have been burnt out of Europe, and until the Old World – and the New – can join hands to rebuild the temples of man's freedom and man's honour, upon foundations which will not soon or easily be overthrown. This is the time for everyone to stand together, and hold firm, as they are doing ... We shall draw from the heart of suffering itself the means of inspiration and survival, and of a victory won not only for our own times, but for the long and better days that are to come.

* * *

There was a touch of mist in the air over southern England on the morning of 15 September. But it cleared quickly and the sun shone through clear and bright. It was excellent bombing weather.

For more than a week, the Luftwaffe had pounded London and other British cities. It seemed certain the German raiders would be over again before the day was out. News rapidly circulated of the horrifying deaths the evening before of women and children sheltering in a church which had been hit by a bomb in London's Chelsea district. No one could doubt there was much grief and devastation yet to come.

An air of expectancy again closed in over Flight Command airfields that morning. Pilots waited at dispersal, their Mae Wests on, their planes primed for take-off by the ground crew. Patrols had gone up from first light and had come down with little to report. Given the fine weather and tense atmosphere, that seemed ominous rather than reassuring. At around 11.00 a.m., coastal radar stations began picking up masses of German planes forming up over their airfields on the far side of the Channel. Thus began the activity on what has come to be known as 'Battle of Britain Day'.

The raiders came over in vast numbers, wave after wave of them. Their mission was finally to deliver the devastating blow against Britain that Göring had repeatedly assured Hitler the Luftwaffe could administer.

Winston Churchill

The [11] Group Operations Room [which he visited on 15 September] was like a small theatre, about sixty feet across and with two storeys. We took our seats in the Dress Circle. Below us was the large-scale map-table, around which perhaps twenty highly trained young men and women, with their telephone assistants, were assembled. Opposite to us, covering the entire wall, where the theatre curtain would be, was a gigantic blackboard divided into six columns with electric bulbs, for the six [11 Group] fighter stations, each of their squadrons having a sub-column of its own, and also divided by lateral lines. Thus the lowest row of bulbs showed as they were lighted the squadrons which were 'standing by' . . . the next row those at 'readiness' . . . then at 'available' . . . then those which had taken off, the next row those which had reported having seen the enemy, the next – with red lights – those which were in action, and the top row those which were returning home . . .

'I don't know,' said Park, as we went down, 'whether anything will happen today. At present all is quiet.' However, after a quarter of an hour the raid-plotters began to move about. An attack of 'forty plus' was reported to be coming from the German stations in the Dieppe area. The bulbs along the bottom of a wall display-panel began to glow as various squadrons came to standby. Then in quick succession twenty plus, forty plus signals were received and in another ten minutes it was evident that a serious battle impended.

One after another signals came in, forty plus, sixty plus; there was even an eighty plus. On the floor-table below us, the movement of all the waves of attack was marked by pushing discs forward from minute to minute along different lines of approach, while on the blackboard facing us the rising lights showed our fighter squadrons getting into the air, till there were only four or five left at readiness. These air battles, on which so much depended, lasted little more than an hour from the first encounter. The enemy had ample strength to send out new waves of attack, and our squadrons, having gone all out to gain the upper air, would have to refuel after seventy or eighty minutes, or land to re-arm after a five minute engagement. If at this moment of refuelling or re-arming the enemy were able to arrive with fresh unchallenged squadrons, some of our fighters could be destroyed on the ground ... Presently the red bulbs showed that the majority of our squadrons were engaged.

Sergeant Tom Naylor

On 15 September, the plotting table [at Hornchurch Sector Station] was in such a mess that it hardly meant anything to anybody. The raids were coming in so quickly and in such large numbers that the whole flippin' system broke down. There was no contact after a squadron took off because most of the pilots just put the switch over and cut their radio right out. They had to concentrate on what was happening around them. They didn't want some Controller on the ground telling them there was a raid over Maidstone when they had three 109s on their tails over Manston. In one way, cutting off those telephones was a good thing because the language that usually came over the loudspeaker from the pilots could be awful, though the WAAFs didn't take a bit of notice.

There were other things that came over the radio, too. There was a young Canadian pilot who obviously had been hit. He came on and said, 'Three-two.' That was his call sign. 'Give my love to mother.' He never came back.

Sergeant Iain Hutchinson

They needed everyone they could find in the air on 15 September. My squadron had taken off, but I didn't have a plane. My aircraft was unserviceable, I think, or maybe it was that I had been shot down the previous day and didn't have a replacement. I don't remember exactly. But I stole a plane from 41 Squadron, which was also at Hornchurch, and went up with them. We did an attack on some bombers and then got split up. I was flying with another Spitfire – a friend of mine in 41 Squadron – watching the sky on my side. The next time I looked around, my friend was gone and there was a Messerschmitt 109 in his place. I'm not sure what happened next, but I was shot down. It's not recorded in the official records, because, not being in 41 Squadron, my name couldn't appear in its list of casualties.

Exchange between Biggin Hill Controller Squadron Leader Bill Frankland and 32 Squadron CO Squadron Leader John Worrall

Frankland: 'Twenty-four bombers, with twenty plus more behind them.'
Worrall: 'Got it.'
Frankland: 'Twenty plus more bombers and twenty fighters behind and above.'
Worrall: 'All right.'
Frankland: 'Now thirty more bombers and a further hundred plus fighters following.'
Worrall: 'Stop. No more information please. You're frightening me terribly.'

Winston Churchill
11 Group Ops Room, 15 September

A subdued hum arose from the floor where the busy plotters pushed their discs to and fro in accordance with the swiftly changing situation. Air Vice Marshal Park gave general directions for the disposition of his fighter force which were translated into detailed orders to each Fighter Station by a youngish officer in the centre of the Dress Circle ... The air marshal himself walked up and down behind, watching with vigilant eye every move in the game, supervising his junior executive hand, and only occasionally intervening with some decisive order, usually to reinforce a threatened area ...

I became conscious of the anxiety of the commander, who now stood still behind his subordinate's chair. Hitherto I had watched in silence. I now asked, 'What other reserves have we?' 'There are none,' said Air Vice Marshal Park.

* * *

There were no reserves, but Park meticulously deployed his squadrons to take on the attackers. They swooped on them as they crossed the English coast. They met them as they flew over Kent. They converged on them as they approached and reached London. They shot many of them down or sent many others limping back to their bases with dead and wounded aboard. They broke up their formations and drove them from their intended targets. They took off, intercepted, returned to base to refuel and re-arm and take off to intercept again. Leigh-Mallory's Big Wing, still operating contrary to

Dowding's tactical prescriptions, struck at the raiders as well and made an important contribution to the day's achievements.

Pilot Officer Boggle Bodie

The morning of 15 September dawned – blue, cloudless sky, fine flying weather.

It was Sunday – what of it? Hundreds of bombers and fighters swarmed over the Channel.

Our turn didn't come until about half-past eleven, when we were ordered to patrol at 20,000 feet; off we went.

I was in my usual position as 'weaver', flying alone 1,000 feet above the rest of the squadron, watching for attack from the rear, or out of the sun. Soon we spotted a formation of Dorniers, and the squadron attacked. I followed, keeping a keen lookout behind, and wasn't surprised to see a dozen or more 109s diving down on us.

By now, the foremost people in the squadron were in amongst the Dorniers, so I told 'em about the 109s and engaged the nearest, but before I could get him in my sights, I was fairly in the soup; they were all round me. They didn't do their job and protect the bombers, but all went for me because I was on my own. I saw the squadron disappearing, dealing most effectively with the fleeing Dorniers, and realised that I was in no position to stay and play with a dozen 109s. Several were on my tail, so I beat it straight down flat out. I levelled out at 12,000 feet; that had shaken 'em off. I was all alone. I called up the squadron on the radio, told 'em I was no longer with them, and beetled off to see what I could find patrolling a few miles south of London.

I saw a blob coming up from the south, and investigated. Boy! Oh, boy! Twenty fat Dorniers, flying wing-tip to wing-tip, ack-ack all round. I was well ahead and above them, so shoved the old throttle open, and dived at them head on.

I picked the chappie who appeared to be leading the bunch, settled him in my sights, and let him have it.

There isn't much time to muck about in a head-on attack. I gave a short burst, then slid underneath his big black belly with only feet to spare, and flashed through the rest of the formation. I hadn't meant to cut it so close, and instinctively ducked as I saw wings, engines, cockpits and black crosses go streaking past my hood.

I had reached about 450 mph in my dive, and heaved back on the stick. I blacked out completely as I went up and over in an enormous loop. My sight returned as I lost speed and the centrifugal force lessened. I was on my back, so rolled over. The speed of dive and pull-out had carried me up ahead of them for another attack.

I saw that my first burst had taken effect, the leader had dropped away and to one side, and was turning back. The rest of the formation were wobbling about, and didn't seem to know quite what to do.

As I dived down again, two Hurricanes turned up and joined in the party. The Huns didn't wait for more, but scattered and fled pell-mell, jettisoning their bombs on open country.

I had helped turn twenty bombers away from London! I yelled and whistled with joy, then pounced on the one I had crippled in my first attack. The Hurricanes were 'seeing off' the others OK, so I left them to it.

He appeared to be having difficulty with one engine. I fixed that by stopping it altogether for him. He looked a bit lopsided then, so I stopped the other one too, and he started a long, steep glide down.

I saw the rear gunner bale out, so went up very close and had a look at the aeroplane. It was pretty well riddled. Eight machine-guns certainly make a mess!

I had a look at the pilot. He sat bolt upright in his seat, and was either dead or wounded, for he didn't even turn his head to look at me, or watch out for a place to land, but stared straight ahead.

Suddenly, a pair of legs appeared, dangling from the underneath hatch. The other gunner was baling out. He got out as far as his waist, then the legs kicked. They became still for a moment, then wriggled again, they writhed, thrashed and squirmed. Good God, he's stuck! Poor devil, he couldn't get in or out, and his legs, all I could see of them, flailed about wildly as he tried to release himself.

It was my fault. I suddenly felt guilty and almost physically sick, until I thought of all the people down below, wives, young mothers, kiddies, huddled in their shelters, waiting for the all clear.

The legs still wriggled and thrashed, 2,000 feet above the cool green fields, trapped in a doomed aircraft, gliding down, a dead pilot at the controls. First one boot came off, then the other. He had no socks on, his feet were quite bare: it was very pathetic.

He'd better hurry, or it'd be too late.

He hadn't got out before they were down to 1,000 feet. He'd be cut in half when they hit the ground, like cheese on a grater. In spite of all he stood for, he didn't deserve a death like that. I got my sights squarely on where his body would be, and pressed the button. The legs were still. The machine went on. The pilot was dead. He made no attempt to flatten out and land, but went smack into a field, and the aeroplane exploded. I saw pieces sail past me as I flew low overhead. I didn't feel particularly jubilant.

Pilot Officer Bobby Oxspring

The German bombers were taking quite a beating from us on that day. Every squadron in 11 Group had intercepted and, at that moment, I saw Douglas Bader's wing of five squadrons – three of Hurricanes, two of Spitfires – coming in from Duxford in 12 Group. That was the day Göring had said to his fighters the RAF was down to its last fifty Spitfires. But they'd run up against twenty-three squadrons for a start, when they were on their way in, and then, when they got over London, with the Messerschmitt 109s running out of fuel, in comes Douglas Bader with sixty more fighters, and got stuck in.

Pilot Officer Peter Brown

They were told we had practically no aircraft left, but there we were – in strength. In no way could they claim air superiority when the bombers they sent over met the weight of fighters we were throwing at them. Our wing probably was extravagant in its shot-down claims that day, but the psychological impact of our being there must have hit the Germans very hard. They couldn't have been very anxious to come back the next day.

* * *

By nightfall on 15 September, the British reported, astoundingly, that 185 German planes had been shot out of the skies, plus more than forty probables, for a loss of only twenty-six British fighters, from which thirteen pilots had been saved. It was a huge exaggeration. It was later learned that only sixty German planes had been shot down. That was still a substantial kill, to which had to be added the many which had wobbled back to base badly damaged. Even more important, the Germans failed in their attempt that day to inflict on Britain the most severe bombardment and destruction that, until then, had ever been visited on any country. It was now undeniable that British air defences remained formidable, that Fighter Command was nowhere near obliteration. By nightfall, the Germans had, in effect, lost the Battle of Britain.

They didn't know this yet. Nor did the British. The fighting and bombing went on. Though less frequently and in smaller formations, German bombers did continue to come over in daylight and did much damage. But heavier, more persistent and more destructive were the terror attacks on London and other cities after dark, when the bombers didn't have to tangle with British fighters, which were still unequipped for night fighting.

Nurse Frances Faviell

After a heavy raid with many casualties ... there was a task for which we were sometimes detailed ... and to which our commandant disliked having to send us. This was to help piece the bodies together in preparation for burial. The bodies – or rather the pieces – were in temporary mortuaries ... It was pretty grim, although it was all made as businesslike and rapid as possible. We had somehow to form a body for burial so that the relatives, without seeing it, could imagine that their loved one was more or less intact for that purpose. But it was a very difficult task – there were so many pieces missing and, as one of the mortuary attendants said, 'Proper jigsaw puzzle, ain't it, Miss?' The stench was the worst thing about it – that, and having to realize that these frightful pieces of flesh had once been living, breathing people. We went out to smoke a cigarette when we simply could not go on – and some busybody saw Sheila smoking and reported her smoking when in uniform and on duty.

Kathleen Taylor

I joined the Women's Voluntary Service in London. My sister did, too. We went around to check up on who lived in which houses and who were likely to be there. In that way, if anything did happen, the air-raid wardens would know who exactly they were looking for. After one raid, the wardens were there a few minutes later asking after the people in two houses which were flattened by bombs. It just so happened that they were all in a shop on the corner at the time. They were safe. Just a trick of fate.

Les Linggard

At the beginning, the local council gave out Anderson Shelters for people to put in their gardens. They were made of very stiff corrugated iron sections. A hole was dug to a depth of two-foot-six in your garden and six feet by four-feet-six wide. The earth they dug out of the ground they put over the top.

The terrible part was there was an earth floor to the shelter and we had a half-dozen people crowded into it. After a full night of bombing, if it started early, which it often did, and went on till 4.00 a.m. or later, when you came out the walls were running with damp. People were worried they'd be eaten up with rheumatism. I can still vividly picture that bloody shelter in the garden. They must have saved a lot of lives, though if there was a direct hit it wouldn't have made any difference.

There were ack-ack guns just down the road from where we were. The first round each night made us jump. Even before the bombing started, fire guard parties were organized for the streets and fire watching was organised in the factories. I was fire watching in the factory where I worked and I was fire guard party leader for my road. That was mostly to deal with incendiaries. You were given stirrup pumps to put in strategic places in the road and you were trained – and you trained others – how to put the stirrup pump in the bucket and somebody pumped and somebody kept filling the bucket up. And you were trained how to keep a fire from spreading, and in the use of an ordinary fire brigade trailer pump. They trained you to go into a smoke-filled room, crawling in on the floor, wriggling on your belly because that was where the air was, in case you had to rescue someone.

Daily Mail, 21 September

London's smallest Tube line, between Aldwych and Holborn, may shortly be converted into the city's largest air-raid shelter, capable of holding thousands of people. This was announced last night as Tube stations were packed with multitudes seeking safety from the raids.

Flying Officer Barrie Heath

We left a lot of vapour trails in the skies. The skies were crisscrossed with them. I wanted to write something rude over the top of London, something to build up the morale of the people down below. But I never got around to it.

Peter Fleming

London Zoo had its fair share of bombs, but casualties to the animals were remarkably light. The possibility of escapes was not over-looked. Within a few hours of the declaration of war, all poisonous snakes, spiders and scorpions had been destroyed in accordance with a decision taken several months earlier. When the bombing started, the lions, tigers, polar bears and full-grown apes were shut up every night in their sleeping dens. It was considered unlikely that the same stick of bombs would make breaches both in these well-built cham-bers and in the iron bars of their outer cages; but against this contingency, the Zoo's Air Raid Precautions staff maintained a small reserve of trained riflemen.

Sergeant Iain Hutchinson

When we went in to London from the airfield, we'd see houses on fire and others that had been destroyed. I must confess that I was more terrified being in London during a bombing raid than I ever was when flying. The worst time in London was during a raid when I had to catch the tube to go somewhere. You heard the bombs coming down. You didn't know where they were going to hit. They all sounded remarkably near. You sheltered yourself as best you could and just waited till the noise stopped. It was a very frightening experience. The thing about fighting was that you were on equal terms with the other guy, so that was OK. But if you were under the bombs, you could only sit and wait. I was very relieved to get back to Hornchurch. But even there, I was more terrified on the ground when I landed to refuel and re-arm during a battle than ever I was in the air. I used to pretend I was looking at the guns of my plane to see if they were loaded, when in reality I was sheltering under the wings till I could take off again.

Edith Siels

I was living at Danehill, beyond 'The Coach and Horses'. A lot of the German planes didn't drop their bombs on London. They dropped them near us on their way back. We understood they weren't allowed to take their bombs back with them, so they dropped them any-where. In the wood behind where we lived, you often heard the explosion of a bomb going off. One afternoon, just after dinner, we heard a terrific bang. Up in the village, a bomb was dropped close to the cemetery. A lot of coffins were blown up. Their handles were found down the road.

Aircraftswoman Second Class Edith Heap

A Ju88 landed on the aerodrome one night. We were walking down to our billet and we thought it was a Blenheim. We used to get all sorts of people landing with us at night. The next morning, we found it had been a German plane. It had got lost. The pilot had landed, left his engine running, and gone to the watchtower. He then obviously realized he was in the wrong place and ran back to his plane. All the guard – a South African – had was a Very pistol. He fired it, ineffectually of course. The German was able to take off again. The guard was so upset at letting him get away, he later shot himself.

United States Ambassador Joseph Kennedy to the Secretary of State, Washington
London, 27 September

FOR THE PRESIDENT AND THE SECRETARY
The night raids are continuing to do, I think, substantial damage and the day raids of the last three days have dealt most serious blows to Bristol, Southampton and Liverpool. Production is definitely falling, regardless of what reports you may be getting, and with transportation smashed up the way it is, the present production output will continue to fall ...

My own feeling is that they [the British] are in a bad way. Bombers have got through in the daytime on the last three days and on four occasions today substantial numbers of German planes have flown over London and have done some daylight bombing ...

I cannot impress upon you strongly enough my complete lack of confidence in the entire [British] conduct of this war. I was delighted to see that the President said he was not going to enter the war because to enter this war, imagining for a minute that the English have anything to offer in the line of leadership or productive capacity in industry that could be of the slightest value to us, would be a complete misapprehension.

Raymond Lee, United States Military Attaché, London
Letter to his Wife, 5 October

I walked past Buckingham Palace where the bomb damage is being repaired, and past Queen Anne's Mansions, hit four or five times, and Westminster and the House of Commons, both damaged. After this the War Office, which had a big bomb. From here past Trafalgar Square, where there are numerous sandbagged pillboxes and barbed wire entanglements, and to Albemarle Street, where two buildings ... are a heap of ruins. Dover Street has a dent in it where a bomb demolished two or three buildings next to Batt's Hotel. Piccadilly Arcade is blocked up completely at one end. Savile Row is fairly battered to pieces; all the glass is out in Bond Street and Regent Street. Not a shop in Conduit Street has any glass in it ... And so on back along Oxford Street, where John Lewis is a burnt-out ruin and Selfridge's huge plate-glass windows have been shattered. Nevertheless, I look at the ruin in the West End with satisfaction, for it marks another of the famous German mistakes. Had they continued to batter the East End and kill and destroy among the slums, there would certainly have been great discontent. As it is, the only complaint the poor people have is that government assistance to the homeless and the provision of deep shelters are not being attended to with necessary promptness.

The Very Reverend W. R. Matthews, Dean of St Paul's Cathedral

We had come through so many nights of air attacks unscathed that we began to think that we were immune. Could it be that the Germans were actually trying to spare St Paul's? We were soon disillusioned, for in the night of 9 October, the Cathedral had its first direct hit and suffered most serious damage. Those who were on the roof that night had the impression that the Cathedral was one of the selected targets. The raid began with the dropping of flares from a great height over St Paul's ... [It was] one of the most beautiful and thrilling spectacles which can be imagined. The so-called 'chandelier flare' contains a constellation of brilliant lights which very slowly fall together, illuminating the whole sky and diffusing vivid and unearthly radiance on the buildings beneath. The shadows that they cast are quite different from any that were ever made by sun or moon ... To get the full picture, you must imagine that a number of chandelier flares are released together and that they are of different colours, orange and red, perhaps, and you must add the angry glow of a fire on the horizon. It may be supposed that we had other emotions than those of pure aesthetic enjoyment, but I believe that few of us were quite unmoved by the beauty. I remember that on such a night the sight of the stars, placidly shining above the man-made glow, seemed to complete the vision with the suggestion of an eternal order behind the confusion.

At 5.55 a.m. on 10 October the Cathedral received a direct hit by a high explosive bomb. It penetrated the roof of the choir and detonated on the crown of the transverse arch immediately west of the apse, tearing a large hole in the vault and lifting the roof from end to end. Its explosion brought down a large amount of heavy masonry, which crashed on to the floor of the choir ninety feet below ...

Joyce Atwood

I can remember travelling by train to Liverpool Street and going out into the smoke and flame after the first very heavy raid in which the area around St Paul's Cathedral was very badly damaged. Because of the smoke, you could see just the cross on top of the dome. Buildings were still burning. The fire brigade had been working right through the night and now their hoses had run dry. There was no more water. I had to get to my office. I was working for the Ministry of Labour and National Service. I walked down roads where, if buildings were burning like that today, the general public wouldn't be allowed anywhere near them. But the memory that holds most clearly was that of huge sewer rats, which had been driven out of the sewers by the smoke or the bombings, lying dead in the gutters.

People did not panic. We were under terrific strain. But I can't remember seeing people in any state where they had lost control of themselves. I saw firemen with eyes rimmed red, worn to a shred from fighting the fires, but I never saw any hysteria. People said, 'Isn't it shocking,' and terrible this and terrible that. But there was no panic.

Mass Observation (public opinion study) asked people how to deal with an unexploded incendiary bomb (which would explode and throw burning fragments in all directions if water was thrown on it). Answers: 'Stand up by a brick wall.'

'Lay on it.'

'Leave it to a warden.'

'Flop a coat over it, or throw it into a sewer, or anywhere
   there is water.'
'Sit back and hold tight.'
'Leave it where it is and run.'
'Keep the thin places of your house patched up.'
'Put on your gas mask.'

FINALE

As suggested earlier, the dates used to mark the various phases of the Battle of Britain are, to some extent, arbitrarily fixed. They provide only a rough guide to the changing patterns of combat in the battle. They are, nevertheless, useful in understanding how the battle developed and finally ended.

The closing phase lasted, more or less, six weeks. This phase began on 16 September when German aircraft losses (particularly in the huge, abortive raids on London the day before) and the failure by the Luftwaffe to cripple Fighter Command (also glaringly obvious on 15 September) meant Nazi plans to invade England had to be seen as only a pipe dream. This phase, and the Battle of Britain itself, can be said to have come to an end in the closing days of October when German daylight raids against England petered out, never to be resumed in any significant way.

The onset of the closing phase of the battle did not ease the intense pressure on Fighter Command. Until the tide clearly turned in October, its frontline squadrons still had to face the enemy in fierce aerial encounters over southern England.

Squadron Leader Sandy Johnstone

We were still going up every day, several times a day. We were still on high alert. We were doing two, three, sometimes four sorties a day. People were coming back and falling asleep, sometimes on the floor at dispersal, or sitting upright in a chair. We were that tired.

Pilot Officer Robert Deacon-Elliott

I was so tired and annoyed at being shot at, I was feeling sick. By then, I really didn't care when I went up whether I'd be coming back or not. And I wasn't alone in those feelings. It wasn't only the interceptions and patrols. It was also the perpetual sitting at readiness, ready to go off in a flash.

Pilot Officer Wally Wallens

When I was in hospital the time I crash-landed with my aircraft shot up and a cannon shell through my leg, the boys in the squadron would come to see me when they had some time off. The hospital was only a few miles from Hornchurch. Sometimes they'd fly past my window and wave to me. Some days, someone wouldn't come past the window and I knew he'd gone and I'd never see him again.

Pilot Officer Bobby Oxspring

They still seemed to believe they could smash Fighter Command. They changed their tactics, but they still wanted to bring us up to shoot us down. They sent over fairly high flying aircraft – Me 110s and Ju 88s – pretty fast aircraft, rigged up with bombs and escorted by Me 109s. They didn't necessarily come into London, but went around Dover and the ports as an enticement for us to go up and get at them.

Squadron Leader Harry Hogan

In fair weather, they still came over two or three times a day. A formation of fifty 109s could draw up practically the whole of our available force. You didn't know in advance whether they were fighters or bombers coming over. You were only given a patrol line or an interception course. Whether it was a bomber at the other end, or a fighter carrying a bomb, you had no idea. Radar couldn't distinguish between them and they were coming in high.

Pilot Officer Jas Storrar

421 Flight was formed to help the radar, which wasn't as effective as it might have been. We patrolled over the French and Belgian coasts and reported back by radio visual sighting of German raids forming. You'd fly as high as you could and follow the raids in, reporting back the number and progress of the raids. We operated singly at first, but when two or three failed to return, we started to do it in pairs to cover each other. Our Hurricanes were especially lightened, without armour, so we could get up high. We weren't supposed to be doing any fighting, just spotting the raids forming up and coming in. You

couldn't always tell where the raids were heading. Sometimes they would split up and go in different directions. But by that time, our radar would usually have picked them up.

Pilot Officer Robert Doe

When the bombers were coming over at night, we, of course, wanted to put up some defence and shoot down as many as we could. On moonlit nights, volunteers were called for. We were vectored out over the Channel to try to get into the bomber stream and shoot them down before they reached England. It depended completely on luck, on whether you saw them or not. It was not terribly successful.

Flight Lieutenant Brian Kingcome

There was the usual fracas when the sky was a mass of wheeling, darting aircraft. And then this strange thing happened which most fighter pilots tell you about. One moment, the sky is full of aircraft. The next moment, it's empty. You're on your own. Everyone's disappeared. You can see one or two aircraft in the distance. But it's as if someone's wiped the slate clean.

It was a beautiful day. I was at 25,000 feet and decided to do an absurd thing. I thought I'd use the occasion to practise a forced landing. I saw three Spitfires behind me and nothing else. So I throttled back and started to glide. I saw Biggin Hill in the distance. My mind was really on the eggs and bacon I hoped to get there.

A moment later there was a rattle and a bang and a crash. Something hit my leg. I looked around and the three Spitfires I had seen behind drew up alongside me and half rolled away. I don't know if they had shot me up or if they had shot someone I hadn't seen off my tail. My aircraft was in a fairly parlous state. There was blood coming out of my flying boot. Being shot didn't hurt at the time. It was just as if somebody had given me a bump. But bleeding to death was the thing one didn't want to do so I baled out.

I was taken to Maidstone Hospital, where the surgeon made an absolute cock of it. He nearly killed me because he tried to find the bullet by following it through the back of my leg without X-raying it. He cut a blood vessel, groping up and down, but couldn't find the bullet. So he stuffed the wound, which was by that time a foot long, full of gauze and wadding, put it in a plaster cast and crossed his fingers. When I came to, the theatre sister said, 'Christ, we never expected to see you again.'

Pilot Officer Robert Doe

I climbed up through cloud, entirely on my own, following a vector from the Controller. What I forgot was that when you're climbing out of cloud, you can be seen from above for the last 500 feet, though you can't see a blind thing till you're clear of it. The enemy formation was slap over the top of where I was coming out of the cloud. No sooner had I broken cloud than I was hit from in front and behind at virtually the same time. Tracer came right over my shoulder into the petrol tank. Luckily, it didn't explode. At the same time, I was hit through the shoulder and got shrapnel through my hand. It was time for me to get out of there. I had always known this situation might arise. I had taught myself – I used to go to bed at night thinking it – that if it did happen, I would hit the stick hard forward, as hard forward as I could, because the safest direction you could move was down. So I hit the stick hard forward and got out of the bullet stream. I managed to release my harness and got thrown out through the roof. I fell for a few thousand feet before I discovered where my parachute handle was – I was a little gaga by then. I was shot at by a German plane, but landed on an island in Poole Harbour, slap on my bottom in a quagmire. My legs were in no state to support me.

A senior surgeon operated on me and did a very good job. He committed suicide a week later. Hospital staff told me he had had a lot of operating failures. It was preying on his mind.

Pilot Officer Bobby Oxspring

When the night blitz began, they put us up at night to try to deal with it, but it was like looking for a needle in a haystack. You couldn't see a thing. We'd go up in singletons and be given specific patrol lines and specific heights. I did a number of these. I could see the bombs hitting London, clusters of them, and the fires below. But I never saw a bomber up there at night. One or two of our chaps did and one or two opened fire and sometimes they shot something down. But I saw only one thing up there at night during the whole of that time – the glow of twin exhausts. I was above it and heading in the opposite direction. I turned to follow it, but it just melted. I didn't know where it went. I couldn't find it again.

Pilot Officer Desmond Hughes

At night you flew a patrol line, just using your eyes to look for German bombers. It took me, I think, 200 sorties before I saw one at night. I was surprised when it happened. It was a fairly bright, moonlit night. I found myself sitting about twenty-five yards from its right wing, just a little below it, looking up at it. It never knew we were there. My gunner, Fred Gash, put his turret onto the engine nearest him, blew an enormous hole in it and it went up just like that. It was a fuel injection engine, with all sorts of little fuel injection pipes, and Fred was firing De Wilde incendiary ammunition. The German never knew what hit him.

We sometimes came across condensation trails at night. I was up around 18,000 feet one night when I came across one of them. I thought, 'That's a German bomber. All I've got to do is follow it flat out and I'll find a bomber at the other end.' What I didn't notice was that I was flying in a circle. When I finally did notice it, I thought, 'Ah, he's taking evasive action.' It wasn't till it must have been my third time around that I realized it was my own condensation trail. I'd been chasing myself.

Sergeant Len Bowman

One foggy evening at Gravesend, when we were at readiness, we went across to the crew room. We used to sit under a blue lamp there to get our eyes accustomed to the dark before we had to take off. Jimmy Green, my pilot, said, 'There won't be any flying tonight, Len, not with this fog.' We were there about an hour when the telephone rang, telling us to scramble. Jimmy looked out the window and said, 'Sorry. We can't take off in this weather. It's too foggy over here.' They said, 'Fair enough.' A half-hour later they rang again. 'What's the weather like over there now?' Jim looked out the window. 'Still too foggy,' he said. This went on for about three hours when I said to Jim, 'Why don't we find our way to the cookhouse for a meal?' I said we could put the other Defiant crew that was going to take over from us on readiness in our place. He said it was a good idea. When we opened the crew room door to go, it was a bright, moonlit night outside. The fog had cleared long before. The blackout material that had been put on the outside of the window had made it look as though it was still foggy. Jim rang up Group and said, 'It's just cleared,' and we took off.

Sergeant John Burgess

For me, the Battle of Britain had three phases. Phase one – when I was naive and thought nothing could happen to me. Phase two – when the battle became a highly dangerous sport and you regarded the Germans as supermen to some degree. They always seemed to be on your tail. Phase three – one day, around the end of September, I was returning to base and saw two aircraft coming up behind me. I turned to take a look at them. They turned out to be enemy aircraft. They had me at a disadvantage. They could have shot me down. But the moment I turned towards them, they both turned away and fled! I suddenly realized the Germans were as scared as I was. It gave us a sense of superiority we didn't have before.

Squadron Leader Sandy Johnstone

When we went up now, we began seeing more and more British aircraft in the sky. This was unusual because previously when we saw anything else up there it was a Hun. Suddenly we were seeing not nearly so many Huns. When they did come over, it very often was only for nuisance raids. They started putting bombs on their 109s. This created something of a problem because they were difficult to find; they came in at low level. We also discovered they were sending over their 109Es, which could fly very high. You used to see them cruising up around 35,000 feet. The Spitfire wasn't much good in combat above 30,000–32,000 feet. So down at Tangmere, the station commander, the other two squadron commanders and myself got together and said, 'Why bother to go up after them. Let's make a maximum height limit for ourselves of 27,000 feet.' That's where our aircraft were still pretty manoeuverable. If the Germans wanted to come down and mix it with us, they could jolly well do so. We were not going to go up after them because they were doing no harm up there. They weren't carrying bombs – with bombs they would have been too heavy to go that high. We cruised around trying to entice them down and a couple of them did come down. They'd just whizz down and go right up again. They didn't wait to fight it out. That's when we began to think the tide was turning.

Squadron Leader Peter Devitt

We were banking up from Warmwell one day to meet a raid coming in to London. We got to somewhere near Guildford, where we should have met that raid, but it had disappeared. We later learned it had turned back, possibly because we had got in the way. Instead of bombing London, they unloaded their bombs on Sevenoaks. I had all my furniture in store at Young's Depository at Sevenoaks and I lost the bloody lot. I got a letter from Young's Depository a few days later saying, 'Regret but due to enemy action all your furniture has been destroyed.'

Pilot Officer Dennis David

We were scrambled from Tangmere – myself and one other – to intercept a suspected enemy coming in towards Manston. They sent us up because we had better weather than most of the airfields in the south, where the fog was right down to the ground, though it was also pretty grim where we were. We got down to the coast and flew along it at under a hundred feet. Near Manston, we were directed towards the French coast, hoping the weather would be better when we got back so we'd be able to find our way home. Then suddenly we were in blue sky – and there was the Ju 88 we'd been sent to find. He saw us at about the same time we saw him. He jettisoned his bombs and turned to go back, but we caught up with him and riddled that plane. I've never seen a worse looking mess. If it got back, it would have been the best advertisement yet not to come to England. The thing is, we were surprised to see it because we'd been having no trade at all.

I was down in Brighton on a bit of leave around then when a 109 showed up, dropped a bomb way out to sea and fired a few rounds before heading back for France. I remember standing there thinking, 'What has he done that for?' I think he just wanted to report back that he'd been there.

Pilot Officer Peter Parrott

Our squadron had taken a beating and had lost a lot of men in August before we were pulled out and sent up to Scotland to recover. We were relieved to go. We needed the rest. But when we came back into the combat area towards the end of the battle, we were disappointed when we were scrambled and couldn't connect up with the enemy. There were still high flying 109s coming over during the day, doing a bit of random bombing from about 20,000 feet, just dropping an egg on the London area. But often we went up several times in a row and didn't see anybody. Once when we did meet some, they didn't want to know. They just turned around and went home.

Pilot Officer Brian Considine

Having lost a stone in weight during the previous weeks, I began putting a few pounds back on again. We began being released from duty in the evenings.

Pilot Officer Bobby Oxspring

Sitting at Gravesend, poking out towards France, we heard Bomber Command and Coastal Command now going over to hit the Germans every night. We knew they were clobbering the invasion barges and laying mines off the ports where the Germans were.

Squadron Leader Harry Hogan

We had new pilots arriving in ones and twos to join the squadron. They came to replace people who were still being shot down and others who were being sent to other squadrons. Some of our men had promotions and moved on to other jobs. Some were sent to back up training units.

The quality of the training was improving considerably. By October, the new men who came to us had already had much more time on Spitfires or Hurricanes than those who had come in August. They came to us far less green. And we were able to give them the coaching and nursing they required in the squadron after they reached us that we hadn't been able to give earlier, during the hectic times.

Flight Lieutenant Frederick Rosier

I had been shot down over France in May and spent some time in hospital. When I returned to the same squadron at Northolt in

October, to command, some of the pilots with whom I'd flown earlier were still there. They had remained with it right through the battle and, luckily, had survived. They'd been blooded, of course, and were different than they had been before. One or two, who had tended to be superficial when I knew them first as young lads, had grown up and become men in those few months. They were more serious. Some, who before had appeared to be not very good, had blossomed out. It was the reverse with others.

The official version is that the Battle of Britain finished in October. It's true that the weather was often bad then. We said, 'Thank God!' when it was bad enough for the Germans not to come over. But as far as our squadron was concerned, the battle just went on and on, petering out somewhat, until we went north for a rest at Christmas time.

Pilot Officer Dennis David

Looking back, I don't see how we won. There were about 650 RAF fighters versus more than 2,000 German aircraft. We had about 1,000 pilots. They had about 3,000. Of our 1,000, only about 600 or so were experienced operational pilots. As the battle progressed, we lost pilots and they lost pilots, but because we were fewer in number, our losses were more serious. At one stage, we were down to less than 350 pilots, which was dicey. That was when it got really critical. I used to look around and think, 'God, this is getting hairy!' We never actually thought we'd lose. But looking back, I wonder how the hell we won.

* * *

As damp, blustery autumn weather closed in over the English Channel, Hitler grudgingly conceded that it would, for the time being, be unwise to try to land his troops on the British coast. Instead, he turned his attention eastward and began plotting the thrust of his forces into Russia the following May.

Officially, the invasion of England was only postponed. But it would never again come under active consideration by the German High Command. If Fighter Command could not be destroyed when it hadn't been ready for the onslaught, it wasn't likely to be overwhelmed when the British were prepared. The Luftwaffe simply was incapable of seizing mastery of the skies over England.

For most people in England, victory in the Battle of Britain had little immediate significance. Most did not even realize the battle was over. Attacks by German aircraft during daylight hours had become a thing of the past, but the massive, horrific night raids on London and other British cities, though doing little to further German objectives, had already begun to transform the way people in Britain lived. The blitz went on through the rest of the autumn, the winter and well into the following spring. It claimed the lives of more than 30,000 civilians, badly injured tens of thousands more, and made more than four million homeless. Large areas of British cities were devastated. And, shattering though it was, the blitz was only a deafening overture to World War Two. That conflict was to thunder on for almost five more years and bring death, destruction and tragedy to millions of people.

Nevertheless, the defeat of the Germans in the Battle of Britain in 1940 was a milestone. Despite Churchill's defiant pronouncements about the determination of his countrymen to resist, had the Luftwaffe been able to overwhelm Fighter Command, or force it to abandon southern England, any target, military or otherwise, in that part of Britain or off its coast could have been obliterated at will by the Luftwaffe. The Germans could then have dispatched and landed the formidable invasion forces they had positioned on the other side of the English Channel. British ground forces, underarmed, undertrained and still reeling from their reverses in France, would have been no match for the German invaders.

Britain might well have been forced out of the war, either through conquest or through being compelled, like France, to sue for peace, the terms of which Hitler would have been in a position to dictate. Nazi Germany, with its instruments of terror, cruelty and oppression, would have been both triumphant and unopposed by any nation on earth. Firmly entrenched throughout Europe, the Nazis would increasingly have been in a position to control the Atlantic sea routes, with unpredictable consequences for America and for the world. The men of Fighter Command achieved far more than they knew.

Winston Churchill

Never in the course of human conflict have so many owed so much to so few.

FINALE

Pilot Officer Hugh Dundas

I suppose we were all quite proud when we heard that. But I also suppose we thought it was a bit of a joke. We didn't take that sort of thing very seriously.

Pilot Officer Jas Storrar

We'd had our baptism of fire over Dunkirk and had taken a terrible beating in the south. We were up in Scotland recuperating when we heard about that speech by Churchill. We thought, 'Aren't they brave chaps down there and thank God we're not there.'

Pilot Officer Robert Doe

It was the first time I realized that we might have done something unusual. I hadn't realized it until then.

Flight Lieutenant Alan Deere

We'd had a hellish day. When I heard about what Churchill said about the many and the few, I said to my friend George Gribble – he was killed in action later – 'By Christ, he can say that again. There aren't many of us left.'

Pilot Officer Barrie Heath

When we heard it up in 12 Group, we thought, 'We're doing bugger all. Why doesn't he call on us to have a bash?'

Anonymous pilot

I thought he was talking about our mess bill.

POSTSCRIPT

Rarely in history can victorious commanders have been treated as shabbily as were Air Chief Marshal Sir Hugh Dowding and Air Vice Marshal Keith Park as soon as they had won the Battle of Britain. Dowding had been due for retirement earlier, but had stayed on to direct the operations of Fighter Command during the battle. Within weeks of winning that battle, he was asked to vacate his office within twenty-four hours (and then asked to stay on for another week because his successor wasn't yet ready to take over). As a sop, Dowding was then given a job to which he was totally unsuited and for which he had no skills – a tour of the United States for the Air Ministry to check on war supplies.

Park, whose 11 Group had done by far the most to repel the German attack, was also relieved of his command, after having held it less than a year. He was treated as if he had botched his job and, at a time when Britain badly needed his hard-earned battle experience in an operational role, he was sent off to run a training group. To add to this insult, Park was succeeded as 11 Group commander by his arch rival, Air Vice Marshal Trafford Leigh-Mallory, whom Park held responsible for not providing adequate cover for his airfields when his own squadrons were otherwise engaged during the battle.

It is true that Dowding – aloof, unsocial, stuffy – had few friends in the Air Ministry. Leigh-Mallory and his protégé, Douglas Bader, had close contact and wielded some influence with senior military and political figures, some of whom had been persuaded that Dowding's refusal to embrace Big Wing tactics had been a dreadful mistake.

No doubt well-grounded criticism could have been levelled against aspects of Dowding's command. He might have required Park and Leigh-Mallory to work harmoniously together for the common good whatever their differences and despite their mutual hatred. More profitable use might have been made of 12 Group's resources, held in reserve not far from the centre of hostilities. Changes in the outdated, dangerous standard Vics of three-flight formation should have been implemented early on throughout Fighter Command. Questions could have been raised about the value of basing fighters on such coastal airfields as Manston and Hawkinge, which were terribly exposed to sneak enemy raids and from which they could rarely achieve height advantage over the incoming enemy when scrambled to intercept.

But Dowding's achievements far outweighed whatever short-comings could have been found in his performance. Aside from saving Fighter Command from being drained away in France before the battle began, he devised and developed from scratch the system for controlling aerial defence forces from the ground over a large area and over a long period of time. He established the system of interlocking Groups and Sectors which received, interpreted and served as a conduit for all available sources of intelligence on enemy raids. And it worked, enabling his frontline squadrons to repel the attack of an enemy far superior in numbers and experience. At the same time, he meticulously husbanded reserves to relieve· those squadrons when necessary and to meet any other incursions the enemy might attempt. In military terms, Dowding, victor of the only major battle ever fought exclusively in the air, was a giant.

Keith Park, brought back into operational service to command the aerial defence of Malta against German attack two years later, employed tactics similar to those he had used in the Battle of Britain, was again successful in repulsing the enemy, and thus made short shrift of the criticism made in the Air Ministry of his performance during the summer and autumn of 1940.

Nevertheless, the behaviour of those in top command with regard to Dowding and Park remains inexplicable, even that of Churchill, who, though other matters occupied his attention, must have known what was being done to them. However, sometime later he reacted with fury when shown an Air Ministry booklet on the Battle of Britain which neglected even to mention Dowding's name! Churchill told the Air Minister, 'The jealousies and cliquism which have led to the committing of this offence are a discredit to the Air Ministry ... What would have been said if ... the Admiralty had told the tale of Trafalgar and left Lord Nelson out of it?'

Dowding was stunned but somewhat restrained in his public reaction to the treatment meted out to him. He had for some time suffered discourtesies and worse perpetrated by the Air Ministry. Park had fewer qualms about revealing how he felt. 'To my dying day,' he said, 'I shall feel bitter at the base intrigue which was used to remove Dowding and myself as soon as we had won the Battle of Britain.'

SCRAMBLE

Squadron Leader George Darley

Dowding was too nice a chap and he came up against a gang of thugs. Leigh-Mallory was very jealous of him. He felt he wasn't getting enough of the limelight and he got a lot of backing in the Air Ministry.

Flight Lieutenant Francis Wilkinson

It was entirely [Dowding's] foresight in being able to see where the strain was going to come, and to be able to take the measure of that strain, which allowed Fighter Command to bear the enormous, almost unbearable load that it had when the fighting came. Stuffy had foreseen that our fighter squadrons were going to be depleted in strength. He had foreseen that Sector Operations Room would be bombed. And he'd made plans for the rapid interchange of squadrons between Scotland and northern England and the south. If it hadn't been for his colossal foresight and meticulous planning right from the very beginning, we'd have had it.

Squadron Leader Sandy Johnstone

After Stuffy was made to retire, the war blew up into a global thing. Great names arose – Eisenhower, Montgomery, Alexander, Bradley. Great battles were won – Alamein, D-Day, the crossing of the Rhine. But they were all courtesy of Stuffy Dowding. None of those people would even have been heard of if Stuffy hadn't been there, if he hadn't won the Battle of Britain. His statue ought to be standing atop a plinth in Trafalgar Square.

Appendix I

THE MAIN EVENTS

1939

1 September: German troops invade Poland.

3 September: Britain and France, honouring defensive treaties with Poland, declare war on Germany. Preparations accelerated for the dispatch to France of the British Expeditionary Force, soon to include the bulk of the British army and several squadrons of British fighter planes and bombers.

5 October: Last substantial Polish military resistance crushed by German invaders.

October 1939–April 1940: The 'phoney war' – little combat despite formal continuance of hostilities.

1940

9 April: Germans invade Denmark and Norway.

10 May: Germans invade Belgium, the Netherlands, and Luxembourg. Over the next ten days, additional British fighter planes are sent to reinforce forces in France.

13 May: Germans crack through French defences and launch an offensive to trap the Allied armies.

16 May: Air Chief Marshal Sir Hugh Dowding warns that sending more British fighter planes to France to try to salvage the increasingly hopeless Allied position there could result in a total British defeat.

19 May: Churchill reluctantly rules that no additional fighter squadrons are to be sent to France.

20 May: German forces reach the French Channel coast, trapping the British Expeditionary Force.

26 May–4 June: Evacuation of most of the British Expeditionary Force from the beaches at Dunkirk.

22 June: France accepts humiliating armistice terms from the Germans. Britain is now alone against Germany.

10 July: The Battle of Britain begins. In the first phase, lasting until 12 August, the Luftwaffe attacks British convoys in the English Channel and English south coast ports to lure British fighters into combat against much larger formations of German aircraft based at newly captured nearby French airfields.

16 July: Hitler orders preparations to be made for an invasion of Britain, to take place 'if necessary'.

19 July: Hitler issues 'a plea for peace' to the British to enable Germany to consolidate its conquests.

22 July: British government rejects the German peace bid.

1 August: Hitler orders acceleration of invasion preparations.

13 August: Phase two of the Battle of Britain begins. German attacks are now directed mainly against British airfields near the coast, radar installations, and aircraft factories. Despite a favourable RAF kill–loss ratio during this period, losses became an anxious concern for the British.

24 August: Phase three of the battle begins. Intensification of German efforts to destroy Fighter Command with massive and repeated raids on key airfields and industrial targets. Night attacks are stepped up. The RAF shortage of pilots grows critical. Pilots are brought into operational fighter squadrons with minimal training.

25 August: Berlin is bombed by the RAF in retaliation for the accidental German bombing of London the previous night.

7 September: Phase four of the battle begins. To retaliate for the bombing of Berlin, the Germans shift their concentrated attacks from British fighter airfields to London. Civilian casualties are heavy and much damage is done, but the reprieve for the airfields permits Fighter Command to recover its ability to meet the German onslaught.

15 September: Huge bomber raids directed against London are driven off by the RAF. Germans suffer very heavy losses on what was later to be known as 'Battle of Britain Day'.

16 September–31 October: Fifth and final phase of the Battle of Britain. Daytime German raids over England gradually cease, signalling the end of German efforts to seize mastery of the skies over England.

17 September: Hitler officially postpones the invasion of Britain 'until further notice'.

EYEWITNESSES

The following were interviewed for this narrative account of the Battle of Britain. All were Royal Air Force Fighter Command pilots during the battle with the exception of those otherwise identified.

D.J. Anderson
Robert Angell (anti-aircraft gunner)
Joyce Atwood (civilian)
Wing Commander John Barnes
Wing Commander Patrick Barthropp
Wing Commander Roland Beamont
Air Vice Marshal H.A.C. Bird-Wilson
Group Captain John Bisdee
Len Bowman (Defiant gunner)
Squadron Leader Benjamin Bowring
Air Commodore Peter Brothers
Squadron Leader M.P. Brown
John Burgess
Peter Burney (radar operator)
Air Vice Marshal G.P. Chamberlain
Philip Coad (gunner, field artillery)
Brian Considine
Wing Commander David Cox
M.E. Croskell
Air Marshal Sir Denis Crowley-Milling
Group Captain John Cunningham
Wing Commander C.F. Currant
Group Captain H.S. Darley
Group Captain Dennis David
Squadron Leader G.G.A. Davies
Squadron Leader Peter Davies
Air Vice Marshal Robert Deacon-Elliott
Wing Commander Christopher Deanesly

Air Commodore Alan Deere
Wing Commander Peter Devitt
Wing Commander Robert Doe
Air Commodore E.M. Donaldson
Group Captain Hugh Dundas
Group Captain G.R. Edge
Wing Commander J.F.D. Elkington
Air Commodore John Ellacombe
Wing Commander John Fleming
Air Chief Marshal Sir Christopher Foxley-Norris
Commander R.E. Gardner (Royal Navy, seconded to Fighter
    Command during the battle)
Wing Commander Richard Gayner
Squadron Leader E.D. Glaser
Group Captain T.P. Gleave
Peter Hairs
Roger Hall
Wing Commander H.J.L. Hallowes
Wing Commander N.P.W. Hancock
Albert Hargraves (bowser driver)
Sir Barrie Heath
Wing Commander H.M.T. Heron
Air Vice Marshal H.A.V. Hogan
Wing Commander Eustace Holden
Group Captain Sir Archibald Hope
Wing Commander G.L. Howitt
Major General B.P. Hughes (Royal Artillery)
Air Vice Marshal F.D. Hughes
Squadron Leader Iain Hutchinson
Wing Commander Bernard Jennings
Air Vice Marshal A.V.R. Johnstone
Cyril Jones (hospital operating-room assistant)
Elizabeth (Cook) Jones (civilian)
Richard Jones
John Kemp
Squadron Leader J.R. Kilner
Group Captain Brian Kingcome
Squadron Leader R.A. Kings
Edith (Heap) Kup (Operations Room plotter)
Lady Kyle (Molly Wilkinson) (Operations Room plotter, cipher
    officer)

EYEWITNESSES

Elaine Leathart (civilian)
Air Commodore J.A. Leathart
Ivy Linggard (civilian)
Leslie Linggard (civilian, fire warden)
David Looker
Wing Commander Peter Matthews
Group Captain A.G. Miller
Group Captain A.D. Murray
Tom Naylor (senior NCO, Operations Room)
Group Captain R.W. Oxspring
Wing Commander Peter Parrott
Dame Felicity (Hanbury) Peake (WAAF officer)
Francis Pecket (groundcrew)
F.S. Perkin
Group Captain G. Powell-Sheddon
Claire (Legge) Quill (Operations Room plotter)
Wing Commander Jeffrey Quill
Air Commodore David Roberts (Sector and Station commander)
Ruth Roberts (civilian)
Ursula Robertson (Operations Room plotter)
Air Chief Marshal Sir Frederick Rosier
Group Captain W.A.J. Satchell
Edith Seils (civilian)
Wing Commander Gordon Sinclair
Derek Smythe (Defiant gunner)
Ann Standen (nurse)
Wing Commander Robert Stanford-Tuck
Wing Commander H.M. Stephen
Squadron Leader Donald Stones
Wing Commander J.E. Storrar
Frederick Taylor (anti-aircraft gunner)
Kathleen Taylor (civilian)
Squadron Leader R.W. Wallens
P.T. Wareing
Squadron Leader Denis Wilde
Sylvia Yeatman (civilian)

DESCRIPTIONS OF AIRCRAFT

Spitfire

The most famous of the British fighter aircraft, the Supermarine Spitfire was extremely fast for the period, with a maximum speed of 362 mph. It was light to handle, the most manoeuverable of all the aircraft involved in the Battle of Britain, with extraordinary powers of sudden acceleration, though it lost some of its vigour at very high altitudes. When asked by Göring during the course of the battle what he could do to help his Luftwaffe fighter pilots, German ace Adolf Galland angered the Reichsmarshal by replying that they could use some Spitfires.

Wingspan: 36′ 10″. Length: 29′ 11″. Weight loaded: 6,200 pounds. Power: 1,030-hp Rolls-Royce Merlin engine. Armament: eight wing-mounted .303 Browning machine-guns. (A brief experiment with cannon instead during the battle proved a failure.)

Hurricane

Though not as widely acclaimed as the Spitfire, the Hawker Hurricane was Fighter Command's main workhorse during the Battle of Britain. Not as fast as the Spitfire (maximum speed 328 mph) and less manoeuverable, it was, nevertheless, a steadier gun platform and could sustain a great deal more damage than the Spitfire without being knocked out of the sky. It was estimated that eighty percent of Luftwaffe losses during the battle could be credited to Hurricane pilots, though that may be partly because the bombers were main Hurricane targets, while the Spitfires were regularly dispatched to tangle with the less vulnerable German fighters escorting the bombers.

Wingspan: 40′. Length: 31′ 4″. Weight loaded: 6,447 pounds. Power: 1,030-hp Rolls-Royce Merlin engine. Armament: eight wing-mounted .303 Browning machine-guns.

Blenheim

The Bristol Blenheim, a twin-engined fighter, modified from a bomber design, quickly proved to be no match for German fighters. It was widely employed against night raiding bombers and for experimentation in the development of airborne radar.

Wingspan: 56′ 4″. Length: 39′ 9″. Weight loaded: 12,500 pounds. Power: two 840 Mercury air-cooled engines. Armament: five .303 machine-guns.

Defiant

A two-seater fighter with a rear gun turret, the Boulton Paul Defiant scored a significant triumph over Dunkirk when German pilots, apparently mistaking it for the Hurricane, attacked it from the rear and lost twenty-seven planes to its rear gunners in one day. But the error wasn't repeated, and from then on the aircraft was extremely vulnerable to attacks by German fighters, having no forward firing gun, which left both pilot and gunner in difficulties in close aerial combat. Withdrawn from daylight duty, it was consigned to night fighting.

Messerschmitt 109 (Me 109)

The main fighter escort for German bombers, the 109 was a sleek, excellent war machine, with direct fuel injection to assist its performance in close combat. Marginally faster than the Spitfire, it was, however, less manoeuverable. This difference had an important bearing on the outcome of the battle. By the time 109s, flying cover for the bombers, disentangled themselves from Spitfires sent to deal with them, Hurricanes sent after the bombers at the same time were often well into their assigned task. Nevertheless, at the most critical part of the battle, Fighter Command pilots felt that 109s always seemed about to swoop down on them, their guns blazing.

Wingspan: 32′ 4½″. Length: 28′ 8″. Weight loaded: 5,520 pounds. Power: 1,150-hp Daimler-Benz engine. Armament: two 7.9-mm machine-guns and two 20-mm cannon.

APPENDICES

Messerchmitt 110 (Me 110)

A two-seater fighter-bomber which established a reputation for performance and invulnerability during the Spanish Civil War, the 110, nicknamed the 'Destroyer', was used primarily as an escort for bombers, supplementing the 109s. Towards the end of the battle, it was also often sent over on bombing missions when it became too hazardous to send over bombers during daylight hours. The 110 was a disappointment to the Luftwaffe during the battle, proving to be no match for Spitfires and Hurricanes, and probably would have been withdrawn from combat by the Germans if more 109s had been available to them.

Wingspan: 53' 4¾". Length: 39' 8½". Weight loaded: 15,290 pounds. Power: three 7.9-mm machine-guns and two 20-mm cannon.

German Bombers

Four types of aircraft did most of the bombing of British targets during the Battle of Britain – Dorniers 17 (Do 17), Junkers 87 (Ju 87), and particularly the Heinkel 111 (He 111) and Junkers 88 (Ju 88). None was fast enough or well enough armoured to cope with British fighters when inadequately escorted by 109s. The Ju 87, the famous Stuka, had been used as airborne artillery by the Germans during their sweep across Europe, diving down ahead of advancing German ground forces to clear the way by wreaking havoc and generating terror with its siren, designed to emit a high-pitched screech as it plummeted down almost vertically on its target. But it was soon apparent that the Stuka was a very easy target for British fighters, and it was withdrawn from the Luftwaffe's assault on Britain.

Appendix IV

ACKNOWLEDGEMENTS

Although the foregoing is based on interviews with men and women who fought the Battle of Britain, some of the material included has been drawn from sources listed here with thanks: *The Ironside Diaries*, edited by Colonel R. Macleod and Denis Kelly, published by Constable; *The Diaries of Sir Alexander Cadogan*, edited by David Dilks, published by Macmillan Inc.; *Skies to Dunkirk*, by Sir Victor Goddard, published by Wm Kimber; *A Chelsea Concerto*, by Frances Faviell, published by Macmillan Inc.; *This is London*, by Edward R. Murrow, published by Simon and Schuster, copyright 1941 by Edward R. Murrow, renewed 1969 by Janet H.B. Murrow and Charles Casey Murrow; *The Nine Days of Dunkirk* and *Dunkirk*, by David Divine, by permission of David Higham Associates Ltd; *Spitfire Pilot*, by David Crook, by permission of Dorothy Hessling; *The Royal Air Force*, by Denis Richards, published by Her Majesty's Stationery Office; *Plague Year*, by Anthony Weymouth, published by Harrap; *Diaries and Letters* of Harold Nicolson, published by Collins; *The Home Guard of Britain*, by Charles Graves, published by Hutchinson; *London War Notes*, by Mollie Panter Downs; the wartime diary of Leonard Marsland Gander, by permission of the diarist; the letter from Flight Lieutenant Frank Howell, drawn from *The Narrow Margin*, by Derek Wood and Derek Dempster, by permission of the authors; *The London Journal of General Raymond E. Lee*, published by Little, Brown and Company; the letter from John Dundas to his brother Hugh, by permission of Group Captain Hugh Dundas; *Readiness at Dawn*, by Ronald Adam, published by Gollancz; The *Memoirs of General the Lord Ismay*, published by Heinemann; *Survivor's Story*, by Sir Gerald Gibbs, published by Hutchinson; the War Diary of Mrs Gwladys Cox, by permission of Alex Mitchell; *The Second World War*, Volume II, by Winston Churchill, published by Houghton Mifflin and Cassell; *Invasion 1940*, by Peter Fleming, published by Collins, by permission of Nicholas Fleming; *St Paul's Cathedral in Wartime*, by the Very Reverend W.R. Matthews, published by Hutchinson; *The Ultra*

Secret, by F.W. Winterbotham, published by Weidenfeld and Nicolson; *The Man Who Won the Battle of Britain*, published by Scribners, by permission of the author, Robert Wright. Material from Crown-copyright records of the British Public Record Office, from files Air 4, 16, 22, 24 and 25, CAB 65 and 66, and WO 199, appear by permission of the Controller of Her Majesty's Stationery Office. Two books invaluable to any person wishing to look further into the Battle of Britain are the aforementioned *The Narrow Margin*, by Derek Wood and Derek Dempster, and *Battle over Britain*, by Francis Mason.

Thanks are due to the following for the loan of books and documents related to the Battle of Britain which might otherwise have been difficult to track down: Air Vice Marshal H. Bird-Wilson, Air Vice Marshal Peter Chamberlain, Air Commodore Alan Deere, Group Captain Tom Gleave, Wing Commander H.M.T. Heron, Edith Kup, Tom Naylor, Group Captain W.A.J. Satchell, Ursula Robertson, Sylvia Yeatman and Wing Commander J. E. L. Zumbach.

INDEX

Page numbers in *italic* refer to quotations

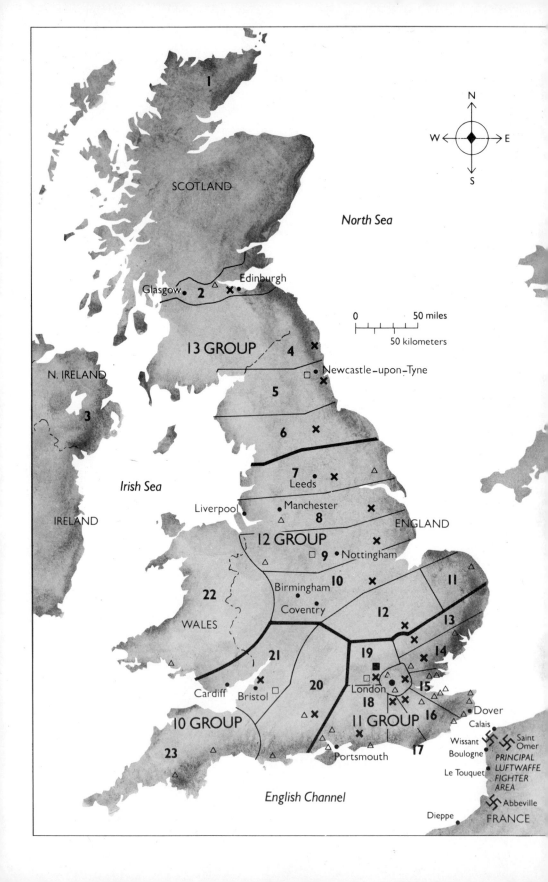